Fresh Voices:

COMPOSITION AT CAL POLY

2019–2020

Volume XIII

Editors
Jason Peters and Dawn Janke

Assistant Editors
Scott Ferree, Gage Greenspan, Rebekah Maples,
Sarah Grieve Miller, Mark Roberts, Dianna Winslow

hayden-mcneil
Macmillan Learning

Macmillan Learning Curriculum Solutions
14903 Pilot Drive
Plymouth, MI 48170
www.macmillanlearning.com

Helmbrecht 1428-6 F19

Sustainability
Hayden-McNeil/Macmillan Learning Curriculum Solutions is proud to be a part of the larger sustainability
initiative of Macmillan, our parent company. Macmillan has a goal to reduce its carbon emissions by 65%
by 2020 from our 2010 baseline. Additionally, paper purchased must adhere to the Macmillan USA Paper
Sourcing and Use Policy.

Hayden-McNeil partners with printers that use paper that is consistent with the environmental goals and values
of Macmillan USA. This includes using paper certified by the Forest Stewardship Council (FSC), Sustainable
Forestry Initiative (SFI), and/or the Programme for the Endorsement of Forest Certification (PEFC). We also
offer paper with varying percentages of post-consumer waste as well as a 100% recycled stock. Additionally,
Hayden-McNeil Custom Digital provides authors with the opportunity to convert print products to a digital
format to use no paper at all. Visit http://sustainability.macmillan.com to learn more.

Contents

Zsolt Biczo/Shutterstock.com

Letter from the Director of Writing: Dr. Brenda Helmbrecht vii

How to Read *Fresh Voices* ix

STUDYING WRITING, RHETORIC, AND ARGUMENTATION AT CAL POLY

Transitioning from High School English to College Composition 1

Transitioning to English 145 2

Composition Course Curricula. 4

    The Writing Sequences 5

    English 145 Curriculum 7

Key Concepts 9

Research and Inquiry: Identifying Effective Sources 25

WRITING WITH IMAGES

Jenny Ashley: *Lampshade Project*. 36

EXPLORING SIGNIFICANT MOMENTS

Image: "Doña Victoria," *by Keilana Sugano*. 41

"How to Handshake," *by Michelle Waal* 42

"So, Where Are You From?" *by Emma Knisley*. 45

"Halves," *by Laura Kuffner*. 51

"'Sumac Kawsay': A New Perspective," *by Keilana Sugano*. 54

"Our Movie," *by Megan Wong*. 58

"Irrevocable Discovery," *by Jenna*. 61

"Finding My Voice," *by Holly Masterson* 64

"The World Is My Nose," *by Grace Kitayama* 67

"Dancing on My Coffin," *by Andrew Baker*. 70

"Becoming the Good," *by Lindsey Shepard* 73

PROFILING A PERSON, PLACE, EVENT, OR TREND

Image: "Pigeon on the Boardwalk," *by Alexander Watkins* 77

"A *Linn*teresting Professor," *by Ryan Takeshita* 79

"Sojourn Grace Collective: A Church, and Yet," *by Abigail Wilkins* 84

"Living in Eden," *by Alex Cushing* 89

"Understanding the Abandoned: An Educator's Immersive Approach,"
by Mackenzie Croxdale 93

"A Farmer, a WAVE, and a Navy Wife," *by Holly Masterson* 99

"Journey to the West," *by May Thiri Kyaw* 103

"The Ultimate Experience," *by John Lazo* 107

ANALYZING RHETORICALLY

Image: "Constructed Perspective," *by Laura Nelson* 113

"Catching Fire," *by Alex Cushing* 115

"Blue Brides," *by Meha Sharma* 119

"Blaming the Victim Is a Crime," *by Stephanie Botto* 127

"A Snapshot of Living in the Syrian Civil War," *by Joshua Schipper* 133

ENGAGING IN PUBLIC RHETORIC AND ARGUMENTATION

Image: "Bodily Movement," *by Laura Nelson* 137

"The OG Feminist: Queen Elizabeth I," *by Leanna McMahon* 139

"Blinded by the Bubble," *by Jaxon Silva* 143

"Voter Registration," *by Kayla Cheyno* 149

"Comfort v. Necessity," *by Bryanna Gay* 155

"Cal Poly Needs More Composting," *by Sarah Bates* 160

"Curving Our Enthusiasm: The Downsides of Grading Curves," *by Kevin Lee* . . .165

"Eyes for the Dark," *by Stephanie Mullen* 170

"Menstruation Nation: Let's Free the Tampons," *by Holly Masterson* 175

REASONING, ARGUMENTATION, AND WRITING

Image: "The Stacks," *by Alexander Watkins* 183

"Not in the Loop," *by Bo Cole* 185

"Putting an End to Single-Use Plastics on Campus," *by Gillian Ippoliti* 191

"Plastics Are Out: Reusables Are In," *by Anna Wannenwetsch* 199

"A Plastic Spoonful of Sugar," *by Catherine Zadorozhna* 208

"We Need Them. Period." *by Bella Amador* 212

"No More 7 a.m. Classes," *by Juliana Brozio* 217

"Solitary Confinement in the U.S. Prison System," *by Fiona Gleeson* 223

"The Death of Marilyn Monroe," *by Kaylee Earnshaw*. 228

APPENDICES

Image: "Invisible Stairs," *by Laura Nelson* 235

Campus Resources: Where to Find Support. 236

    Your Instructor's Office Hours 236

    Resources for Multilingual Students 236

    Mustang Success Center 237

    Veterans Success Center 237

    Disability Resource Center 237

    Writing and Learning Center 237

    Kennedy Library: Resources for Research 239

Defining and Avoiding Plagiarism 241

General Education Course Objectives 243

Composition at Cal Poly: Catalog Course Descriptions 245

The Graduation Writing Requirement 248

"Look Here:" URLs 249

Submitting Your Work to *Fresh Voices,* 2020–2021 256

Acknowledgements

The *Fresh Voices* editors extend sincere gratitude to both the College of Liberal Arts and the English Department for supporting this project.

In particular, the editors appreciate the English Department staff—Susan Bratcher, Gregg Parras, and Jenni Hailer—for their assistance with essay submissions. We especially want to thank Jenni Hailer for cataloguing submissions, communicating with students, and helping to organize the *Fresh Voices* Awards Reception each fall.

Finally, the editors wish to recognize our amazing Cal Poly students, especially those who have submitted their work to this collection. Without their investment in writing and writing education, this collection would not be possible. Keep using your voice to impact the world around you!

Letter from the Director of Writing

At Cal Poly you will…Learn by Doing…and Learn by Writing…

Dear Student:

Welcome to *Fresh Voices*, a collection of writing that showcases the effort, commitment, and talent of students who completed Cal Poly's first-year writing courses.

The essays featured in the collection are typical of the intellectual engagement and critical thinking promoted in Cal Poly's first-year writing classes. We value the work of these writers for many reasons. We especially think the essays in this collection:

- Explore issues about which the writers truly care.
- Demonstrate sophisticated and unique approaches to the same assignments you are likely to encounter in your composition courses.
- Grapple with contemporary questions and issues.
- Employ distinctive and interesting rhetorical strategies to engage readers.
- Cultivate distinct voices and styles.

In short, these writers have something to say!

And we think they have something to teach you about writing at Cal Poly.

As the Director of Writing, my goal is to ensure that you experience current and innovative approaches to writing and rhetoric instruction. Indeed, one of Cal

---

ASK YOURSELF:

"What can these essays teach me about my own writing?"

STRATEGIES FOR DEVELOPING YOUR WRITING:

- Carefully consider your instructor's thoughtful feedback.

- Regard revision as an opportunity to learn more about your writing.

- Keep an open mind.

- Let go of the idea that you write best "under pressure."

- Ask for help if you want more guidance or are struggling.

- Use writing to learn more about topics and issues you care about.

Poly's stated University Learning Objectives (ULO) is "effective communication," which means that you will be developing your writing skills throughout your Cal Poly career. You may soon find that writing at the college level requires you not only to demonstrate knowledge of the skills you developed in high school, but also to experiment with new approaches to writing.

At Cal Poly, you will be asked to write essays that move beyond the five-paragraph structure (or other formulaic approaches to writing) you may have previously relied upon. Instead, you will have an opportunity to choose an organizational strategy that suits your topic, use language and punctuation that most effectively convey your meaning, address your audience with sensitivity, and select essay topics you care about. All writers make choices, and when you write at Cal Poly, we want to help you make choices that will ensure you are communicating effectively with your readers. Try to absorb and engage with the new approaches to writing you may experience in your classes.

Perhaps you have been waiting to take your writing in new directions. Now is the chance to start fresh. If you commit to and reconnect with your writing, I predict that you will make incredible strides this year. **You will learn a lot by writing at Cal Poly!**

The *Fresh Voices* editors and I welcome you to composition at Cal Poly.

Dr. Brenda M. Helmbrecht
Director of Writing

How to Read *Fresh Voices*

Regardless of whether you excel at or struggle with writing, this collection can help you transition into your college composition courses.

The essays in this collection will offer you new ways to approach your writing, perhaps in terms of how to craft an introduction, how to integrate quotations, or even how to locate evidence to support your position. Most importantly, studying these essays can help you bring greater complexity and depth to your writing—two traits that are highly valued in *all* of Cal Poly's courses. In other words, focus on the rhetorical choices the writers made so that you can make thoughtful rhetorical moves in your own writing. Effective writers consider how the language they use affects the people around them—and we expect the same of all Cal Poly writers. We believe the essays in this collection will offer a range of perspectives and experiences to learn from.

We're excited by the wide range of student life experiences and perspectives represented in this year's collection. The University recognizes that for many students, English is only one language among many. We live in one of the most diverse areas of the world, with more than 200 languages represented in California, including many endangered indigenous languages. Perhaps you or your family knows one (or more!) of these languages, and perhaps your voice is influenced by its styles and traditions. We hope that by making space for a wide array of language and culture in the pages of this book, we will inspire Cal Poly pride in all of those eager readers in our families and our communities, in San Luis Obispo, throughout California, as well as our *familias del otro lado*.

While your instructor may assign essays from each section of this collection, you probably won't be responsible for reading the whole book. Still, we encourage you to take the initiative to read essays from *Fresh Voices* that haven't been assigned for class. For instance, if you earned AP credit for GE A1 and moved directly into GE A3 (English 145/148/149), make sure to read about the A1 class so you have some understanding of the skills your A3 instructor will assume you have developed. And, if you are assigned to read two essays in a section of this book that has six essays, take the time to read a few more.

Most importantly, use these essays to help gauge how you approach your writing by comparing your choices with the choices your peers have made. Do you write about topics you care about? Do you challenge yourself to take new stylistic approaches to your work? Can you feel your "voice" in your writing?

The editors did not select these essays because of the grade they earned or because they are perfect (frankly, we don't know what grades these essays received and neither does your writing instructor). Our intention is not for you to imitate these essays but to use them to help you develop your own writing style and process. In other words, read the essays in this collection with an eye toward your own writing. See the essays as a kind of *bridge* connecting the writing projects you have already created and the projects you will complete at Cal Poly.

At the end of the collection, you will find important information about campus resources that can provide additional support for your writing and research, including the university's Writing and Learning Center and Kennedy Library. You may also want to become familiar with the "Defining and Avoiding Plagiarism" section. And finally, at the end of collection, you will find information for submitting your work to next year's *Fresh Voices*.

Studying Writing, Rhetoric, and Argumentation at Cal Poly

TRANSITIONING FROM HIGH SCHOOL ENGLISH TO COLLEGE COMPOSITION

You will likely see some similarities between the classes you took in high school and the composition classes you take at Cal Poly. This is by design. English 129/130, English 131/132, English 133, and/or English 134 are not intended to be complete departures from your high school courses. Rather, your college writing courses offer you an opportunity to build on the skills you have been developing for the past few years. You will be asked to complicate and challenge the ways you may already think about writing.

While you might find some overlap with previous courses you have taken, your Cal Poly instructor's expectations will probably be higher. **In short, you will be held accountable for your rhetorical choices.** Your instructor will assume that when you write, you are making informed choices, and they will evaluate the effectiveness of those choices. In effect, you won't just be regarded as a student. **You will be treated like a *writer*, or someone who can learn and benefit from honest and careful responses to their texts.**

First-year composition courses at Cal Poly position writing as a mode of inquiry. In other words, by writing about a subject, you learn more about specific issues, about your audience, and about yourself as a writer.

> Writing goes beyond reporting information; writing actually creates knowledge.

The Beaten
by Alexander Watkins

In this new role, you will be expected to assume many responsibilities. For instance, you will be expected to:

- Attend class every day and on time.
- Keep your phone tucked away.
- Bring your book(s) to class.
- Contribute to class discussion.
- Ask questions if you don't understand something.
- Interact respectfully with your peers.
- Complete all your coursework.
- Turn in your work on time.

If you felt restrained in your high school English classes (perhaps timed-writing and high-stakes exams dominated the courses), try to regard writing courses at Cal Poly not as classes you *must take,* but as opportunities to really improve your writing. A positive mindset toward writing can help you successfully navigate the many writing projects you will encounter throughout your career at Cal Poly—including upper-division writing intensive courses, your senior project, and the Graduation Writing Requirement (which is discussed in the "Appendices" section at the end of the collection).

TRANSITIONING TO ENGLISH 145

English 145: Reasoning, Argumentation, and Writing builds on the concepts you began exploring in English 133/134: Writing and Rhetoric. For instance, in English 133/134, you began to study rhetoric and likely wrote a persuasive paper. English 145 will continue to study persuasion but will do so by exploring more advanced rhetorical and argumentative concepts, like stasis theory, logical fallacies, and reasoning. English 145 will help you see the complexities of argumentation, a foundational skill for your personal, professional, and public life.

During ENGL 145, your instructor will invite you to deepen your understanding of the conversation that surrounds all of us as academic writers. To meet this goal, you will most likely complete one or several research-intensive assignments that require you to fully examine an issue. In other words, you will take the research methods that you learned in English 133/134 and build on them to consider critically the full scope of an issue.

As such, the course will push you to examine viewpoints that you may never have considered, explore topics with which you might be unfamiliar, and vet arguments and scholars you come across during your research. The deepening rigor of the class encourages you to move from deploying rhetorical strategies that persuade audiences by any means necessary to deploying those strategies ethically and at a more advanced level.

The Goals of Argumentation

In a dispute, debate, or even court case, the goal of argument is to win. Furthermore, in these contexts, there tends to be only two sides of an issue (i.e., for/against, guilty/innocent). In comparison, the goal of argument in academia has a different purpose: advancing knowledge for the benefit of humanity in general and for the greatest number of stakeholders.

In your college courses and beyond, try to regard argumentation as a tool for discerning and explaining what is currently known, identifying gaps and edges of that knowledge, synthesizing existing knowledge in new ways, devising strategies for discovering new knowledge, and combining new knowledge with existing knowledge to fill in gaps and/or push the edges of our knowledge into new territory. In short, argument is a creative tool, not a destructive weapon.

In an attempt to distinguish the kind of argument used in creating new knowledge from the kind of argument used in debate, we identify below the characteristics of scholarly argument.

Scholarly argument:
1. Assumes the possibility of growth and change;
2. Invites participants to reconsider their perspectives in response to the sound reason and evidence of others; and
3. Seeks common ground—shared beliefs, values, and assumptions—on which to begin and continue dialogue. When an individual does not seek common ground to support a claim, or does not offer reasons that others can accept, reasoned argument is not possible.

Two frequent barriers to finding the common ground necessary to engage in scholarly argument are ideology and opinion.
- *Ideology* refers to the belief systems, worldviews, and lenses for interpreting experience that we acquire as we grow and learn. Everyone is affected by ideology; it is a natural facet of human consciousness. Ideology can become a problem—a barrier to rigorous, rational argument—when people believe their lens is the only correct one, that it's the natural, universal, and right way to see everything.
- *Opinion* is a position resting on purely personal criteria. Without shared criteria for approaching an issue, people will not be able to find the common ground to accept each other's reasons and evidence.

Writers risk confirming bias when they look only for evidence that supports their ideologies or personal opinions, deliberately ignoring evidence that challenges their own positions or supports opposing positions.

Scholarly Argument as Entering an Ongoing Conversation

In addition to using argument as a tool for creating new knowledge, scholars view argument as an ongoing conversation; they engage in research to discover what is already known about an issue and who is already in conversation on the issue. Since the goal of scholarly argument is to advance what we know, one reason scholars engage in research is to avoid repeating what has already been presented. They also develop their own *ethos* by demonstrating familiarity with other scholars and their texts.

To present your own argument as a contribution to the existing conversation, it is important to make use of the work of others, to consider their expertise and the currency of their work. Considering relevant information about the rhetorical context for their arguments, like the places and dates of publication, further reinforces the value of their contribution to the ongoing conversation and your own right to join in.

In *The Philosophy of Literary Form* (1974), twentieth-century rhetorical scholar and cultural critic Kenneth Burke explains the connection between argument and conversation using the relatable experience of entering into a conversation at a party:

You come late. When you arrive, others have long preceded you, and they are engaged in a heated discussion, a discussion too heated for them to pause and tell you exactly what it is about...You listen for awhile, until you decide that you have caught the tenor of the argument; then you put in your oar. Someone answers; you answer him; another comes to your defense; another aligns himself against you....
The hour grows late, you must depart. And you do depart, with the discussion still vigorously in progress.

COMPOSITION COURSE CURRICULA

While courses are shaped by the instructors' unique approaches to teaching writing, each section still tends to follow a parallel curriculum, ensuring that every class meets the same learning objectives (which you can find in the Appendices). Nearly all first-year writing classes share common goals: close reading of texts and clear and effective communication through writing.

"Writing and Rhetoric" and "Writing and Rhetoric for Multilingual Students" focus heavily on developing an effective writing process. Through various assignments, you will learn to:

- Brainstorm, draft, and revise essays with different rhetorical purposes. For example, instructors might assign their students a personal narrative, a profile, an analysis essay, and an argument;
- Become more aware of the rhetorical effect your work may have on an audience;

- Develop fluency with the rhetorical appeals (*ethos*, *pathos*, and *logos*);
- Enhance your ability to develop your essays through observation, interviews, and research;
- Think rhetorically about organization, style, voice, development, analysis, and cohesion;
- Arrange your essays to flow with logical and effective transitions;
- Vary sentences with effective punctuation—especially with semicolons, colons, and dashes; and
- Avoid faulty grammar.

The papers you write may not be exactly the same as the assignments described below; however, you likely will be writing papers that are comparable in purpose and approach to those presented in this collection.

The Writing Sequences

Exploring Significant Moments

This narrative essay is often written during the first week or two of class. In many of these essays, students reflect on their experiences as writers, drawing attention to the importance of developing a writing process, the challenges of writing, and the sense of accomplishment they experience after recognizing their development as writers. Other essays will explore a significant moment or experience in the writer's life that helped shape him/her.

Please note that these essays go beyond just telling a story: they each have a discernible focus and purpose. On the one hand, you may find yourself nodding in agreement as you read these essays because you may have had similar experiences in your own life. On the other hand, you may be unable to directly relate to a writer's narrative. As a reader, your role is to find ways to connect with these writers' experiences. As you read, use these points of similarity and difference to help you revisit moments in your life. Moreover, consider how these essays can affect how you write about your own experiences.

Profiling a Person, Place, Event, or Trend

In the profile essays included in this volume of *Fresh Voices*, students carved out distinctive approaches to the assignment—approaches that permitted them to explore exceptional elements found in cultures, places, and people surrounding them. Topics for the profile sequence vary by instructor: some instructors select a theme, such as the environment or media; other instructors ask students to use this assignment to become better acquainted with an aspect of someone's life, a well-loved place, or even a social trend. For many instructors, conducting an effective interview—and learning how to accurately represent someone else's point of view—is an essential component of this essay.

You will find that this assignment challenges you to synthesize multiple texts and viewpoints: your analytic response to your interviewee's work, the interview itself, and, when appropriate, your own experiences and responses. If you choose to profile a place or a trend, you will also learn to incorporate field notes and other outside sources. In addition, you must account for and write to an audience that does not have knowledge of your essay's subject matter. In other words, you need to present your own "insider's perspective" about the profile subject. But remember that regardless of who or what you profile, this essay is created and shaped by you. In other words, your profile subject needs to speak *with* you as a writer, not *for* you.

Analyzing Rhetorically

Learning how to rhetorically analyze a text is one of the most important skills you will learn in this course. Whether you are studying an advertisement or a speech, identifying the strategies used to persuade an audience helps you better understand how an argument is conveyed.

In particular, your class will make a distinction between two concepts:

Summary ➡ **What** a text says

Analysis ➡ **How** a text conveys its message

Breaking a text down to its individual parts helps you better understand how the text makes meaning for its readers. Depending on the kind of text you analyze, you will be looking for different elements.

While analytic papers can be composed individually, analysis is also part of every writing sequence. For example, you may have to analyze your profile subject's work, environment, and thoughts. And, when writing your public rhetoric and argumentation paper (below), you will need to carefully analyze the evidence you use to support your claims. You will find a more in-depth discussion of analysis below.

Engaging in Public Rhetoric and Argumentation

For this sequence, students choose a public issue and write a persuasive essay supporting their viewpoint on it. The persuasive essays in this collection cover a broad range of subjects, yet you will see one common feature: the authors have a personal stake in their chosen topics.

In writing your own public rhetoric essay, you will learn that a well-written and fully supported argument requires you to conduct research both to support your own claims and to fairly depict opposing viewpoints. You will also learn to use the rhetorical appeals of *ethos*, *pathos*, and *logos* (defined in the following pages) to persuade and connect with your chosen audience. Regardless of the topic you choose, it's generally best to select a focus that matters to *you*, something you want to understand better and learn more about. Try not to approach your topic with a firmly held point-of-view; proving what you already *think* you know isn't the goal of this essay. Indeed, it's important to understand the distinction between an opinion and an argument. Rather, as you conduct research and learn about your topic, your stance towards the topic may shift. Rhetorical inquiry and engagement require this kind of flexibility.

Final Project

Each section of English 133/134 completes the course with different final projects. For instance, some classes conclude with presentations, others use portfolios, and some classes require unique projects like 'zines or a letter written to someone who can effect change in the world.

Regardless of the final project you are assigned, you will be expected to draw from everything you have been taught throughout the quarter. This assignment can be regarded as the capstone to the course in that it offers you an opportunity to demonstrate all that you have learned.

English 145 Curriculum

English 145: Reasoning, Argumentation, and Writing draws on the skills you developed and refined in English 133/134 and moves into a more nuanced understanding of reasoning and argumentation. In English 145, you will learn to

- Understand inductive and deductive reasoning;
- Recognize logical fallacies and avoid them in your own essays;
- Make claims that are supported with relevant evidence;
- Think critically about the texts studied in class and about your own arguments;
- Examine your own assumptions and biases when developing an argument;
- Construct your own cogent arguments;
- Conduct more in-depth research; and
- Develop more complex forms of refutation.

> After successfully navigating both English 134 and English 145, one student suggested:
>
> *"The main difference between English 134 and 145 is that English 134 is very focused on writing while English 145 is more focused on critical thinking and how to analyze arguments. Expectations for the student's level of writing and critical thinking were definitely higher in English 145."*

Looking Ahead

Picture this: you're a year or two out of college and you've got a decent entry-level job working at a company you like. You've learned and demonstrated an ability to execute the essential functions of your job, and in a general way, you're satisfied. And yet, you sense that you can do more for the company, offer more. You're ready to move up, both in terms of responsibilities and pay.

Soon enough, your boss invites you to a meeting, one that's generally attended by employees higher up on the corporate ladder than yourself. In the meeting, people are discussing a project with which you're familiar; perhaps your entire division has been working on it in some form or another. Being a part of the meeting feels good to you. The coffee is amazing, the leather on the chairs is downright supple. And the people in the room are *smart*; they don't all agree with one another, but they make solid points and explain those points in detail. They go back and forth sharing different ideas and perspectives. The whole experience is darn near intoxicating. You think to yourself, "I could get used to this," and then your boss turns to you and asks, "What do *you* think?"

- *Why* do you think what you think?
- *What* informs your positions, claims, opinions?
- *Where* do you find information?
- *How* did you arrive at your conclusions?

Every head in the room turns and looks at you as if to say, "Yeah, what *do* you think?"

English 145 is designed to help prepare you for this kind of moment. The course curriculum moves you beyond a conception of argument as a kind of paper that you write *toward* an understanding of the principles related to engaging in ongoing, high-level conversations. In addition, English 145 is designed to help you succeed in the instances that follow the "what do you think?" moment, when people inevitably challenge your perspective or ask to know more. Ultimately, what you think—your perceptions, your beliefs, your opinions, and your perspectives—is up to you. If you approach English 145 seriously, the course will help you determine those ideas, consider them, and share them effectively with others.

KEY CONCEPTS

The concepts discussed below are covered at different points in the writing courses you will take.

Rhetoric

In its most basic terms, rhetoric generally refers to written, verbal, and visual persuasion and communication. While you may have studied rhetoric in your high school English class, you will approach this concept through many different angles in your college composition classes.

According to Aristotle, rhetoric is the "ability to observe, in any given case, the available means of persuasion." In short, rhetoric refers to your ability to make effective choices when speaking and writing. Yet the word "observe" here is also key: it refers to your ability to look at how rhetoric is used on you, even when you are not consciously aware of it. With this definition in mind, you will study how rhetoricians—including you—persuade people to consider their point of view.

In her book, *Still Life with Rhetoric: A New Materialist Approach for Visual Rhetorics* (2015), rhetoric and writing scholar Laurie Gries suggests that something becomes rhetorical when it has the "ability to induce change in thought, feeling, and action; organize and maintain collective formation; exert power, etc…. all things have the potential to become rhetorical as they crystallize, circulate, enter into relations, and generate material consequences." When you study rhetoric, you are looking at the real-world implications of the words people use, the choices they make, and the positions they hold.

Consider rhetoric this way: Every time you sit down to write, you must account for the ways in which you want your audience to respond to your text. What means are available to you as you seek to persuade people to change their position on an issue? If you lose track of the rhetorical situation and forget to consider how to best to communicate with and persuade your reader, your essay may not affect your readers the way you intend. In effect, every act of writing becomes an act of persuasion.

The Rhetorical Appeals

Throughout your courses, you will encounter three rhetorical concepts that may be new to you: *ethos*, *pathos*, and *logos*. We have borrowed these terms from Aristotle, who long ago argued that every writer who wants to communicate effectively with his or her audience must account for these appeals.

Ethos: Credibility

When we use the term *ethos*, we are referring to a writer's or a text's credibility, reliability, and trustworthiness. After all, audiences are most persuaded by writers who have the knowledge to write intelligently about a given subject and who presents information accurately and fully. In other words, writers must develop a strong *ethos* in order to develop a rhetorical relationship with their audience. Conversely, audiences tend not to trust writers who leave out relevant information or who don't work with reliable sources.

For instance, if a writer continually relies on web pages with no clear authors or publication dates, the argument may not be convincing (see the section on "Identifying Effective Sources"). However, if a writer uses sources that have a track record of presenting information without a great deal of bias and that promote writers who conduct trustworthy research, the writer's *ethos* increases, and the audience is more likely to be persuaded.

Ethos can also be developed when writers simply share a relevant personal experience that has given them insider knowledge. For example, if you want to write an essay about water politics in California and your family owns a farm that struggles to obtain an adequate amount of water, it would make sense to share that information in your essay in order to build credibility as a writer. There are many ways to develop your *ethos,* some of them quite subtle. You will study these approaches in your course.

Pathos: Emotion

Readers are most invested in and persuaded by ideas to which they have a deep emotional connection, and when writers appeal to their readers' emotions, writers are deploying *pathos*. Even Aristotle, who believed rhetoric shouldn't rely on manipulating readers' emotions in order to persuade them, conceded that a rhetorician will only be effective if they can garner an emotional reaction from the audience. Effective rhetorical moments, then, touch readers on a deeper, expressive level. When considering your essay's use of *pathos,* you must decide *how* you want your readers to feel. Moreover, how do you persuade a reader to feel as intensely about a subject as you do?

To ensure that readers share your emotions when reading your work, you must first attempt to predict the elements that will encourage your readers to engage with your writing on an empathic or sympathetic level. When writing, you must account for the beliefs, values, and other personal attributes that may trigger an emotional response in your audience. Do you want your readers to feel anger? Frustration? Sadness? Joy? Do you want them to feel motivated to go out into the world and make changes? When deciding which words best convey your ideas, don't forget the emotional impact of language.

As a reader, you must also develop a critical awareness that enables you to determine if an argument overuses *pathos*. In other words, if an argument relies on your emotive response to persuade you and forgoes any other means of persuasion, you should be suspicious of it. The key here is balance. There is a fine line between persuasion and manipulation, but it's a distinction that every skilled rhetorician must make.

Logos: Reason

Though a piece of writing must make some use of *pathos*, emotions must still be balanced with logic and reasoning. *Logos* refers to the *entire structure* of an argument. Does the argument overall make rational sense? Have you selected the kinds of sources that will encourage your reader to be persuaded by the logic of the argument?

Look for smaller ways to build a logical argument, too. For instance, using language like, "everyone knows…" or "in today's society" automatically forces the reader to question your logic. After all, is there anything that "everyone knows"? Can you really account for everyone? Who or what does "today's society" really refer to? As you conduct research and structure your essays, keep in mind that audiences like to see information presented rationally, logically, and carefully. Sweeping generalizations about people, culture, and issues will probably not persuade people, in large part because generalizations are not steeped in careful logic.

Deploying the Rhetorical Appeals

You will learn that every effective essay has *ethos, pathos,* and *logos* coursing through it, and the most effective arguments also account for *kairos*. *Kairos*, translated from Greek, means the right or opportune moment.

Kairos: The Right or Opportune Moment

When you make an argument can be as important as *how* you make it. When considering *kairos*, you must consider the current cultural and social context surrounding your argument. Indeed, effective rhetoricians learn to take advantage of the circumstances surrounding their audience, giving their argument a sense of immediacy. For instance, if you wanted to develop an argument that focused on bringing high-speed rail to California, it would be important to research what is happening with that issue *right now*. How can you use this moment in time to advance a position on a particular topic?

Look at it this way: if you are writing an argument about a highly technical subject, you may find yourself relying on *logos* more than *pathos*. Yet, even texts about technical subjects require writers to invite people to care about them.

For instance, in an essay about the treatment of orcas at SeaWorld, you may incorporate evidence that approaches the topic logically by citing scientific studies of orca whales' behavior in the wild (*logos*), evidence that frustrates your reader by offering an account of the small spaces in which the mammals are held (*pathos*), and evidence from a trustworthy, independent source on the subject, which heightens your credibility (*ethos*). Finally, if you had made such an argument soon after SeaWorld Orlando's orca, Kayla, died suddenly in January 2019, you would have been responding to a strong *kairotic* moment for bringing public attention to the issues surrounding her captivity.

The Rhetorical Situation

You will be able to use the appeals more effectively if you keep in mind the entire rhetorical situation, which can often be represented by **Aristotle's rhetorical triangle:**

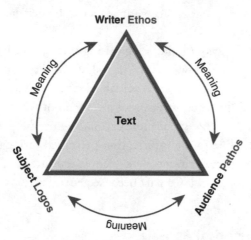

Kairos surrounds the entire argument

As you can see, the arrows here represent meaning. In other words, the rhetorical triangle tells us that a writer must account for the ways in which meaning moves simultaneously between the three points—the writer, the subject, and the audience. Note that each arrow moves in two directions, indicating that meaning also moves in multiple directions (not just one direction).

In other words, the audience you are writing for should influence how you present the subject, and both of those elements should influence your *ethos*. As you write, let these relationships shape your texts. After all, if you forget about your audience as you write and only focus on your subject and your *ethos*, your meaning will not be communicated in the way you intend.

Summary, Analysis, Synthesis, and Evaluation

Summary reproduces a text's original meaning without generating new or original thinking. For example, one could write a summary of the film *Spider-Man: Homecoming* and include brief descriptions of its key elements, such as plot, themes, and main characters. The important thing to remember about summary is that it does not include evaluation of how those elements work together. Summary is intended to be informative rather than analytical.

The purpose of engaging in *analysis* is to discover as much as possible about the nature, structure, and function of a thing—a text, an object, a speech, a film, etc. During the analytic process, we isolate a thing's constituent components and discover patterns and relationships among them. For example, we can analyze the film *Spider-Man: Homecoming* by breaking it into components such as lighting, digital effects, musical score, and so on. Fundamentally, analysis is about how the parts of the whole interact; it always attempts to respond to the question, "How does it work?"

In contrast, the word *synthesis* refers to concepts like combining, putting together, and composing. In its very nature, synthesis is the opposite of analysis. Instead of breaking things apart, synthesis considers the results of multiple analyses in relationship to each other, combining their elements to create new knowledge. To extend the example of the film analysis, we can synthesize the results of our *Spider-Man: Homecoming* analysis by weaving them together with an analysis of *Guardians of the Galaxy Volume 2* to generate a new understanding of the aesthetics of the Marvel Cinematic Universe.

> **Summary:** restate or reproduce a text's original meaning without changing it.
>
> **Analysis:** break a text apart into its constituent parts to understand how the parts function and create the text's meaning.
>
> **Synthesis:** weave together materials produced by the analytical process to create new knowledge.
>
> **Evaluation:** consider the implications, consequences, meaning, or significance that stem from analysis and synthesis.

Evaluation is the final step in a critical thinking sequence. It draws conclusions about meaning or significance of the analysis and/or synthesis process. When a critical thinker evaluates something—especially the results of analysis or the findings of an experiment—the thinker considers the results or findings in terms of the question, "Why does this matter?" One might phrase that question in a variety of ways, but evaluation always moves toward articulating meaning: "What is the value of this result?" or "What is the significance of these findings?"

Making Effective Rhetorical and Stylistic Choices

Too often, we think about writing only in terms of correctness. We become consumed with what's right and what's wrong, and we risk forgetting that, as writers, we have control over our own writing choices. While there will certainly be an emphasis on grammar and mechanics in your composition courses, you may be asked to think about these concepts through a stylistic lens.

Style can be regarded as a rhetorical concept that is less about error and more about the choices you make as a writer. Of course, you should understand the grammar conventions, but you also can make stylistic choices that push against the conventions. Whatever stylistic choices you make, you need to account for how those choices affect the text and the reader (consult the rhetorical triangle). For instance, we know that a fragment is not a complete sentence and that we generally need to write with complete sentences. But what if, for once, you don't want a complete sentence. Just a fragment. Is that okay?

What if you want a one-sentence paragraph?

Or what if you want to use "I"? Or you directly want to address the reader with "you"? Maybe you want to stop relying on commas and periods and instead want to try semicolons, colons, and dashes. The more stylistic variability you bring to your writing, the stronger it will be.

As you develop your writing style, work to make conscious, deliberate choices. Style is something at which writers work; it's not innate. If a reader asks why you used a fragment, you need to be able to explain what effect you wanted that fragment to have. Perhaps you wanted to create a kind of rhythm in your text.

As you continue your development as a writer, you undoubtedly will make good choices, and you will make some that are a little shaky—but that's okay. Style takes practice, and perhaps even more importantly, it requires you to take some risks with your writing. Sometimes the safest choice isn't the best one.

Accounting for Your Audience

In order to develop the most effective arguments, writers must have an informed understanding of their audience. For instance, your audience could be a specific person, such as a government official, a family member, or a community leader. Or, you may be seeking to persuade a group of people, such as a business, a political organization, or a group of consumers. It's important to identify whom you are seeking to address when making rhetorical choices. After you have settled on a topic (though not necessarily a position) begin analyzing your audience.

Consider the following questions:

- Who are the stakeholders of this issue? What is at stake for them?
- How might your argument impact your readers' lives or interests?
- What is important to readers? What are they passionate about, and what values do they hold?
- What motivates your readers? How can you motivate them to take an interest in your position?
- What role do the readers play in your life, if any? What roles do they play in society in general? Are they in a position to effect change?
- What specific problems can you solve for them? Or do you want to present them with new ways to think about a problem?
- How can your audience distinguish your position from the positions of others who write about the issue?
- What makes this an opportune moment (*kairos*) for addressing your audience on this issue? Why does your argument matter *now*?

Speaking to and about Readers

In the past, the pronoun "he" was often used to refer to all readers, regardless of their gender. Yet at this point in time, if a writer uses "he" to refer to everyone in an audience, some readers likely will feel excluded.

LOOK HERE:

In March 2017, the Associated Press included *they, them,* and *their* as singular, gender-neutral pronouns to their stylebook.

Language is a living organism: it's constantly growing and changing as we find new ways to communicate with each other. Because the English language does not have a gender-neutral singular pronoun, the language is slowly adapting to account for new ways to use pronouns. In January 2016, the American Dialect Society chose the pronoun *they* "as a gender-neutral singular pronoun" for the 2015 Word of the Year. The society settled on this specific definition:

> **they:** gender-neutral singular pronoun for a known person, used as a non-binary identifier

Readers tend to regard *they* as a plural pronoun, and in some contexts, it is plural, but writers increasingly use *they* to refer to a singular person. You will see *they* used as a gender-neutral pronoun in this very book. In effect, you need to think carefully about using inclusive language, such as gender-neutral pronouns, in your writing.

Using *they* in a singular sense is often a conscious choice a writer can make, one that rejects standard gender binaries. If you make this choice in your writing, consider using a footnote or endnote to alert your readers of this decision so they fully understand your intentions. You may also want to discuss this choice with your instructor.

Conducting an Interview

The key to conducting a good interview is to craft questions that enable you to capture your interviewee's candor and insights as fully as possible. As the interviewer, *you* are not the focus of the interview; rather, think of the interview in terms of collaboration and discussion. Try to meet with your subject in a setting that can reveal something about her profession, pastimes, or beliefs. You can set the tone for the interview by asking important questions when your subject

is laughing, smiling genuinely, and just seems relaxed—moments when she is comfortable discussing tricky subjects. While uncompromising and unflinching questions can make for a dramatic essay, you still have a responsibility to approach your interviewee respectfully. Ideally, after the interview begins, step back and let your subject take hold of the interview by offering thoughtful responses to your carefully crafted questions.

While you can conduct an interview via phone or IM, it's always best to talk face-to-face. So, if you are interviewing someone who is not in close proximity, try a video conferencing service, like "Skype" or "Google Hangout" so you can track your interviewee's facial expressions and mannerisms.

Writing Interview Questions

Learning to ask carefully crafted, thoughtful questions is a life skill that will benefit you in your classes, in job interviews, and in conversations with interesting people. It's also important to learn how to do primary research, so you don't always rely on outside texts to understand an issue. As you develop interview questions for any research project, keep in mind your own credibility (*ethos*) as an interviewer. How can you:

- Present yourself professionally?
- Appear confident and relaxed?
- Establish trust with your subject?
- Learn from your interview subject?

LOOK HERE:

The "Blank on Blank" series offers animated interviews with actors, musicians, writers, and other memorable public figures. Watch a few and pick up some more tips!

Writing questions for an interview can be tricky. Knowing which questions to ask and how to ask them makes all the difference. The following are five simple tips to help you write interview questions.

1. *Avoid asking "double-barreled questions."*
   Keep your questions very clear. For example, the question, "Do you think he is telling the truth and that he deserves to be set free?" contains two questions. The respondent will most likely just answer one of them, and you may not get the information you want. Try to separate your questions.

2. *Refrain from asking biased or leading questions.*
   Avoid asking questions that are slanted towards one opinion or viewpoint. A good interview question is neutral and allows the respondent to offer his or her own response to an issue. Your questions should not influence the respondent's opinion.

3. *Avoid questions that assume a specific response.*

   Some questions subtly assign opinions to the interviewees. Note this question, which is preceded by a statement: "A lot of people are angered by this crime. Are you one of them?" This question seems to assume that the interviewee should be angry. But what if she isn't? You can move the discussion forward by simply asking, "Do you believe a crime took place?"

4. *Keep your questions short and clear.*

   Sometimes brevity is most effective. Long, detailed questions may confuse your subject, and you may not get a detailed response in return. Write questions that are short and concise. The stylistic choices you make are essential; the slightest grammatical or punctuation mistake can change a question's meaning.

5. *Ask questions beginning with WHY, HOW, WHAT, and WHEN.*

   Your interview may not reveal much information if you rely on questions that elicit "yes" or "no" as a response. Instead, create open-ended questions to which you don't know the answer. Give your subject space to think carefully and thoughtfully about a question and be prepared to go off-script and ask follow-up questions if you want to know more about your subject's responses.

LOOK HERE:

Some advice from a pro...

In his recently published *New Yorker* article, John McPhee discusses his experiences interviewing people during a fifty-year career as a journalist. He advises:

> If I am in someone's presence and attempting to conduct an interview, I am wishing I were with Kafka on the ceiling. I'd much rather watch people do what they do than talk to them across a desk. I've spent hundreds of hours in the passenger seats of their pickups, often far from pavement, bouncing from scribble to scribble. Under a backpack, and hiking behind environmentalist David Brower, I walked across the North Cascades, up and down the switchbacks, writing in a notebook....
>
> Whatever you do, don't rely on memory. Don't even imagine that you will be able to remember everything verbatim in the evening what people said during the day... From the start, make clear what you are doing and who will publish what you write. Display your notebook as if it were a fishing license. While the interview continues, the notebook may serve other purposes, surpassing the talents of a tape recorder. As you scribble away, the interviewee is, of course, watching you. Now, unaccountably, you slow down, and even stop writing, while the interviewee goes on talking. The interviewee becomes nervous, tries harder, spills out the secrets of a secret life, or maybe just a clearer and more quotable version of what was said before. (50)

Work Cited

McPhee, John. "Elicitation." *The New Yorker*, 7 Apr. 2014, pp. 50–57. You can find McPhee's entire article here.

Approaches to Argumentation

Aristotelian Argument

This style of argument is associated with the Greek philosopher and rhetorician Aristotle (384–322 AD). This approach to argumentation—and specifically the refutation—could be characterized as adversarial; a rhetor using Aristotelian argument sees the interlocutor as an opponent and seeks to "win" the argument. This rhetor sees the opposition as wrong and may mock or belittle the opponent's arguments in order to emerge as the victor.

Rogerian Argument

This approach is based on the writings of Carl Rogers (1902–1987), a psychotherapist who applied his findings on interpersonal communication to communication between individuals—and even nations—in conflict. Rogerian Argument, in contrast to Aristotelian Argument, is less confrontational and more compassionate; this rhetor tries to understand and empathize with the opposition, often making concessions rather than attempting to persuade utterly. A person practicing Rogerian Argument shows respect for the interlocutor, seeing them, despite the disagreement, as a person of good will.

Toulmin Argument

Stephen Toulmin's (1922–2009) approach to argumentation breaks a text/argument into six parts: claim, warrants, evidence, qualifiers, rebuttal, and backing. As Toulmin sees it, an argument is effective when the audience shares assumptions and values about the topic; a rhetor, therefore, incorporates warrant(s) to connect the claim and the data to the audience. Also key to Toulmin's approach to argumentation is the inclusion of both qualifiers and rebuttals, which enable reasoning to account for complexities of rhetorical situations. Because this method breaks an argument into six parts, it is particularly helpful for analysis.

Inductive and Deductive Reasoning

The two forms of reasoning you will encounter in ENGL 145 are inductive and deductive.

Inductive Reasoning

Inductive Reasoning is a form of reasoning in which one makes a generalization based upon one or more examples. Prediction, analogies (associations), statistics, causal inferences, and arguments from authority or tradition (precedent) are examples of the generalizing nature of inductive reasoning. Inductive reasoning weighs the *probability* that its conclusions follow from its premises. It is important to understand, however, that inductive reasoning attempts to reach beyond the examples or premises on which it is based.

Because inductive reasoning's very nature is to reach further than the examples or premises upon which it is based, we never say of inductive reasoning that it is true; we only say that it is strong or weak, sound or unsound—an assessment depending on premises that are factual, verifiable, comprehensive, or representative.

- An **inductive argument** is strong if the premises are accepted to be true; it is improbable that the conclusion be false if the premises are true.
- A **weak inductive argument** does not follow probably from the premises, OR the conclusion is true regardless of whether the premises are true or false.
- A **sound inductive argument** is both strong and has true premises; additionally, the premises in a cogent argument must not only be true, but the premises include important aspects, conditions, or examples in order to reach the stated conclusion.
- An **unsound inductive argument** is weak, has one or more false premises, or both. An unsound argument ignores some crucial aspect, condition, or example in order to reach its conclusion. Thus, an unsound argument may be weak or strong, but it may overlook something essential.

Inductive arguments may be strengthened or weakened by the inclusion of a larger sample or additional examples within the premises, which is why we think of them as concerning mere *probability*.

Deductive Reasoning

Whereas the nature of inductive reasoning concerns whether the conclusions *probably follow* from the premises, deductive reasoning concerns whether the conclusions *necessarily follow* from the premises. Mathematical arguments (as distinct from statistical arguments), geometrical arguments, definitional arguments, and syllogisms are examples of types of deductive arguments.

Because the conclusions must necessarily follow from the premises, instead of saying these arguments are *strong* or *weak*, as one might about a *probabilistic* reasoning situation, deductive reasoning is assessed using the terms *valid* or *invalid*.

- In an **invalid** deductive argument, it is possible for the conclusion to be false, even if the premises are true.
- In a **valid** deductive argument, it is impossible for the conclusion to be false given that the premises are true.

You might be surprised to hear that an argument can have true premises and a true conclusion but still be invalid. This situation occurs when the terms of the argument shift among premises or commit other structural errors that offend the integrity, consistency, and cohesiveness of the argument.

Identifying and Avoiding Logical Fallacies

You will primarily study logical fallacies in English 145. If a persuasive text relies on a fallacy to persuade an audience, that logic itself needs to be questioned and examined. Often fallacies attempt to redirect an audience's attention away from poor reasoning. As a writer, you will need to learn to identify fallacies in the texts you read, and you will need to develop arguments that are not inadvertently supported by fallacies.

Some logical fallacies can be directly tied to the rhetorical appeals. Below you will find some fallacies that can affect the use of *ethos*, *pathos*, and *logos*. You will likely study these fallacies and many more in your class.

Logical Fallacies

Logical fallacies occur when the relationship between your claim and your reason(s) is logically unsound.

Non Sequitur

This Latin phrase translates roughly as "does not follow." Basically, all informal fallacies are a form of non sequitur. The term is useful for identifying a complete gap between the claim made in an argument and the reasons/evidence offered. If another type of fallacy more accurately identifies the nature of the gap, then use that fallacy for pinpointing the problem in the reasoning. If you do not see any relationship between the claim and the reasons/evidence—which can occur when irrelevant reasons are offered or when the connection between the reasons and the claim is not clear—then identifying the fallacy as a non sequitur is useful.

Hasty Generalization

This is a broad generalization based on too little evidence. Generalizing is a common error in inductive reasoning—moving too quickly from a limited sample (experience, data set) to a generalization. Stereotypes are a form of hasty generalization. However, not every faulty inductive generalization is a hasty generalization. If a data set is large and collected over time, but it is not relevant or representative, the generalization will not follow from the sample, but it is not a hasty generalization. It will be a different type of fallacy.

Post Hoc

The Latin phrase *post hoc ergo propter hoc* means "after this, therefore because of this." A *post hoc* fallacy occurs when a sequential relationship is presented as a causal relationship without any other reason to support the causal connection. For instance, claiming that eating at In-N-Out made someone sick because they were throwing up and running a high fever two hours after they ate there is a post hoc fallacy. The person could have already been coming down with the flu.

Begging the Question/Circular Reasoning

Begging the question is the fallacy of making a claim in which the reasons offered simply restate the claim in slightly different language. When a claim is arguing by definition and the reason involves a synonym, the reasoning is circular. Sound reasoning has something more than the claim itself as its support. For instance, if someone claimed, "Capital punishment is murder because it is the intentional taking of a human life," the definition of murder is the reason offered. In other words, the claim basically says, "Capital punishment is murder because it is murder."

False Dilemma (either/or fallacy)

Binary thinking is very common in debate structures. When one argues that only two options are possible—implicitly or explicitly presenting them as mutually exclusive—they are usually committing the false dilemma fallacy. Rarely are issues and situations so simple that we must choose only one option. We often need to look at the murkier, messier parts of an argument to truly understand it.

Slippery Slope

This fallacy involves projecting an inevitable causal chain that will lead to catastrophic effects. The fallacy occurs in assuming that it is not possible to intervene in the chain, preventing the slide into disaster. Note that this fallacy involves a negative slide; it is the doomsday fallacy, not the promise-of-utopia fallacy!

False Analogy

Sometimes a comparison between to events, positions, experiences, etc., is presented as the reason to accept a position or viewpoint. Yet, if the two things being compared differ in some clear and defining ways, then the analogy is false. Analogies by nature are not perfect, but they do need to identify relevant relationships when they are used to persuade. When making an analogy, we need to be careful not to gloss over glaring differences in order to make the analogy work.

Loaded Label/Definition

This fallacy uses a label or definition to influence a reader's view through connotation. Loaded labels can tap into the reader's ideologies/biases/prejudices/assumptions. They can be either negative—calling an estate tax a "death tax"—or positive—calling a food item "all natural." Loaded labels can also be used to change the meaning of an activity depending on who is doing the activity. For example, on not changing one's mind—you are stubborn; but I am firm—being called "stubborn" has a much more negative connotation than being called firm.

Equivocation

A speaker or writer can implicitly shift the meaning of a word or phrase within an argument so that the conclusion depends on a different meaning of the word than what was used in the premises. This fallacy exploits the ambiguity in words to mislead the audience.

Ethical Fallacies

Ethical fallacies occur when an argument targets the person making the argument rather than the reasoning of the argument. Such an approach attempts to draw attention away from the actual reasoning of the argument. This move can damage the credibility of someone with an opposing argument and ends up damaging one's own credibility. Particular ethical fallacies are as follows.

Appeal to False Authority

Any appeal to authority in which the person's expertise/credentials are not directly relevant to the topic/claim. The most common form of this appeal is found in advertising when celebrities are used to endorse a product or issue about which they do not have expertise. However, we also find this fallacy when someone references an authority without establishing the actual expertise of that person or group. For example, if someone wanted to argue for the environmental benefits of electric cars based on the views of Jane Doe, who has a Ph.D. and drives a Prius, it could be an appeal to false authority if Jane Doe's Ph.D. is in early childhood development, not environmental studies. If a celebrity has first-hand experience with a product, false authority is not at play.

Ad Hominem ("to the man")

Attacking the person rather than an argument—or directing the argument against someone's character rather than against their reasoning—attempts to redirect an audience's focus away from an argument's weaknesses. If the person's character (*ethos*) is the issue, or if it is a relevant issue, then addressing aspects of character is not a fallacy.

Poisoning the Well

Discredits an opposing view or argument in advance, such as in introduction of the opposing person. For instance, if we introduced (a hypothetical) Senator Smith by highlighting the ways her slash-and-burn economic policies have consistently reduced aid to the poorest in our nation, we would be influencing how the audience saw this person before she even uttered a word.

Straw Man

Oversimplifying an opponent's position to make it easier to refute, counter, or discredit. This is not a legitimate way to develop an argument. Any presentation of an opponent's reasoning that is not accurate, fair, and complete constitutes a straw man fallacy. Taking quotes out of context is also a straw man fallacy.

Pathetic Fallacies

Pathetic fallacies involve appealing to the emotions of your audience rather than their reasoning. *Pathos* is an important element in a well-developed persuasive argument, but it needs to support, rather than displace, *logos*.

Appeal to Pity

Substituting emotion for more relevant or objective grounds as a primary reason for accepting a claim or adopting a course of action should be avoided.

Appeal to the People (ad populum)/Appeal to Stirring Symbols

Appeals to the fundamental beliefs, biases, and prejudices of the audience. Doing so asks them to rely on the feeling of and desire for solidarity with a specific group to function as support for a claim, rather than reasons and evidence. This fallacy is often found in visual rhetoric, advertising, and political speeches. Moreover, this fallacy is not limited to patriotism and "flag waving"; it is common in religious groups, corporate entities, regional/hometown issues, and school competitions.

Appeal to Tradition

A variant of the ad populum fallacy, appeals to tradition assert as a reason for continuing to do something the fact that it has always been done that way. This fallacy assumes that the ways of the past—of the preceding generations—are better, if not completely correct.

Bandwagon Fallacy (appeal to popularity—not ad populum)

An assertion that the sheer number of people doing something is a sound reason for accepting a position or course of action.

Appeal to Ignorance

The absence of definitive proof should not be regarded as a reason for accepting or rejecting a claim. For example, asserting that the absence of definitive proof against the existence of UFOs is not a reason for accepting the assertion of their existence. The appeal to ignorance is not the same as a legitimate call for caution. For instance, claiming that GMOs should be considered dangerous until they can be proven safe is a call for caution based on the pattern of past advances in science turning out to have unforeseen negative consequences.

Studying Writing, Rhetoric, and Argumentation at Cal Poly

Red Herring

Based on the practice of distracting hound dogs from chasing after their legitimate quarry by masking the scent of the real prey with the scent of herring (stinky, smelly fish). In argument, the distraction can take the form of either an unrelated inflammatory issue or of an irrelevant aspect of the issue that draws the audience away from the main claim.

CONSIDER THIS:

Learning to understand (vs. recognize) fallacies is a key component of becoming an effective rhetorician. Below, try to articulate what distinguishes the fallacies in each pair from each other:

1. Ad hominem vs. straw man
2. Ad hominem vs. poisoning the well
3. Appeal to ignorance vs. appeal to tradition
4. Post hoc vs. begging the question
5. Slippery slope vs. red herring
6. Appeal to false authority vs. appeal to tradition
7. Ad populum vs. appeal to false authority
8. False dilemma vs. hasty generalization
9. False dilemma vs. begging the question
10. Loaded label vs. ad hominem
11. Appeal to pity vs. red herring
12. Equivocation vs. false analogy
13. Straw man vs. loaded label
14. Bandwagon vs. ad populum
15. Red herring vs. non sequitur
16. Post hoc vs. hasty generalization
17. Post hoc vs. non sequitur
18. Non sequitur vs. hasty generalization
19. Slippery slope vs. bandwagon
20. Slippery slope vs. non sequitur

RESEARCH AND INQUIRY: IDENTIFYING EFFECTIVE SOURCES

When conducting research, your first impulse may be to turn to Google. You type in a few key words and you can pull up all kinds of source materials. But, be careful in using this approach: not all sources are created equal. It's important to become a critical reader of sources. And, while Google can be helpful, you should also become acquainted with the Kennedy Library's searchable databases.

Below you will find information that can help you identify sources with good *ethos*.

LOOK HERE:

Check out Kennedy Library's Research Guides for 82 different disciplines.

Why and How We Research

Different disciplines use different citation styles or sets of conventions that dictate how to refer to, write about, format, and list sources used in research. Engineering, biology, psychology, history, and even *The New York Times* have developed their own styles.

Differences in style are not intended to give researchers headaches; instead, they are systems that reflect the principles and priorities of the discipline or publication.

The Sciences: In the sciences, you might collect a huge data set or sample—the bigger, the better—then analyze the data, report your findings, synthesize those findings, and draw conclusions about their significance. But, the audience reading your report can only assess how you describe your process for collecting data—they seldom go out and gather a gazillion white flies in an iceberg lettuce greenhouse themselves.

When an experiment is methodically carried out and the report clearly articulates the method and results, that experiment is more likely replicable. A hallmark of scientific research is replication: if an experiment can be replicated and produce the same (or reasonably similar) results, it is regarded by the scientific community as strong and reliable. Therefore, in the sciences, one might see a citation at the end of a statement that lists studies or experiments by the last name of the primary researcher and the year it was published. Often, you'll see multiple names and years in a string, indicating that the finding referenced was validated multiple times by different researchers.

The Humanities: The humanities cares about replication, too, but those disciplines tend to show the replication differently. In the humanities, the paper or argument itself is the experiment, and the data is the collection of sources and becomes the foundation for one's thinking about a topic. Essentially, a paper in the humanities provides the readers with the context, tools, and explicit reasoning needed for the readers to track and assess the strength of the argument, its evidence, and its conclusions as they read.

In any discipline: Contrary to the practices that produce many "night-before high-school papers," collegiate and post-collegiate research takes for granted that one's thinking comes *from* one's research and analysis of sources; a true researcher doesn't go find sources that "support" the claim one already believed (or hoped) before doing any research to test that theory. That's called *confirmation bias* (or "cherry picking"), and it is bad science, bad reasoning—it's just plain sloppy. Scholarly work, whether undergraduate, graduate, or professional, seeks to add to the existing body of knowledge and perspectives, to develop a diverse and varied array of approaches to the world, and to do that, one must be rigorous in one's research methods.

So, the first thing researchers do when becoming interested or beginning to educate themselves on a topic is...research.

They cast a wide net, looking first for the basics, but then branch off into unexpected quarters, looking for various patterns, categories, anomalies, approaches, and gaps as a means of understanding their subject both broadly and deeply.

In other words, whether in the sciences or the humanities (or engineering, or architecture, or agriculture, or business fields), researchers collect data. Furthermore, the data they collect has to have a measure of variability in it: that variability—that diversity of circumstances, characteristics, qualities, or perspectives—functions analogously to the "control" in a scientific experiment. The data used in an experiment ought, as well, to be vetted to ensure its credibility. Evaluating one's data or sources is crucial to effective argumentation.

Fake News and Bias

The 2016 Presidential election saw the proliferation of online news stories that were not supported by actual facts or evidence. Social media users and news organizations began complaining about the influence that fake news was having on the election. The term "fake news" was quickly taken up by President Trump and his administration as a descriptor for news reporting that he felt was unfairly biased against his campaign and his administration, even if that reporting was a factually accurate report done by a reputable news organization, such as *The New York Times.*

The problem of evaluating the quality of online content, however, is not new to the presidential election. In late 2016, Stanford University released "Evaluating Information: The Cornerstone of Civic Online Reasoning," a report of an 18-month long study of students' abilities to evaluate the quality of online information. The report's authors note that the results of their study "shocked [them] into reality." They write, "Many assume that because young people are fluent in social media, they are equally savvy about what they find there. Our work shows the opposite" (7). They warn that "young people's ability to reason about the information on the Internet can be summed up in one word: bleak" (4). As major media outlets have moved online, they now must compete with independent "citizen journalists" and conspiracy theorist websites for an audience. This confusion over fairness, accuracy, and legitimacy in news reporting has affected the way we are experiencing and understanding major world events.

Because evaluating and using source material is an important part of the work you will do in college, you need to become adept at identifying the motives and biases behind the information you encounter in your research. This includes your ability to discern legitimate news reporting from various forms of "fake" content.

A Note about Bias

Bias is unavoidable. Rhetoric teaches us that information has a real-world usefulness and value, so people will always want to protect it, promote it, suppress it, or announce it in ways that serve their interests. Bias in a news story doesn't necessarily make a story fake. Inaccuracies in reporting are inevitable and don't necessarily make a story fake, either. Your job as a researcher and writer is to be able to identify the biases in an argument and to verify the accuracy of the information presented, giving the argument credit where it is merited and criticism where it is deserved.

In the following pages, you will find five different kinds of online content that are all demonstrably fake. These go beyond questions of bias and factual error in reporting. You have likely encountered these kinds of content already in your online use, perhaps without realizing it.

Sponsored Content

We all know an ad when we see one—logos, slogans, glossy images, and clever text that together convey an overall image or feeling to represent a company or product. However, not all advertising is so obvious. Some ads are disguised to match the form and function of the publication in which they appear, so that they don't stand out as advertising. This kind of advertising is called "sponsored content" or "native advertising" (because it looks like a natural part of the publication). The Federal Trade Commission requires that such disguised advertising be labeled in the corner or bottom of the ad with a word like "Sponsored," "Promoted," "Ad," "Suggested Post," or "Sponsored by" with the

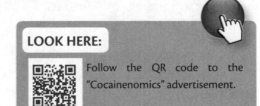

LOOK HERE:

Follow the QR code to the "Cocainenomics" advertisement.

name of the company that paid for it. You've probably seen "Promoted" tweets in your Twitter feed, or "Suggested" posts on Facebook. These are examples of native advertising on social media. Look at "Cocainenomics," a piece of native advertising appearing in the *Wall Street Journal*. It appears to be an investigative multimedia report about cocaine trafficking, but if you look closely, you'll see that it was created by Netflix to promote their exclusive series *Narcos*.

Satire

Some content is intentionally written to be fake, with the expectation that readers will be able to identify it appropriately. Often such content is humorous in tone but attempts to draw attention to real social issues in a way that encourages critical thought. The most famous historical example of literary satire is Jonathan Swift's "A Modest Proposal," published in 1729. Swift wanted to bring attention to the excesses of mercantilism as the economic relationship between Britain and Ireland at the time. Mercantilism led to severe impoverishment in Ireland while at the same time contributing to

LOOK HERE:

Interestingly, political satire tends to be biased in favor of liberal politics and against conservative politics. To know more, take a look at the article "Waiting for the Conservative Jon Stewart" published in *The Atlantic* in 2015.

LOOK HERE:

Follow the QR code to the online satirical news site, *The Onion*.

the great wealth of Britain. In his satire, Swift recommended that the poor in Ireland should just begin selling their children to the British as a way out of their poverty!

More recent examples of satire include *The Daily Show*, *The Colbert Report*, and the online newspaper *The Onion*. The danger of getting your news from such satirical sources is that they can make compelling and persuasive claims without needing to be factually accurate. Visit their websites and see whether you can identify the underlying social or political commentary implied by some of their humorous writings.

Clickbait

"8 Things You Should Never Feed to Dogs"

"This 2-Year-Old Was Left Home Alone. What He Did Next Will Leave You Speechless"

"20 Foods to Eat That Will Help You Live Longer. #17 Will Shock You!"

Since online advertising revenue is based on the amount of web traffic a website generates, "clickbait" emerged as an advertising strategy to manipulate viewers into visiting a website by using enticing but misleading headlines and images. Websites like Upworthy and BuzzFeed are well-known for generating content using clickbait methods. While clickbait content isn't necessarily fake, it is greatly distorted and exaggerated. As Jonah Berger of the University of Pennsylvania noted to *Wired* magazine in 2015, "a headline has more chance to [receive clicks] if the sentiment expressed in its text is extreme, towards the positive or the negative side." While clickbait has declined as an advertising model in recent years, a distressing trend is that these same strategies are being used by the digital outreach departments of some established news organizations. Keep in mind that if a news headline or image conjures up strong emotions or a sense of curiosity in you, it may be intentionally exaggerating or distorting its content in order to drive you to a website for the advertising revenue.

LOOK HERE:

Here are a few examples of major news outlets using clickbait strategies for writing headlines for their online stories:

 NBC: "A fifth grader who jumped to his death was upset over this, police say"

The New York Times: "Is Donald Trump a Threat to Democracy?"

 CNN: "14-year-old girl stabbed her sister 14 times, police say. The reason will shock you"

 The Atlantic: "How Trump's Speech to the CIA Endangered America"

Fake News

You may have heard Donald Trump refer to major media outlets such as *CNN, ABC, NBC, CBS, The New York Times,* and *The Washington Post* as "fake news." However, his criticisms usually center on how these media outlets are neglecting to cover certain stories, or how they are framing stories in deceptive or biased ways (see "A Note about Bias"). The editorial choices of any media outlet certainly deserve examination, analysis, and critique, but those choices do not necessarily make them fake. Fake news is something entirely different.

Fake news websites advertise themselves as legitimate news sources—often pretending to be the website for a local TV news affiliate or a local newspaper—but the news source itself does not actually exist. There's no newsroom, no pool of reporters, no access to a news wire, no editorial structure. It's just a website made to look like a real source. These sites post hoaxes and disinformation parading as actual breaking news.

On November 5, 2016, three days before the 2016 presidential election, the Denver Guardian website posted the story, "FBI Agent Suspected in Hillary Email Leaks Found Dead in Apparent Murder-Suicide." The story claimed that a federal agent who had been investigating Hillary Clinton's email server use had been found dead. The story was shared more than 500,000 times on Facebook and garnered 1.5 million views. The only problem is that it was completely fabricated (this was later confirmed by its writer and by the owner of the Denver Guardian website).

LOOK HERE:

Here are a few important resources for learning more about the problem of fake news:

 "Inside the Macedonian Fake-News Complex," *WIRED* (February 2017)

 "We Tracked Down a Fake-News Creator in the Suburbs: Here's What We Learned," NPR's *All Things Considered* (November 2016)

"PolitiFact's Guide to Fake News Websites and What They Peddle," *PolitiFact* (April 2017)

What's more, the Denver Guardian is not an actual newspaper (which is why we are not italicizing the title). If you visit the site today, it's just an empty template. If you were to visit it in November 2016, however, you would have seen a legitimate-looking front page, complete with local Denver weather and links to several real Denver resources. The website is owned by Jestin Coler, an Internet entrepreneur who lives in Los Angeles and runs several imitation news websites through his company Disinfomedia.

The fake news problem is not limited to this one company, and it is not going away anytime soon. For example, the small town of Veles in Macedonia has an entire fake news industry run largely by local teenagers. The organizers of the Deploraball, an unofficial inaugural ball held in Washington, D.C., to celebrate Donald Trump's presidential inauguration, are also Internet entrepreneurs responsible for much of the Trump campaign's social media presence. They have launched a company called Warfare Media, which is sure to continue to exploit the affordances of fake news for its clients.

Disinformation

On April 4, 2017, the Syrian government of Bashar Al-Assad launched a chemical weapons attack on its own people in the town of Khan Sheikhoun, dropping bombs that contained a sarin-like gas and killing 58 people. Almost immediately, Al-Masdar, a Syrian media outlet sympathetic to Assad and his Russian allies, published a story online claiming that reports of the attack were a hoax and that the attack never happened.

By the next day, a number of "alt-right" Twitter influencers, most notably Mike Cernovich (@Cernovich), were amplifying the Al-Masdar story online using the hashtag #syriahoax. Digital forensics labs at the Atlantic Council and the International Center for Counter-Terrorism at the Hague both confirmed that the #syriahoax hashtag was initiated by a network of Russian social media accounts, eventually making it the #1 trending hashtag on Twitter. The Atlantic Council found that a mere forty accounts were responsible for 15% of the 20,000 tweets using that hashtag over a six-hour timeframe.

This kind of concerted effort to suppress or distort the truth is a type of propaganda called disinformation. Many U.S.-affiliated conspiracy theory websites, most notably Infowars.com, have joined in the efforts to disinform. You can find a similar disinformation campaign concerning the death of Seth Rich, a DNC staffer, using the hashtag #hisnamewassethrich and another concerning an alleged government cover-up of a pedophilia ring being run out of a Washington, D.C. pizzeria using the hashtag #pizzagate. See what social media has to say using these hashtags, and then research what makes them examples of disinformation.

Reading a Works Cited Page

A list of works cited is the starting point for both assessing the nature, quality, and critical thinking implicit in other people's projects and beginning your own project. When considering your own approach to research, the Works Cited list isn't the last thing you construct. Rather, it's the first thing you assess as you engage in others' research and determine the validity and reliability of their studies, and it's the first thing you begin to compile as you begin your own project.

To go deeper into a piece you are reading, note the interesting sources the author(s) used and track them down to compare the way that you read them, in their original context, with the manner in which the published piece presented, represented, and used those sources in its own experimental context.

When you do that, you're replicating the experiment. What's more, when you undertake that approach to collecting and assessing your data, you've begun the process of building a strong, solid foundation from which to develop your own thinking about the subject. And that's what scholars do. Researchers find; scholars learn not just to find things but also to use critical thinking methods and practices *in order to think rigorously about what they find*—and, ultimately, scholars seek to figure out something new.

Studying Writing, Rhetoric, and Argumentation at Cal Poly

CONSIDER THIS:

When examining a list of sources used—your own or a list published by another researcher—try applying the following questions as a means of assessing that list's creativity, criticality, breadth, and depth:

1. Based on the list of sources, what do you infer to be each author's topic?

2. Based on the list of sources, what do you infer to be each author's position on their topic?

3. To what extent does the list of sources seem to indicate valid, credible sources given the author's topic?

4. To what extent does the list of sources seem to indicate an appropriate variety of source *types* given the author's topic?

5. What other directions or subjects could the author research to develop depth and breadth?

6. To what extent does the list of sources indicate a balanced perspective on the topic?

MLA Citation Style

In the spring of 2016, the Modern Language Association (MLA) updated the guidelines for citation entries on the Works Cited page. The biggest difference between the 7th and the 8th edition is that in the newest version, entries for all sources feature the same elements in the same order regardless of the type of source (previously the citations varied based on the type of source being cited). This "plug and play" method is meant to simplify the process of creating and reading citations.

The format of the Works Cited page remains unchanged. "Works Cited" appears at the top center of the page; the entries should be in alphabetical order based on the first element; and all entries have a hanging indent and are double spaced without any extra spaces between entries.

The following template includes an explanation for each element in a citation as well as the punctuation that should follow the element. In MLA 8, there are no longer placeholders for missing information (e.g., in MLA 7, a missing date would have been signaled by n.d.). If information is missing, elements are simply eliminated.

As you develop Works Cited pages in your composition courses, use this MLA template as a guide.

Author.

If a source has only one author, the name appears with last name first and first name second; for example, **Smith, John**. If there are two or three authors, the second and third authors' names appear first name, then last name; for example, **Smith, John, Susan Brown, and Paula Price**.

"Title of source."

If your source is found within another source, it should appear in quotation marks immediately after the author(s). Common sources that appear here include chapters, songs, essays, articles, poems, webpages, dictionary definitions, etc.

Title of container,

MLA uses the word "container" to indicate a source that contains another source; containers need to be italicized because they are major sources. Containers include books, albums of music, magazines, journals, anthologies, websites, etc.

Other contributors,

This is typically a source that has editors or translators and takes either **Translated by** and **Edited by**.

Version,

"Version" refers most commonly to the edition (e.g., **10th ed.** or **Spring edition**).

Number,

"Number" refers to sources published in a numbered sequence. The most common source with both volume (e.g., **vol. 2**) and issue (e.g., **no. 3**) numbers is a scholarly article from a database journal. For television shows, the season and episode numbers (e.g., **season 2, episode 21**) belong in this element.

Publisher,

The publisher is the entity that publishes the work. For books, it is the publishing house or press. For websites, it is often the copyright holder or whoever runs the website.

Publication date,

This is the date of publication with as much detail as provided. Dates are written with the day first followed by month then year (e.g., **28 June 2015**).

Studying Writing, Rhetoric, and Argumentation at Cal Poly

Location.

MLA uses "location" with a different meaning than it has in the past. In MLA 8, think of location as where you find the source. For print sources, the location would be the page numbers (e.g., **pp. 33–43**). For websites, it is the URL (e.g., **www.calpoly.edu**), though a web address is not strictly required. For database sources, it is the name of the database in italics (e.g., *JSTOR*) and the use of the Digital Object Identifiers (DOI) is encouraged. All digital sources, whether a website or a database source, may include an access date (e.g., **Accessed 12 Mar. 2017**), especially if the location is public or unstable.

Writing with Images

"Pictures are supposed to be worth a thousand words. But a picture unaccompanied by words may not mean anything at all. Do pictures provide evidence? And if so, evidence of what? And, of course, the underlying question: do they tell the truth? [...] A captionless photograph, stripped of all context, is virtually meaningless. I need to know more."

Errol Morris, Documentary Filmmaker
"Liar, Liar, Pants on Fire," *The New York Times*

We are bombarded by images every day. We laugh at memes shared on Instagram and Facebook, traverse realistic fantasy worlds in our video games, and sort through "gifs" and "listicles" on *Buzzfeed*.

We encounter image-based modes of communication on television, online news and gossip sites, and films *so often* that we may not even pause to ask critical questions: Who created these images and why? Whose agenda do these images serve? How should I respond?

LOOK HERE:

To read more about the relationship between captions and images, check out this Errol Morris essay at the *New York Times* site.

Analyzing visual rhetoric allows us to understand the explicit and implicit arguments that images make about culture and society. The act of examining an image isn't a passive process; images need more than a casual, quick glance to understand them. The sheer pervasiveness of images means they require critical reflection and analysis. Synthesizing images carefully and effectively into written work requires careful planning and decision-making.

Images and writing have much in common: they are intricately bound as they seek to entertain, to educate, and to persuade. After all, readers may not be persuaded by written arguments alone. When an image is effectively paired with text, the reader may get a fuller understanding of an issue. Understanding how images persuade will enable you to approach the images you encounter every day—including the images you create—with a more critical eye.

As members of a visual culture, we must learn how to navigate, interpret, and analyze the messages conveyed to us via imagery. Many writing classes ask students to study images through a rhetorical lens, which means that students explore how images make rational arguments (*logos*), how they evoke an emotional response from a viewer (*pathos*), and how (when used effectively) images can enhance a writer's or speaker's credibility (*ethos*). An image may also carry its own *kairos*.

As you engage with *Fresh Voices*, focus on the relationship between the images and the writing. How do the images enhance the written arguments? How do the visuals heighten appeals to *ethos*, *logos*, and *pathos*?

JENNY ASHLEY: *LAMPSHADE PROJECT*

Jenny Ashley is a photographer on the Central Coast. She has exhibited her work throughout the U.S. and internationally, most recently in New York, Los Angeles, Barcelona, and she has a forthcoming solo exhibition at CECUT Cultural Center in Tijuana, Mexico. The photographs on the following pages are taken from her *Lampshade Project* series, one of two photo series in which she addresses women's struggles for equality in their personal and professional lives. From Ashley's artist statement:

> Have you ever felt overlooked? Silenced? Trapped? My photography explores these struggles and offers me a way to be seen and heard. I approach each photograph as a potential movie set or cinematic stage, and I enjoy curating the design of the set, as well as the wardrobe and props, much of which seems to trap the women in a bygone era. What my "Mad Women" series and my "Lampshade Project" have in common are that the woman in each scene is somehow overlooked or limited to a very narrow gender role, like perhaps a quiet housewife or a sexy object. Even in 2019, after decades of believing women can "have it all," there are still so many societal and relational trappings that aim to keep a woman in her "place," whether that be something seemingly inconsequential like dismissing her ideas in a business meeting or something more overt like overlooking her for a company position because the current industry or office dynamic is still a man's world. My photography is a way for me to join the voices of resistance and to visually say, "nevertheless, she persisted."

You can view Jenny Ashley's work locally. Check her website, jennyashleyphotography.com, for details.

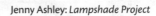

"Vacuous," *Lampshade Project*
Jenny Ashley

"House Beautiful," *Lampshade Project*
Jenny Ashley

"Blinded," *Lampshade Project*
Jenny Ashley

"Boudoir Betty," *Lampshade Project*
Jenny Ashley

CONSIDER THIS:

- Ashley describes her approach to each image as "cinematic." Where do you see Ashley using cinematic techniques to compose her shots? How might the images combine to suggest a story? What's the effect of having the feeling of a scene or a story but not having the whole story?

- Of course, the detail that most immediately strikes the viewer is that the women are wearing lampshades, preventing us from seeing their faces, yet some of the photographs are composed like portraits. How do the lampshades convey the women's own emotional experiences of these scenes? Why is the use of a lampshade significant? How would the effect of the photo be different if the women were wearing, for example, masks? (Incidentally, Ashley has another photo series titled "Masks & Monsters").

- Connect the stories and feelings of these photos to Ashley's artist statement. How do these photos represent Ashley's rhetorical stance on the role of women in society? What stylistic choices does Ashley make that help convey that stance? Can we connect the *Lampshade Project* photographs to the rhetorical concept of agency?

Writing with Images

Exploring Significant Moments

*A collection of moments, both mundane and profound,
shapes who you are and how you understand the places you inhabit.
Which moments have molded you into the person you are today?
Who and what has shaped you as a writer, a thinker, a learner?*

*In the following essays, writers explore significant moments in their
lives and reflect on how those moments helped them discover new perspectives or use language in new ways. For example, Keilana Sugano writes
about how the summer she spent in Ecuador with the Global Glimpse
leadership program helped her discover the meaning of life.
As you engage in this sequence, which relies on description and
storytelling, consider how these writers shape the thinking and telling of
significant moments in their lives and how you might do the same.*

Doña Victoria
by Keilana Sugano

How to Handshake

Michelle Waal

Reflective Memo: *I had mixed feelings about writing this first essay. Part of me loved it, because I enjoy finding the small and simple moments that have really made an impact in my life. I like thinking about these experiences and exploring what they mean to me. On the other hand, I struggled with my focus on this essay. I was not too sure if my story was truly getting my point across to the readers. Handshakes do mean a lot to me, but I had a hard time explaining why they are so significant to me in words on paper. In addition, I had a hard time finding places to use descriptive and vivid language due to the fact that my story mainly consisted of dialogue and reflection. It was very nerve-racking writing my first college essay. I'm not quite sure if my writing is developed enough yet for college-level English classes. I always did well in my high school writing classes, but the stakes seem much higher now.*

When first meeting someone, what do you normally do? Do you greet them "Hello," ask them how they are, or give them a casual, nonchalant wave? For me, a little wave and a slight, shy smile would usually suffice. Making a noticeable first impression did not seem important to me. Why would it matter if I most likely would only be meeting this person once? However, to my surprise, I learned that the first interaction you have with someone can mean a lot more than may be realized. Ever since I sat down with my Papa three years ago, he made this clear to me, and the way I greet people was forever changed.

Despite my previous thinking, my Papa, comprised of 90 years of knowledge and experience, taught me the significance of making a memorable impression when greeting one another. Being that my Papa is an older man, he sees life through an old-fashioned lens. Not growing up and being immersed in the booming tech world has made him avoid digital interaction. He's all about face-to-face interaction and communication and has emphasized the value of this to me numerous times. He's a classy man, the quintessential gentleman, the perfect husband, the most caring father, the most loving Grandpa, the head honcho that brings all the families together. Whenever he smiles at me, it's genuine and delicate, making me feel like the luckiest granddaughter in the world. Although at times he can be quite stubborn, his intentions are always for the best. Every time I see him, he can't help but to teach me the ways of a "proper lady." When I am being educated or criticized, he always leans in close to my ear, making sure I hear every word that comes out of his soft-spoken lips. "No elbows on the table" and "don't talk with your mouth full" are common sayings that he preaches day in and day out. While my common response to these lessons would usually be a slight nod and a vague glimpse of acknowledgment, one lesson left me thinking. I didn't realize in the moment how important this lesson would be, but it has changed how I see myself and how I want others to see me. The moment I am referring to is the day I was taught a gesture that most people do subconsciously: a handshake.

"Michelle, shake my hand," Papa ordered. I extended my arm and lightly grasped his rugged, wrinkled skin, worn out from years of living. As soon as I did this, his eyebrows furrowed, the wrinkles on his forehead increased tenfold, and he made a slight frown.

Baffled by this reaction over a handshake, I snapped back, "What did I do wrong?"

"Are you scared of hurting my hand?"

"No, of course not. But it's just a handshake, what's the big deal if it's not firm?"

"There's your first mistake," he retorted, "See, a handshake tells a lot more about a person than you think. It's the first gesture you make when you meet someone new. For this reason, it can indicate a great deal about what type of person you are, such as whether you are portrayed as being confident or shy. Let me show you how to properly shake someone's hand."

I was unaware just how much of a science there apparently is to shaking someone's hand. My papa immediately went into detail about what must be done and what one should be focusing on when they are about to shake another person's hand. He went over the procedure, step by step, as if it were a lab experiment.

"Step 1," he started explaining, "point your thumb upwards and extend the other fingers out in

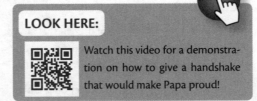

LOOK HERE:

Watch this video for a demonstration on how to give a handshake that would make Papa proud!

front. The thumb and the index finger should make an 'L' shape. Step 2: When you are about to come into contact with the other person's hand, the focus of the hand's movement should be on finding the spot between the thumb and the index finger. This is the direction the hand should go in. Step three: Once the other hand is grasped, the thumb should fold over the other person's thumb. Step four: Move the other person's hand up and down two times."

After he explained the proper techniques and steps, we practiced, over and over again, until my handshake was deemed acceptable for him. Throughout the whole process, he emphasized to me that the handshake should be firm and forceful, not dainty and light.

"Make yourself known," he said, "Allow others to see just how confident and assertive you are."

Little did I know how much of an impact this simple lesson and the advice that came along with it would have on the way I interact with people. My Papa's words have stayed with me to this very day. I've applied his handshake techniques everywhere: meeting the head of an investment firm in the spring, during my job interview this past summer, and more recently, when I introduced myself to my new professors and peers at Cal Poly. Knowing that I have a strong, firm handshake has no longer made me afraid of approaching powerful people or new acquaintances. My handshake masks the true fear and anxiety that I feel inside. Rather, I feel more prepared and comfortable to open up to others about who I am when I perform this initial gesture. The handshake has already left an indication about who I am as a person and more importantly, how I see myself, as well. I want others to immediately get the feeling that I am a person who is confident, brave, and fearless. I want them to be aware of my presence. I want them to remember who I am. I want them to look forward to getting to know me better. And a powerful handshake, as I learned from my Papa, can do just that.

Michelle Waal is a Business Administration major.

CONSIDER THIS:

- How does the writer's use of dialogue help to construct the narrator and Papa's ethos while also moving the narrative forward?

- The essay develops a personal narrative by first centering the essay around Papa. It then uses this description of Papa to reflect on the narrator's own personal qualities. How does the essay connect Papa's qualities to the narrator's in order to show the impact that Papa has had on them?

- The paragraph outlining steps for how to give a proper handshake seems not only to be Papa's instructions to Waal, but also Waal's instructions to readers so that they might develop their own handshake. Consider other creative ways that an essay can address its audience indirectly.

So, Where Are You From?

Emma Knisley

The snow-capped mountains of Colorado. The tree-covered valleys of Connecticut. The coastal bays of Maryland. The rolling hills of Virginia. The expansive fields of Missouri. The golden coastline of California. I am from each of these places and can't pick just one. These landscapes have equally shaped me for the last 18 years, and I owe my perspective on life to the sensations and circumstances surrounding them.

Scrubby bushes rustling as the dry wind skims over the land. Snow glistening at the top of a distant peak. The silence of nature, broken only by a big black dog barking once at foraging deer and quickly hushed by quiet voices. The smells of pine needles and wood smoke permeating the air. The only light coming from the stars shining clearly in the crisp mountain air.

These were the sensations of my early years. I don't remember much of Colorado but visiting always brings back a rush of nostalgia for the serenity of our house on the mountain. The sight of snow-capped peaks and the dry dusty feeling of a breeze at altitude leave me with a yearning to be back in the place where I first breathed life. Through all the places I have lived, Colorado has always been my origin, where my roots lie and where I hope to return. My time there was spent growing, primarily, but also learning, adventuring, discovering the world, and occasionally being buried by four feet of snow. I learned about the beauty of nature by seeing it outside my window, the mountains stretching out before me the only reality I had ever known.

At four years old, a knock on our door woke me up from a nap. I heard an unfamiliar deep voice and my mother responding with urgency. Soon I was hustled into the car with the dog, my parents, my brother, and two hastily packed bags. Not understanding, I questioned my family the whole way down the mountain. A fire, they responded. We needed to evacuate. I didn't comprehend until we rounded a corner and a fierce blaze came into view, stretching over the mountainside like a fiery blanket of unbridled fury intent on consuming everything in its path. I stared with wide eyes at the image of something I had only before seen in my fireplace eating up the massive trees as if they were no more than twigs. We turned another corner and I lost sight of the fire, shocked but somehow already falling asleep again to the sound of my parents making grim phone calls to our family down in Denver. The two weeks we spent down in the city were full of tense moments in front of the TV permanently set to the news, watching the fire creep steadily closer to our home, getting calls from our neighbors and friends informing us of the losses of all their belongings, and knowing each time the phone rang that we might soon be next. "We'll be okay," said my parents, "we are all we need." I still didn't really understand what was going on, but when we got the call saying the fire had been stopped only feet from our property line, I picked up enough from my mother's relieved crying to figure out that we were going back home and everything would be back to normal. As we drove back up the mountain, however, the landscape was unrecognizable. Charred remains of forests were all that was left of the scenery I had grown to love and the view from my window was of blackened mountain sides and smoky skies. It would never look the same.

From the mountains and raging wildfires of Colorado, I learned respect for the beauty of nature and its overwhelming power to destroy.

Hills covered in vibrant trees, every shade of red, orange, yellow, and purple. Leaves crunching under foot and rustling as cool breezes wind their ways through the forests. The smell of people grilling and the sound of children playing in a cul-de-sac, riding bikes in endless circles. A red-tailed hawk soaring above the picturesque town and landing on a nearby branch to observe. Pumpkins littering doorsteps and the taste of warm apple cider after a day spent exploring the wooded hill behind the house.

This is how I try to remember Connecticut, full of New England small town charm and an easy childhood. The majority of my life was spent here, but I don't have too many distinct memories of those years in our quiet town in the Farmington River Valley. I spent my days living out a cookie-cutter child-hood—almost too perfect. I was best friends with my next-door neighbors, and we played together every day. I started school and enjoyed the challenge. I was known as a quiet girl, smart and obsessed with horses. I walked down to the bus stop every morning, catching falling leaves in the fall, throwing snowballs in the winter, and counting caterpillars in the spring. I spent my summers at the town pool, drinking lemonade and enjoying the fact that I knew everyone there. A day of boredom could be easily cured by exploring the woods in our neighborhood or pretending the spaces under the boughs of the giant forsythia bush in my back-yard comprised a mansion.

As I grew older, however, the boredom couldn't be alleviated so readily and knowing everyone at the town pool became more of a curse than a gift. Now I associate Connecticut with the intense monotony of my life there and the sense of vague despair I began to recognize in its residents. It came to represent a place I needed to get out of, and I eventually grew to hate the feeling of being closed off from the world in our little town, simultaneously protected and trapped. I wish I could remember Connecticut only as the New England paradise that I once knew it as, my town as perfect as Stars Hollow from *Gilmore Girls*, which was based off of it. Instead I tend to remember the bitterly cold winters and the unbearably humid summers spent confined inside for fear of frostbite or being eaten alive by mosquitoes. I remember the feeling of wishing to be somewhere, anywhere else.

From the quaint small-town charm of Connecticut, I learned that I wanted more than just a quiet routine life.

Wide city streets bustling with men in carefully pressed suits. Cherry blossom petals floating through the air and coating the ground, warm breezes filling the air with their sweet scent. The Capitol building rising imposingly over the city, reminding the world of its power. Chanting masses taking to the streets to fight for their causes. The sound of a Metro train whooshing up through dirty sidewalk grates.

This fast-paced atmosphere unique to Washington D.C. shaped my high school years. I learned about government not just in school but by being immersed in it, understood politics by seeing the ebb and flow of power affect the people around me. I watched as the 2016 election ripped the nation in two and participated in marches with hundreds of thousands of people fighting for gun control. At my internship in the House of Representatives, lights hummed and C-SPAN played quietly in the corner as I clicked through seemingly endless streams of messages from constituents and "batched" them into subject areas. Around me, other staffers chatted about their lives and the upcoming House votes interchangeably, as if they were of equal importance. I walked through the halls of Congress gathering signatures for bills and passing by our nation's leaders and influencers. I answered calls from enraged and upset constituents, only months after the election. I attended hearings and briefings and wrote

LOOK HERE:

The House of Representatives has college internship opportunities.

memos for my Congresswoman to review. These actions seemed insignificant at the time, but I realize now that my mindless tasks still had an effect on the entire nation, no matter how small. Tiny little me, short and awkward, was carrying a government ID badge and walking the halls of the U.S. Capitol. Suddenly, I was a little more than the quiet girl who rode horses and didn't speak up much.

From the fast-paced atmosphere of power in D.C., I learned that I mattered.

Flat fields stretching out as far as the eye can see. A grey sky pressing heat down onto muddy paths. Crows cawing loudly at pickup trucks chugging along straight two-lane roads. Dark storm clouds amassing behind the columns of a college campus, eerily abandoned for the summer. People licking ice cream cones, window-shopping. A wide river, flowing smooth and unperturbed along its winding route. The sound of tractors starting up for a day's work.

Exploring Significant Moments

This was my first impression of Missouri, where my dad took a job the summer before I left for college. Needless to say, I was apprehensive of leaving my beloved bustling city and East Coast way of life for the Midwest. All I could picture of Missouri was farmers with incredibly exaggerated accents plowing their fields. I wasn't too upset about moving because my academically-minded father was excited to teach sports journalism at the University of Missouri, and I was about to leave the East Coast for college anyways. But I struggled to see myself fitting in at all in this new place. I could only imagine myself back in Connecticut, bored out of my mind, alone and far from my friends. Basically, I was expecting the worst.

My father and most of our furniture moved out to the "Show-Me" state early and my mother and I followed at the end of the summer, setting out from D.C. with a U-Haul trailer full of the rest of our belongings. After three very slow, very boring days of

LOOK HERE:

Every state has its own special qualities. Check out the QR code and find out the best things about your home state!

driving, we pulled off the highway for our final destination: Columbia, Missouri. I say we pulled off the highway as if it were a real exit, but instead it was a tiny, barely paved road jutting out from the interstate without even an exit lane. I assumed my mom was pulling over because something was wrong with the car. Why else would we be turning onto what was obviously just a useless access road? I realized too late that this was the way to our house as my mom, ever sarcastic, exclaimed, "Well, here we are!" The "road," really more potholes than pavement, stretched away from us through impossibly flat fields lined with scraggly trees and looping telephone wires. Was this really it? I think I shivered a little looking out at it. My vision was coming horribly true. As we bumped along the road, we gradually ascended a very slight hill. I was still in a daze looking out at the fields, but my mom's voice brought me back as she pointed ahead with a smile, "Look." A few miles ahead of us a small city had popped up seemingly out of nowhere. I will never forget the relief I felt at that sight of civilization, or at least what passes for civilization in Missouri.

I only spent a couple weeks there before driving on to California, and a couple more weeks during Thanksgiving and Winter breaks. However, the more I experience of the town the more I am surprised by what it has to offer. Columbia, it turns out, is a thriving college town with a dynamic and artistic downtown. Being totally alone there gives me the time to thoroughly explore the locally owned stores and quirky coffee shops that make up the downtown streets. Not knowing a single person other than my parents there is oddly refreshing. No one knows anything about me. No one saw my awkward middle school years or remembers my embarrassing Halloween costumes. No one knows about that time I thought side bangs were a good idea or when I was obsessed with One Direction. I have the chance to reinvent myself, to be more than I first appear just like my new home in the Midwest. There are definitely a lot of farmers plowing their fields, but Missouri is far from the empty wasteland devoid of sophistication that I had pictured.

From the surprising energy of Missouri, I learned that a first glance doesn't always tell the whole story.

Velvety green hillsides dotted with trees stretching down to sandy beaches with waves loudly rushing towards shores. Rocky spires, the remnants of volcanoes, reaching up to the clouds. A car, racing alone along the highway with the mountains to one side and the ocean to the other, hands sticking out the windows and faint music pumping through the speakers. The smell of salt air and the noisy cawing of seagulls. A warm sun beating down on students chatting hurriedly between classes.

This classic California vibe is, to me, a paradise. I know in my gut that coming here for college was the right choice every time I step outside and feel the sun beating down on my bare arms in the middle of January. The sensation of being warm and surrounded by breathtaking nature combined with the independence of col-

LOOK HERE:

Architect David Adjaye, who designed the Smithsonian's National Museum of African American History and Culture discusses how place shapes identity.

lege makes me feel like I can do anything. One long weekend my best friend and I made the spontaneous decision to take a road trip down to LA and go to Disneyland for her birthday. We packed a bag, rented a Zipcar, grabbed some friends, and were off. It was nothing like the meticulously planned trips I had taken with my family. We had no idea where we were going to stay, how long we would be there, or if our parents were going to kill us for being so reckless, but it didn't matter. I was driving along the coast, going 75 miles an hour on an empty road and absolutely in awe of the beauty of the landscape through the windshield. The windows were down, the sun was shining, and I was screaming along to my favorite cheesy boyband songs with my new favorite people. My hair was flying around getting tangled almost beyond repair, but I didn't care. I was smiling so hard I could barely sing. It felt like a scene in a movie. In that moment, nothing could hurt me. I was invincible.

From the stunning vistas of California, I got an intoxicating taste of freedom and a life free from worry.

Each set of surroundings I've encountered has forced me to adapt to conditions entirely different from the last, to take in a place that was unfamiliar and make it familiar. I strive to protect nature, because I saw its destruction firsthand in Colorado. I seek out adventure and change, because I didn't find them in Connecticut. I embrace politics and know the effect small actions can have, because I witnessed them in D.C. I look deeper below the surface of people because of what I found after taking a second look at Missouri. I take the time to let loose and be impulsive, because I felt how it gave me strength in California. When people ask me where I'm from—as if it will tell them everything they need to know about me—I have no idea how to answer. I've lived in a lot of different places, and each of them defines a part of me. I am a nature-loving Coloradan. I am a Nutmegger with big dreams. I am an influential Washingtonian. I am an open-minded Missourian. I am a free-spirited Californian. But all together, I am me.

Emma Knisley is an Environmental Management and Protection major.

CONSIDER THIS:

- Knisley plays with organization by incorporating descriptive, italicized paragraphs to segment the essay into sections for each of the different places that define her. What effect does this structure have on the reader's understanding of the essay? What other creative organizational strategies can be used to impact one's writing?

- Although this is a narrative essay, it incorporates brief profiles of the various places that Knisley has lived. How does Knisley use these profiles to depict her personal identity?

Halves

Laura Kuffner

My sophomore year of high school, my mother abruptly announced that we were moving to Japan to be closer to my aging grandparents. A month later, just two days after packing my entire life contents into four cardboard boxes labeled "BEDROOM" in pungent Sharpie and sending them and their haphazard duct-tape job across the Pacific Ocean, I found myself on a crowded subway platform in Yokohama, Japan, jittery with nerves that inevitably come with moving half-way across the world to find yourself commuting to the first day of 11th grade in an unfamiliar country, alone.

Admittedly, Japan isn't entirely unfamiliar to me. I was born in Tokyo and am half Japanese, or "hafu." My childhood is colored with soft, simple memories of blinking Japanese vending machines; unicycles, their leather seats sticky under the summer sun; and starlit, cricket-filled nights glued to the sumo match on the television screen. I attended a public school near my grandparents' home for five consecutive summers, and I return to Japan every year.

Following my parent's divorce when I was eight, I have lived exclusively with my Japanese mother.

However, I am also half-American; my family moved to the states when I was a toddler, and I grew up across Portland, Oregon; Pittsburgh, Pennsylvania; and Palo Alto, California.

Several summers ago, I attended a family reunion in Texas, and amidst the mason jars of chewing tobacco, smoky sunset hot dog cookouts, and garishly neon floral-printed swimsuits hung to dry on a tree by the lake, I was reminded that I am equally from this, too. I have never spent more than three years at a single school and have always struggled straddling the line between my Japanese and various American identities. In Japan, I am American. In America, I am Japanese. In both places, I am an "other." Culture is made up of the nuances of the local community, and in the countless times I have been uprooted and replanted in new and different cultures, I have lost touch with all of them.

That morning, I remember weaving through the crowd of half-asleep blurs, catching glimpses here and there, echoes of my childhood in Japan that left quickly-fading imprints like footprints in the sand. The crisp, neatly pleated white of a collared shirt. The persistent blinking red light of the vending machines lining the walls. The smooth, scuffed handrail of the escalator as I descended into the masses jammed onto the platform. I was intoxicated by the sheer number of people that ebbed and flowed from each passing train, spilling into the platform and rearranging themselves in neat lines, heading into the bright white sunlight that stood in stark contrast to the dimly lit underground.

I took a deep, shuddering breath and refocused. I was ready to start over, to erase my garbled childhood memories of Tokyo and fresh prints of America, and begin again, from square one, as I always had. Looking down at the primary colors I was wearing amidst the muted neutrals on everyone else, I half-laughed to myself. At least one thing I was certain would remain the same: I would still be an "other" in a place I only partially belonged to.

LOOK HERE:

Follow this link for an in-depth look at Yokohama Chinatown in Japan.

I exited my train at the right stop—"Motomachi-Chukagai," the low, staticky voice over the intercom informed me—and found myself pointed in two opposite directions: exit 1–3 or 4–6. If I was truly Japanese, I would've quietly examined the subway map and went on my way, but my years stateside had poked gaping holes in my ability to read Japanese. If I was truly American, I would have blithely plunged ahead in English, blundering my way into receiving directions from a startled passerby, but my Japanese values of self-sufficiency and conformity told me that such an approach was disrupting the natural order of things, the rhythm of the writhing dance that played out before me. So instead, the girl that was from everywhere and nowhere at all decided to do what she had done in every other place prior. Like a puzzle piece trying to jam itself into the wrong spot, I took a shallow, shaky breath and blindly ascended the closest escalator to the street along with everyone else.

As soon as my eyes adjusted to the blinding morning sun that glinted off unlit neon signs, promising the smoky smells of nightlife, I knew I had made a mistake. In trying my hardest to follow the crowd, I had taken the wrong exit, and ended up in Yokohama Chinatown, a world improbably more foreign than Japan or America usually felt. The seemingly endless morning crowd I had found solace in underground were now nowhere to be seen, likely unwilling to nip down to Chinatown on a Monday morning for a keychain souvenir. I tried to retrace my steps, my heart rate quickening as each turn revealed yet another unfamiliar façade. Imagining the looks on my new classmates' faces when I rushed in inexcusably late and decidedly American, I turned to the only other thing that, through all the cities and schools and years of being "other," had remained unchanged: I called my mom.

Thirty minutes and several more wrong turns later, I arrived to my first day of 11th grade at a brand-new school an hour late, panting, my dreams of starting the year on a good note squashed.

Upon reflection, I think following either of my Japanese or American instincts that morning would have taken me to school on time. I was so adamantly against being "othered" again, tired of not knowing, eager to discard my half-formed, partially-congealed past skins, that I lost my sense of

LOOK HERE:

The mission of Cal Poly's Cross Cultural Centers is to offer services and programs to support our students under the shared values of family, diversity, learning, growth, and advocacy.

self entirely. But really, my identity isn't flawed or lacking; it is just split cleanly into two. I am not "hafu," or "half," as my label suggests, but whole—even if that whole is a messy sort of cultural conglomerate that values Japanese ideals of the greater good while embracing spunky American individuality and celebrates both Tanabata and Fourth of July with equal, if slightly misinformed, gusto.

These days, I am learning to accept my otherness as a kind of beauty and strength. There is beauty in having fragments of my soul spread thin across all the homes I've lived in, schools I've attended, and lives I've led. It takes a certain strength—one I am slowly learning to use—to be an unashamed "other" in all the rooms I only partially inhabit.

Laura Kuffner is an Architecture major.

CONSIDER THIS:

- Note how Kuffner's account of accidentally heading to Yokohama Chinatown manages to convey the overwhelming feeling of being in a major city. Which descriptive details and narrative moments do you think help to create this feeling?

- In Kuffner's last line, she describes finding the strength to claim her identity "in all the rooms I only partially inhabit." In addition to being thought of as "credibility," the rhetorical concept of *ethos* is often described as "a dwelling place," a way of using language to create a space where you can live with others. Do you see evidence of Kuffner's struggle to establish her own *ethos* or "dwelling place" in this essay?

"Sumac Kawsay": A New Perspective

Keilana Sugano

The summer before my senior year of high school, I discovered the meaning of life high among the peaks of the Ecuadorian Andes. It was there that Mother Nature baptized me in the waterfalls of the Rio Pastaza, my innocence and wonderment at the beauty of the world washed away, carried swiftly by the cold, clear waters that run down to the mighty Amazon. The icy spray awakened me soaking my being to the soul… I was anointed a Global Citizen, inspired to study indigenous cultures of the world, socioeconomic impacts affecting developing countries, roots of injustice and to bring about positive change.

Before my transformative journey, my junior year in high school was the roughest by far as I attended the funerals of my three remaining grandparents and a cousin. My interest in school diminished and I began questioning the meaning and value of life. Perhaps by coincidence or maybe it was my good fortune and destiny when my Journalism teacher nominated me for a program called

LOOK HERE:

Global Glimpse provides opportunities for high school students to participate in international travel programs that focus on service learning and leadership. Check out Cal Poly's International Center for opportunities to study abroad while attending the university.

Global Glimpse which promised to "increase academic engagement," "foster life-long learning," and "empower students." It was as if the brochures were speaking directly to me, lifting my spirits as I filled out the lengthy application.

With the Global Glimpse acceptance letter in hand I faced the challenge to raise two-thousand dollars to pay my way for an immersive experience in rural Ecuador. I took a job in the school cafeteria working recess and lunch breaks knowing that the five weekly hours of pay were a good start but I needed to do much more.

I opened an eBay account and was amazed at what people would buy, stashing away a modest sum of money for my used stuff.

With the payment deadline approaching, I threw myself into becoming an expert cookie baker. I baked like mad, whipping up larger and larger batches in the non-stop oven. I perfected the cookie business—analyzing quality, quantity, profit, packaging and marketing—all fed by my fever to fundraise for my Global Glimpse excursion. I sold cookies singly, by the dozen and by mail. Donations came along with words of encouragement. I focused on the positive and celebrated every success one batch at a time, just in time to meet my financial goal. Little did I know, at that moment my hard work, focus and determination would pay me back with a lifetime of inspiration.

My journey began with a glimpse of a totally different world, far away and unnoticed. The days I spent as a Global Glimpse delegate to Riobamba, Ecuador presented stark contrasts between the lives of the indigenous Quechua people and that of my own. As I labored in the fields with our host, Doña Victoria, I marveled at her ancient culture and traditions, alive and well, as they have been for generations. I was amazed at the strenuous work this 60-year-old woman single-handedly accomplished each day. We walked the half-mile from pastures outside her house to her small animal enclosure with heavy bundles of grass on our backs for her cattle. With machete in hand, I harvested Aloe Vera hauling the heavy 5-foot-long leaves to feed her cows. Her Andean red corn looked sparse in the field, yet we were able to harvest several bushels of the produce back to her house to prepare for market. Doña Victoria's pet sheep, Martina, resembled the Quechuan equivalent of a pet dog, following her everywhere and bleating plaintively anytime she was out of sight! Struggling to keep up with Doña (and Martina) throughout the strenuous days, I anxiously found opportunities to speak Quechuan, her native language, from the few greetings and numbers I had memorized. Her smiles and nods of acknowledgement were warmly rewarding, and I felt the rush of compassion for two people working together for a common goal, yet from worlds apart.

Over a lunch of soup and potatoes, I struggled to comprehend my life with no hot water, electricity, car or cell phone…none of the essentials for life as I knew it. Doña Victoria related to us the moving story about her challenges in life: how her parents died when she was young, raising her younger sister and brother, the lack of land, small crops under the four seasons in Ecuador, farm work, household chores and little time for her artisan craft of weaving beautiful textiles which she was famous for in her community. In an attempt to lighten the mood and to bond between our worlds, I showed Doña Victoria my handwritten phrases in her native language. She simply stared at the paper in my hands and when she looked up, our eyes met, and her lost expression was all that was needed to tell me that she couldn't read. Bravely, I tried to represent my world with an apologetic smile, but my emotions betrayed me as I bowed my head from the weight of the incomprehensible truths. Before I could disconnect from her world, Doña Victoria touched my hand softly, our eyes met again, and she smiled as she took the paper from me, folded it gently, and deftly tucked it in her skirt pocket with a nod. Instinctively, she knew how to change my perspective and with that change somehow it healed me. In that moment, with that simple gesture, my world became forever connected to Doña Victoria's. A woman who had very little in the way of education and possessions, gave me peace. Freeing me from guilt over who I was and what I had, instead I understood the simple truth and the pure beauty in Doña Victoria's life, and this instilled my hope for humanity.

This transformational journey into the world of rural Ecuador provided me with glimpses of the truths about poverty and the global economy, the value of education, and the plight of indigenous peoples of Ecuador. These glimpses provided a vision which I will not let be unseen. In my schooling, I will recall the experiences and draw parallels between the lives of the Quechua people and my own. As they struggle with harvest, I will challenge my coursework with fervor. As they rely on their social structure and community for survival, I will seek peers and relationships that solidify my base. As they gaze up at the stars at night and think their ancient thoughts, I will be studying those thoughts in my curriculum of anthropology.

Throughout my stay, Doña Victoria taught me the native Quechuan phrase "Sumac Kawsay." It seemed to be important to her and was an emphatic point that she repeatedly made, curiously, in many different contexts.

Returning home, not waiting to decompress rather wanting to define my amazing experience, I hit the internet. I learned that "Sumac Kawsay" describes a way of doing things that is community-centric, ecologically-balanced and culturally-sensitive, bearing much more significance than the literal Spanish translation "buen vivir," or good living.

To my astonishment, I learned of the significance of Doña Victoria's casual lessons in Sumac Kawsay. In 2008, Ecuador became the first country in the world to incorporate Rights of Nature into their constitution, recognizing the inalienable rights of ecosystems and requiring the government to address violations of these rights. By translating Sumac Kawsay into law, Ecuador acted to reverse the damage done by their extracting economy, preserving both nature and culture.

My time spent immersed in rural Ecuador inspired much reflection of my beliefs and values. I incorporated my thoughts and feelings into my new reality, my premise for the meaning of life: it is a perspective of Sumac Kawsay.

This perspective is the embodiment of life. It is a vantage point framed by beliefs, values and relationships. It is a view from within our selves encompassing our truths in life. This perspective defines who we are, what we do and what is important to us and in our societies. My perspective has been redefined with the understanding of the concept and teachings of Sumac Kawsay. My life has taken on new meaning with a vision to advocate for indigenous rights, engage with people like Doña Victoria, and pave ways for them to join us in our globalized world without sacrificing their traditions.

In my curriculum of Anthropology, I am on a path of studying the people and boundaries that form us into foreign bodies, that separate us and the many factors that make us different. In my Cultural Anthropology class, we place great importance in the analysis of each society and utilize many different lenses of perspec-

LOOK HERE:

Cal Poly's newest residential community, yakʔitʸutʸu, is named in honor of the indigenous peoples of San Luis Obispo. Check out more information on the Northern Chumash Tribe of this region.

tive. A major tenet for this area of study is that we cannot truly understand a different people if we let our own ideals, our ethnocentrism, interfere with our judgement. However, my scholastic commitment does not end with learning to better understand the uniqueness of a society. In my heart, I know first-hand that people from seemingly worlds apart can find commonality in simple ways, such as a nod and understanding smile. My Sumac Kawsay life drives me to study people, cultures and causes and to apply my knowledge to innovate sustainable methods of aid to benefit humanity. There are many problems the world faces today, but Sumac Kawsay has allowed me to discover the characteristics of a harmonious world as well as define the meaning of life for me:

Life is the environment, life is sustainability, peace, equality, compassion, social justice and bringing positive social change. The responsibility to live responsibly. Life has just begun for me.

Keilana Sugano is an Anthropology and Geography major.

CONSIDER THIS:

- This essay balances the techniques of *showing* and *telling* in order to depict the author's experience in Ecuador while reflecting on the meaning Sugano took away from the trip. Identify distinct passages in the essay when Sugano incorporates dialogue or action and when she relies on narrative summary to tell her story. How does Sugano transition between the two techniques of showing and telling?

- As you read in the opening section of this book, *kairos* refers to a writer's use of an opportune moment to convey information or make an argument. How does Sugano take advantage of *kairos* to demonstrate how the ancient Quechuan philosophy of Sumac Kawsay is relative today?

Our Movie

Megan Wong

Reflective Memo: *When asked what my story was, something that was impactful on my life, I thought of all the things I had done and learning to overlook society's perception of the homeless was something that forever changed me. At first, I did not know how to get my point across as I did not wish to sound condescending or rude. Although this was an obstacle, I found that writing my essay came naturally as I truly believed every word I wrote. Additionally, my favorite aspect of this piece was how I used an extended metaphor of a movie throughout this essay as I thought of myself to be a protagonist in this situation, attempting to figure out how to accept people different from me. This was difficult at first and was something I really struggled with. However, throughout my piece, one can see how genuine the homeless are and how much I loved them and saw them as people better and more accepting than myself.*

There is a movie that plays in my head when I see them. A movie that plays in my head when I think of them. A movie that plays in my head when you say the word "homeless." This movie—this gut-wrenching, heartbreaking movie—is about my favorite people: Rachele, John, Lloyd, and others. They are homeless.

San Diego is fourth on Forbes' list of cities with the largest homeless populations and as a native San Diegan, I see the effects of homelessness: streets lined with countless tents and boxes caked with dirt but held together with duct tape, humans on the verge of starvation blowing into their hands just to keep warm, people urinating on themselves because there is nowhere else to go. This is the movie that plays in my mind. This is our movie.

Our movie began four years ago. It begins with my naive heart believing that I could feed a few people and leave feeling accomplished and sympathetic. Homeless men and women shuffle into a shelter where I am volunteering and one by one, I fill battered mugs with water and hand out lukewarm bowls of pasta. My heart opens to each person as they greet me with a loving smile and a grateful look in their eyes. And as if the hands of reality slap me, as if someone takes a dagger to the bubble I am living in, I realize my childlike mindset; the bubble pops. These people who have nothing possess something I lack: humility. The simplicity of water and pasta can be so much more than a meal. For the water rejuvenates the soul and the pasta warms the heart. Thus, after a night of serving more than three-hundred homeless, my heart was not filled but open and broken; I was no longer blind to the world around me. That night when I got home, this tragic movie played relentlessly and overwhelmingly in my mind. No, I would make our movie have a happy ending. My mission no longer became one to merely feed the homeless, but to get to know them, to know their story and to be more than just a person, but a friend. To touch their hearts with compassion and allow them to change me in the process.

Scene two begins: I stuff various pairs of socks with thoughtfully chosen memory verses that helped me through adversity and Quaker Oats granola bars to soothe the sounds of a "hangry" stomach. These balled-up socks are placed inside the glovebox of my car, in-between notebooks in my backpack, inside my purse that follows me everywhere. I am ready now.

Eventually, one pair of sock finds its way into the warm and welcoming hands of a homeless woman, a place where the sock belongs. As Rachele realizes how much I care for her, she breaks into a tear-filled smile. She tells me, "You saved my life." "Rachele," I say, "you saved mine."

Scene three starts at five a.m. on a Saturday morning. I groggily stumble out of my bed into my car and buy a few dozen donuts. By seven a.m., I am in downtown San Diego watching the sun float above the clouds while breathing in the morning air now permeated with the aroma of sugar and dough. And as if the universe sends us to each other, I meet John, a homeless man with a name that matches that of my only uncle. Holding John's cracked hands, his eyes light up as I tell him the story of my uncle and hand him his favorite donut, a maple bar. He tells me, "This is all I have to eat today. Thank you."

Scene four is my favorite scene. A man is dancing in the middle of a homeless shelter, so I walk to him, curiosity overtaking my thoughts as I wonder what makes him dance. "The second I saw you," he says, "I started dancing. My name is Lloyd." Lloyd has cancer and he breaks down, sobbing into my now wet shoulder,

LOOK HERE:

If you're interested in volunteering at a homeless shelter in SLO County, follow the QR code to CAPSLO and learn how you can help.

my clothes now smelling like him. I hold his hand, wipe his tears, and he kisses my wet shoulder. For hours I sit with Lloyd and console him. "I will never forget you," he tells me. I tell him, "And I'll never forget you." This man who dances through cancer teaches me something: that actions as simple as speaking to someone and understanding them can have such a deep impact. And I know that through all my interactions with the homeless, I showed them my love and care; and they showed me their selves, whether it be humbleness or unfazed gratitude.

There is also scene five, and six, and seven...

You see, our movie is never-ending. For the past years, I have dedicated my life to creating the best movie possible for this homeless community. Being the giver of rolled-up-socks-and-donuts does not exactly roll off the tongue and is not exactly the most profound label. However, it has allowed me to grow within myself while doing my best to spread positivity and humility within a community that has been a part of my hometown for as long as I can remember.

Thus, I stayed up late creating more socks, I woke up earlier to buy more donuts, I held more hands, I leapt into more tent-lined streets, and I walked with them. I spoke with the homeless and I knew them. I did this so at the end of each night, Rachele, John, and Lloyd knew someone was thinking about them, praying for them, loving them.

Every sock I made, every donut I gave out, every hand I held, and every eye I looked into, I looked into with purpose. Everyone needs a purpose, and mine was to show compassion to those who needed it while giving them a piece of myself.

Megan Wong is a Business Administration major.

CONSIDER THIS:

- In order to depict the narrator's experience helping the homeless, Wong uses the extended metaphor of a movie to break up part of the essay into "Scenes." How else could this comparison to a movie be developed? What other extended metaphors could you use to alter an essay's organizational structure or emphasize its purpose?

- This essay develops a strong sense of *pathos*. Look back through the essay and note the details and descriptive moments that have the strongest emotional impact. Is it clear who Wong envisioned as her audience for this piece?

Irrevocable Discovery

Jenna

For many people, a life changing moment comes about from accomplishing something they thought impossible or overcoming some unbearable loss; for me, it came while I was gaming in my pajamas late on a Sunday night. Colors splashed across the screen of my laptop, illuminating the wall behind me and refracting a mirage light around the dimmed room where I sat. This went mostly unnoticed by me as I had long since been sucked into the monitor on my desk. I was ignoring the college applications I had to do by spending the last hours of my night playing a silly dating-sim game I found online. After a few days of conversation, one of the characters I had been talking to told me a secret that she kept from most people, one that roused something I buried in myself a while ago. That she had been born physically male. That she had been taking hormones for years to look more feminine. That she was transgender.

Of course, I had heard about trans people before then—it's impossible not to at least once when you live on the internet—but being "transgender" was just a label that ended up on people that didn't quite look male or female. It was just this title that was bestowed upon people without much meaning behind it. This two-minute conversation at just before midnight with a cartoon character that didn't exist had just brought a sledgehammer down on what I knew about trans people and left my mind swimming from the implications. I slid my mouse up to the corner of the screen, closing out the game and opening Google. One curious search quickly became five, then fifteen, then twenty. I went through Wikipedia pages, Reddit posts, and forum threads in a rush to read every minutia of detail I could find about what it meant to be transgender.

By the time I had finished my flurry of research, the sky had gone from black to grey. I clicked my laptop shut and leaned my chair back until it hit the wall with a light tap. My eyes were heavy from the hours of reading from a screen, but I kept them locked open, star-

LOOK HERE:

Check out the National Center for Transgender Equality.

ing up into the ceiling, focused on some point miles beyond it. For the first time, I honestly asked myself if that could be me. I had had dreams of being a girl for years, but quickly shut them down with thoughts of "That's just a fantasy," and "Maybe if it was possible in real life, but it isn't." But sitting right here in front of me was mountains of evidence to the contrary. If I could be a girl in real life, would I? Could I actually be transgender?

Yeah, maybe I could.

The next few days passed by in a haze, like someone had been spiking all my meals with morphine. It was a pleasant fog that hugged the corners of my brain. I tried to stay focused, I really did, but I couldn't seem to stop the thoughts that encompassed my head, the thoughts that maybe I could actually do this. A handful of my friends noticed that I was in an unusually good mood, but I was both too distracted and too nervous to tell them the truth; for the moment, my discovery would remain a secret. I had found hope for the future, something I didn't know I needed so badly until it fell into my lap. No matter how high school ended up or where I got accepted for college, I could count on the peace of someday being the person I had dreamed of. When I got home Monday evening, the corners of my mouth were sore from being pulled up all day. Then, as follows every high, came the inevitable crash.

It only took two days for the reality of the situation to hit me in the chest like a bucket of cold water. I had a dream for the future, but I didn't have the first clue on how to reach it. On top of managing school work, college apps, a social life, and a newly discovered

LOOK HERE:

The Trevor Project offers resources on coming out.

pain from not being able to express who I wanted to be, I had to figure out what this new revelation meant for my future. I figured out I could be/was a girl, but I couldn't just tell my friends about it; if they didn't turn out to be a lot more liberal than I thought they were, I might lose the majority of my support network in one fell swoop. And my parents were a whole 'nother animal; my mom seemed pretty cool, but I had absolutely no idea what my dad's response would be. Best-case scenario, they're supportive, if a little unsure of what it all means; worst-case scenario, their differences in opinion lead to fights over my future and I either get kicked out or just leave to escape the turmoil, leaving my sister behind to face the domestic cataclysm alone. Of course, the worst-case scenario didn't happen and probably never would have, but those were the options I thought I faced.

In the end, there really wasn't much of a story to tell. I put off coming out until I turned 18, but it was only to my immediate family and I was too nervous for much to really come of it, I didn't even ask for them to call me by a different name. My mom was immensely accepting. My dad did his best to understand. Near the end of senior year, I had started taking hormones, and by summer, I didn't really have much to show for it. I graduated alongside my peers with the same name, face, voice, clothes and pronouns that they had all been accustomed to over the four to twelve years I had spent with them in school. As I look back on it now, I can't help but wonder if everything would have turned out better if I had just come out to everyone back then, but there's not much point in dwelling on the past.

Arriving at Cal Poly, I still wasn't sure who I could trust to come out to, but I had a blank slate on which I could make something new of myself. Nobody would have to relearn a name they had used for years—besides one person, but they're also trans—so I could start out my college experience being the person I had hoped to become. I actually ended up putting off coming out to the people in my dorm for most of the first quarter, but life has improved. While I still struggle with people trying (and often failing) to guess my pronouns, and figuring out which bathroom to use is a topic that could fill up its own essay, I can finally make strides towards that glimmer of a future I saw sitting in my pajamas late on a Sunday night.

LOOK HERE:

Respecting others' gender pronouns sets a positive example for our campus community. Check out the Pride Center's webpage on why pronouns matter.

Jenna is a student in the College of Engineering.

CONSIDER THIS:

- Notice that Jenna's narrative is structured both chronologically, but it is also structured around her decisions to come out to a wider and wider network of relationships. She begins the essay with herself and then moves outward from there as she contemplates coming out to family, friends, and college roommates. Do both of these narrative structures seem balanced? Or do you tend to notice one more than the other?

- Jenna uses the narrative technique of pacing to control how her story unfolds. At times, she condenses a lot of time into a few sentences, while other passages amplify a few seconds over the course of an entire paragraph. How does this sense of pacing impact your ability to identify the most significant moments of Jenna's story and your ability to identify with how she experienced those moments?

Finding My Voice

Holly Masterson

It was dropped onto my desk like a nuclear bomb. As it fell, my eyes dropped to the grade and my ego dropped three levels. My first D.

This couldn't be my paper...this never happens to me... I'm an A student...

After confirming my name in the upper right-hand corner and finally passing the denial stage of grief, I decided to face the facts and read the comments. My eyes dashed around the many red, scribbled notes covering each page. "Did you even proofread?" was among the first.

LOOK HERE:

The online science and technology news portal Phys.org summarizes a 2013 study about the effects of the red pen on student learning.

I felt a knife piercing into my heart and twisting around.

Of course, I'd proofread my paper. Who turns in an essay without proofreading first? I felt like a complete failure. I couldn't help but feel as if all of my previous English teachers that liked my work had been lying all along.

This story is a familiar one in the anxiety-inducing classroom of the eighth-grade Literature teacher, Mrs. Niksch. As a very sensitive person, I took it pretty hard. That night I went home and avoided my Mom like the plague. I knew she wouldn't be angry with me, but I felt as if I'd disappointed her. I remember sitting on my bed with a blanket around me, doing my homework, when I saw her shadow in the doorway.

"Holly..." She spoke in a low, concerned voice. "What's wrong, baby?"

After a few unsuccessful back-and-forths of "everything is fine" and her not believing me for a second, I finally held up the D paper in shame.

"That's it?"

I nodded gravely.

"Oh Lord, send me. I thought something horrible happened at school."

I looked back up at her incredulous, how would this not be considered a horrible event?

It took a few hugs as well as a few pushes into reality, ("This is a bit ridiculous, you know.") but she eventually convinced me to give Mrs. Niksch another shot. She told me to go in during lunch and talk to her about what I could do on my next essay to improve.

Doing exactly that would become the best advice anyone could've given me.

Although she was tough as nails, I have never had a more helpful teacher than Mrs. Niksch. Her personality is as unique as her brutal teaching style. Her dark brown eyes seemed to look behind yours and into your skull, watching the cogs work, deciding whether or not you were telling the truth. She wore a fedora every day and would take it off periodically to rub her forehead in visible pain when a student was being obnoxious. She would then silently point to a small jar on her desk labeled "ashes of problem students." She had three metal hoop earrings in her left ear that would jingle as she spoke. She was significantly cooler than anyone in our eighth-grade class. We all knew it.

When I went in to talk to her that day it took ten minutes for me to make it through the door. I took a deep breath, said a little prayer, and entered the room. She sat at her desk with a pen to her forehead, then looked up at me. Her dark eyes scanned me up and down, assessed that I was nervous, and quizzically asked what was wrong. I held up the paper.

"Ah. Sit down. Let's go over this."

After a long lunch period, as well as 30 minutes of the next class when she had a prep period, she helped me find the beginnings of my writing voice. She explained that the problem in my essays was that I was copying what sounded to me like a professional, fancy-pants voice; I wasn't speaking like

LOOK HERE:

 Follow the QR code for an article in *Inc. Magazine* that reveals four steps for finding your voice.

myself. This along with some serious help in the grammar department was the most help any teacher had given me, and not only that, but it was on her own time. This humbling experience gave me a new appreciation of both literature and writing.

After a few weeks of working hard on the next essay, I received a C+. My grades may not have improved dramatically that year, but I did learn about how to use my voice on paper (as well as a valuable lesson on deflating the blown-up ego my thirteen-year-old self had acquired). Getting to that point was difficult, but the payoff was more than worth it. Eventually high school rolled around, and I often found myself sitting in front of the computer planning essays. The vast blank space on the document intimidated me, but once I began writing, the words just seemed to fall right out of my mind and onto the pages.

During these moments, I would replay that scene in Mrs. Niksch's office. I would see her sitting at her desk, taking off her fedora, and saying to me: "Let me help you find your voice." She would tell me to write in the unique ways that my brain guided me with, and to never let anyone else tell me it was wrong. She would remind me to be confident in my own way of writing and to use it to speak out. It took a significant amount of time to find it (and to polish it), but now that I have my voice, it has become my dear friend. It explains my opinions better than any other voice could, and it shows people who I am. My voice is a vessel of expression that allows me to identify myself on paper.

Holly Masterson is an Animal Science major.

CONSIDER THIS:

- How does the writer use dialogue to enhance the narrative? What other narrative techniques does Masterson incorporate to engage readers?

- Like Masterson, many of us can think of at least one teacher who has had a lasting effect on our lives. If you were asked to write a narrative in tribute to a teacher who changed your life, about whom would you write? What would you say?

The World Is My Nose

Grace Kitayama

Reflective Memo: *I had fun writing this essay. The hardest part for me was coming up with a topic to write about. I actually came up with the topic idea when we did our freewrite in class. I think I could have been more creative in my sentence structure. I am still not very confident using semi-colons, colons, or dashes in my writing, which is something that I can work on in my next essay. I also feel like I need to work on keeping the tempo of my story consistent throughout the essay.*

The first page of my essay I was really proud of because I thought it was the most interesting. However, in the end of my essay when I described the technical details about ADD, I felt like the story got bogged down and boring, but I felt the need to keep those details in the story because I thought they had important context that was needed to understand my essay. I need to learn how to make the whole essay or story I write engaging, or else no one will want to read it.

If you ever want to blow someone's mind, tell them that their eyes are constantly looking at their nose, but their brain chooses to ignore it. It's true. If it weren't true, we wouldn't be able to get half the work done that we need to do because we would spend most of our day trying to look past our noses. Now imagine living your life when your brain simply refuses to ignore your nose. How would it feel? Distracting? Yes. Frustrating? Certainly. Hopeless? At times. In a sense, that's what my brain does, except with everything.

My brain has trouble filtering out all of the information around me.

This is why it has always been so hard for me to pay attention. I had tried all the tricks to stay focused in class: my back to the window, sitting in the front row, turning off my phone, keeping my desk clear, even cutting sugar and caffeine out of my diet to avoid jitteriness. It didn't matter. My attention always got pulled away from me. It would get split between the scratch of my classmate's pencil on the paper next to me, the ticking of the clock, or the conversation happening next to me. Worst of all, my internal monologue would drone on relentlessly about things it shouldn't—Is that a bruise on Jeremey's jaw, or is it a hickey? I wonder where Taylor got her balayage done? Aaron definitely showed up to class high today. I wonder if Mr. Bocksnick was cool in high school? Probably not. He's bald. I wonder if his kids worry that they'll be bald when they're his age. I would be. I have two bald teachers this year, and I had none last year... And so on. In this metaphor, if the world was my nose, my uncooperative brain was me, and I was noticing my nose all the time. It could be insufferable, but I had learned to cope with it to the best of my ability. I used noise-cancelling headphones, secluded myself to the quietest corners of the library to study, and would visit teachers after class to ask for help. For a while, I could get through school with good enough grades so that I could at least pretend that my brain was ignoring my nose.

Then in my sophomore year of high school, my nose got bigger. Classes became harder and more demanding. My grades immediately began to suffer and none of my old tricks helped. I knew it always would take me longer than most to get my homework done, but there seemed to be no resource on my high school campus that could help me understand some of my subjects.

The worst part of the semester hit me when I received my final report card—one C in Chemistry and one B in English. I was shocked. I was pissed off. I knew I wasn't the fastest learner in school, but I was a hard worker and that had always been enough. I had worked with my Chemistry teacher after school and with a Chemistry tutor during lunch. And English? English was my thing. I was always the teacher's pet in that class because I was the only one who would do all the reading. How had I let this happen? No one gets into a respectable college with a C on their transcript. But what more could I do? What did all of my friends have that I didn't? How come everyone else could see past their nose except me? That's when I thought that maybe I was different. Maybe I wasn't struggling because I am a bad student. Maybe I was struggling because I'm a different one.

After I gave the idea much thought, I went to see a doctor and asked her about ADD. She explained to me that ADD manifests itself differently in girls. It's not disruptive behavior so much as passive lack of participation that often takes the shape of daydreaming or zoning out. She also

LOOK HERE:

For more information about ADD, explore the official website for the Attention Deficit Disorder Association.

told me that she doesn't view ADD as a disorder but as an adaptation. It's instinctive to be hyper sensitive to sounds and quick movements out of the corner of our eye. However, over time, we've been conditioned to pay attention to one thing for an extended amount of time, and that is just inherently harder for some people than it is for others. She told me that we could look into it, and thus we began the year-long process of working towards a diagnosis. After months of surveys, character witnesses, tests, and meetings from teachers, coaches, school administration and family, I was diagnosed with ADD. I remember how silly I felt during the whole process. I hated putting all these people through so much trouble just for me, and at times wondered if it was even worth it. Nevertheless, it did help. Now I qualify for accommodations during class that allow me to be more successful while still being challenged.

However, it's still an uphill battle. There are people who doubt me and tell me things like "you don't seem like you have ADD" or "you don't have ADD, you just need to try harder." My favorite comment being, "you're so quiet, how could you have ADD?" Though the comments can be bothersome, I understand people's reluctance to believe that I have ADD. From the outside, everyone's nose looks normal. Sure, some are bigger or smaller, but we all have them, and if you've always been able to see past it, then it's hard for you to imagine what life would be like any other way. You probably don't even think about it. It's the same thing with ADD. Though my brain actually does filter out my nose, it doesn't filter out anything else, but that's okay. I learned to work harder than others to achieve my goals, and I get to view the world a little differently than most people. The world is my nose, and it's a beautiful one at that!

Grace Kitayama is a History major.

CONSIDER THIS:

- In Kitayama's reflective memo, the writer contemplates whether the end of the essay gets "bogged down" with details. Do you agree? If so, can you think of strategies she might have deployed to help strike a more effective balance between the creative tone with which she began the essay and the technical details she added toward the end?

- Essay titles should help readers predict an essay's content, reflect its tone, and capture readers' attention. What steps can writers take during the title-writing process to meet those goals? Discuss with a partner the title of Kitayama's piece. Did it draw you in? Does it establish a certain tone? What does she accomplish by circling back to the title in her concluding line?

Dancing on My Coffin

Andrew Baker

"It's not tragic to die doing something you love."

Mark Foo, accomplished surfer and Hawaiian local

5:29 A.M. I pull into a parking spot with faded white lines that have not been painted over in years. After putting my truck in park, I open the door and take the deepest breath possible. The smell of salt water and a little bit of sewage fill my nostrils (this beach parking lot sits right next to a storm drain). Warm and toasty from my car heaters, the cold ocean breeze overwhelms my body. My bare feet hit the rocky gravel ground, cutting the end of my toes, as I jump out my driver's side door. The crash of waves breaking hundreds of yards away rage on in my ears. Visibility is low as the sun has not risen over the mountains; I peer into the abyss where I know the water lies and can only dream of what lies ahead.

My best friend parks his old beat up pickup truck right next to mine. We make eye contact, happy to see each other in the early hours of the morning but say nothing. We hold a mutual understanding of what we have come here to do. I grab the cold rusty metal lever holding down my 9'6 board in my small five-foot truck bed and unlatch it. I turn my board perpendicular with the car and hop on the bumper of my truck. I whip out a brand-new bar of my fresh surf wax, I scrape the top of my board until the light tan top, once resembling the beaches of Tahiti, turns to a darker gray full of bumps. Perhaps one of the most difficult tasks of the morning: I slide my damp wetsuit on, which smells of crusty salt water, sweat, and a bit of piss. After this grueling task, I grab my board and head into the direction of the beast.

First light appears, and I face the water. Outlines of the waves become visible and white wash scurries towards me as my feet sink deeper into the wet sand. A cold rush runs up my spine as the chilling water engulfs my legs up to the knee. I take my board out from

LOOK HERE:

Follow the QR code to learn about the Surfrider Foundation and its efforts to protect the world's oceans.

under my arm and throw it into the ocean. With a powerful push from my lower half, I spring myself onto the board right in the direction of rolling waves.

Left stroke, right stroke, left stroke, right, left, right. This tiring repetitive motion moves me closer to my target. As I paddle, bursts of the frigid morning water splash into my face. My hands are already numb from being in the water. I approach a wave and push my board right into it, floating over the hump, giving me the feeling of an amusement park ride as I go down the backside. Finally, sitting two-hundred yards out, I make it to the reef. Reefs tend to be where waves break and a perfect spot for a surfer like myself to rest. I sit up on my board, my feet dangling off the edge to what seems like a bottomless pit. Anything could be below me, but I do not have a care in the world.

Waiting for what seems like days, I peer on the horizon and see what I have been waiting for so patiently. A mystical dark blue wave, barely lit up by the early morning light, rushes towards me. This is it. I shift my body to the back of my board and spin myself to face the beach. I look to my right to see the sun just peaking above the mountains that lay in the distance, a beautiful sign for a surfer. I start to paddle furiously towards shore as the wave comes upon my backside. The cold water rolls over my body, I push my board into the wave, and I kick my feet to the front of the board.

Now. The most joyous part of surfing. The dance. I stand upright on my board, straight into the morning air, my body still aching from being up at the crack of dawn. I cut through the wave at high speed. I feel the cool ocean breeze hitting my body. I parade my feet up towards the front of the board. Moving my left foot, then right, then left, until both feet stand on the very front tip of the board. I am standing on the edge of the world, water rushing below me as I ride this wave for what it seems like forever. I move my feet back to keep my balance, then move them forward again to hopefully get the undisturbed view of the flowing water, shooting underneath my board. I move my feet back and forth so fast and often, it is like I am dancing the tango. The board is my stage, and Mother Nature is my partner.

What seems like centuries later, I can tell the wave is coming to an end. The wave is walling up, and I seem to have no other choice but to go down with it. Near the end of a ride, if you are not far enough outside, the face of the wave, or the front, becomes a flat "wall" and there is no way to

LOOK HERE:

Baker begins his essay with a quote by surfer Mark Foo. Check out more about Foo in an excerpt from the documentary *Riding Giants.*

escape it. The walled-up wave is beautiful yet so dangerous. I stick out my hand and let the edge of my pruned fingertips glide along the face in hopes to have one more mystical moment before everything comes crashing down. As I explore the wave with my touch, I feel as if God came down from heaven and is holding my hand through Mother Nature.

SPLASH! The avalanche of white-water crashes on my head and knocks me off my stage. The dance is over. However, now I must pay the price for seeking out this dangerous wave. My board, once my beautiful stage, has become my coffin. I am thrown underneath the wave and start to roll in circles like clothes would in a washing machine. The wave, this wonderful dance partner turned dangerous beast, holds me under. My body screams at me to gasp for air, but I know I cannot. I curl into a lifeless fetal position to protect myself, and lay there underneath, at the pure mercy of the beast. I might only have been below the surface for no more than seven seconds, but as any surfer can attest, it feels much longer. Finally, I feel the beast let go of his death grip. I move my arms in the breaststroke motion to raise myself towards the surface. My head breaks through the glass surface that is the cold icy water and my lungs fill. I am given life by Mother Nature and rebirthed into the world with this breath of fresh air.

I perform this dangerous dance, also known as surfing, all the time. I seek the thrill it provides every wave I catch. Crashing, falling off my board, and understanding I am in the ocean where I am not atop the food chain, are all challenges I face. These conditions are all side effects to surfing, and I live and die with them. I learned to love the wipeout at the end of the wave, equating it to my payment to Mother Nature for letting me ride her beautiful waves. Surfing is a dangerous game, but it lets me feel alive more than anything else can. Riding a wave holds a deeper love in me more than anything else has before, a love I would die for. Hopefully the day does not come soon, but if I were to pass away amongst the waves, I could die with content in my heart.

Andrew Baker is a Business Administration major.

CONSIDER THIS:

- Writers incorporate epigraphs (quotes or phrases placed at the beginning of a text) for a variety of purposes. Take a look at the quote Baker uses to frame his narrative and consider what purpose it serves. Does the quote by Mark Foo set a particular tone or encapsulate the theme of Baker's essay? Once you've followed the "Look Here" link to more information on Mark Foo, does the epigraph carry more weight as a stylistic choice?

- Metaphors are used to draw comparisons between two seemingly different subjects or concepts, and often they are difficult to sustain throughout an entire text. At times, writers over-emphasize those comparisons and risk losing their readers. Beginning with the title, Baker deploys the use of metaphors. What message(s) does Baker convey through those metaphors as he explores surfing as a significant moment in his life? How well does he balance the use of metaphors throughout his essay?

Becoming the Good

Lindsey Shepard

As I stood behind the deep red velvet curtains in my unimpressive high school auditorium, I could feel my heart beating into my throat. Frazzled production managers who seemed to bypass the concept of personal space weaved a microphone cord under my blazer and adhered it firmly to my face. In that moment, I felt like an intellectual warrior, being suited for battle, ready to open the minds of the hundreds of people waiting to hear me speak. Okay, maybe not a warrior. I don't think warriors wear periwinkle blazers and floral stilettos into battle. Nonetheless, I was essentially jumping under a lens of scrutiny and judgement held by my San Diegan community. Hundreds of eager people were waiting to dissect every word I was saying, not to mention the web surfers who could find the professionally taped version on YouTube for the rest of eternity.

After being yanked through the narrow walkways and over old set pieces, I was eventually in the wings, looking out at the faces of the crowd. I could hear the dying applause after my somewhat generous introduction signaling my cue to walk on stage. I felt an immense rush to run away as fast as I possibly could. Flight is the one prehistoric trait that I just can't seem to shake. Yet somehow, someway, I trekked onto that stage with confidence and poise. After that point, I may have blacked out a bit. All I can remember from those twenty minutes was the blinding auditorium lights and the barely audible yet deafening hum of a microphone. Then, after what seemed like years of endless suffering, I could feel the roaring applause, my shaking legs, and an immense sense of pride for accomplishing my first professional milestone—my very own TED Talk.

LOOK HERE:

After reading Shepard's essay, take some time to watch her TED Talk.

This story began in the midst of subdued conversations between stone-aged couples whose faces gleamed with wrinkles conveying lives lived with passion and a constant waft of aged espresso beans. Delicate happenings like these contrasted with eccentric employees who had too many jaded tattoos and fresh piercings to count. As I sat at the childlike yet artistically crafted tile table that I always did, I had a potentially life-altering decision to make in this coffee shop: whether to accept the proposal to give a TED Talk at my high school. I would be representing my school as the only student in the production, surrounded by outstanding community members who were experts in their fields. I continued to thumb through my worn-out copy of *On the Road* more as a therapeutic effort than as an attempt to process any of the black ink words my eyes were reading. Damn, I loved that book. Yet still I was questioning how I would be able to speak to a crowd with any sense of credibility or importance. Who was I other than a high school senior with no idea where her life was headed?

This is a relatively typical crossroads a teenager comes to: Am I good enough for the task at hand? I shut Kerouac's masterpiece and entertained the crippling doubts that clouded my ability to come to a decision. Staring at that copy of *On the Road*, I realized the answer had been right in front of my eyes this whole morning. If Kerouac could drop out of his first year of university and go on to become the icon of an entire literary generation, then who's to say I'm not credible enough for a fifteen-minute TED Talk? Subconsciously, I was nodding my head to this stream of consciousness that arose. "Yes!" I thought, "How could I not have seen this before?!" In retrospect, that was a bit of a far-fetched conclusion. Nevertheless, it propelled me to take a risk. Something about finding that connection caused me to recognize the potential for greatness in myself.

Bravery is a word I hadn't given much thought to prior to my senior year of high school. I never thought of myself to be particularly brave. In fact, I tended to avoid situations that called upon bravery. After accepting the offer to present a TED Talk, it was something I began to consider. Through months of early morning dress rehearsals and endless criti-

LOOK HERE:

University professor and author Dr. Brené Brown says "sometimes the bravest and most important thing you can do is just show up." For more inspiration, consider watching Brown's Netflix special, *The Call to Courage*.

cisms, I came to realize that moments of bravery come when using your voice. I learned to be confident in intimidating situations, especially when I was on a stage practicing in front of some of the smartest middle-aged people I'd come by in my life. My voice was my most influential power and being aware of this, everyday situations where a lone voice was needed became apparent to me. I began to exercise the power of speaking for those who needed it most. Whether it involved walking out of my second period class to join the Parkland inspired gun control protest out front of my school or voicing concerns to my principal in a meeting about unjust disciplinary actions against fellow classmates, my voice became a defining factor in who I was. Manifesting my own bravery took much more than giving a speech to hundreds, it took facing real life situations. It is easy to use your voice on your own behalf but using it for a higher purpose is when it actually matters. Suddenly, giving a TED Talk seemed like an easy feat. That's the funny thing about a voice, it is most difficult to use when you're not the one who needs it. All along, the bravery I needed to give this talk was already inside of me, almost like a superpower that went unrealized for all eighteen years of my life.

Though I am very proud of my TED Talk, I am even more proud of who it indirectly caused me to become. It was a largescale production that called upon the most vulnerable part of me to be shown: my voice. More importantly, it brought me to understand what true bravery looked like in my life. True bravery lies in taking initiative in the present. It is in every minor injustice you notice and choose to speak up for. Whether you draw inspiration from a dusty old Kerouac book or facing a large audience head on, I encourage you to find your voice and use it to be the good.

Lindsey Shepard is a Wine and Viticulture major.

CONSIDER THIS:

- Re-read the first two paragraphs of Shepard's essay and discuss with a partner what strategies she deploys to hook readers. How do the descriptive elements she incorporates at the outset of the essay set a particular tone? Does that tone shift at any point, and, if so, what is gained or lost in the transition?

- In this section, you've been invited to turn the gaze inward and examine how significant experiences have impacted you. In the next section, you'll have an opportunity to turn outward and profile an important person, place, event, or trend that impacts the world around you. Shepard drew inspiration from author Jack Kerouac as she worked toward finding the courage to use her voice. What people, places, events, or trends have influenced you and the world around you?

Profiling a Person, Place, Event, or Trend

You can learn a lot by asking people questions and observing closely the surrounding environment. How does observing a person, place, event, or trend help you understand more about yourself and the world around you? How does your angle of vision shift when you take the time to zoom in and zoom out on a particular subject?

Profile writers gather information and then purposefully select details they hope will communicate to readers what compositionist John Trimbur refers to as a "dominant impression." What information do you need to share with readers in order to create an objective portrayal of a subject that also conveys the value you see inherent in it? A profile writer succeeds when they provide enough description and objective information so that readers can understand the significance of the topic through the eyes of the writer while also having the space to form their own impressions. The writers featured in this section have done exactly that— how has their subject altered their perceptions and yours?

Pigeon on the Boardwalk
by Alexander Watkins

Profiling a Person, Place, Event, or Trend

CONSIDER THIS:

Profiles give readers an "insider's view"—a close-up perspective on a certain subject; they present information about the subject and convey (sometimes subtly) the writer's impression of that subject. How does the close-up of the pigeon by Animal Science major Alexander Watkins capture a particular essence of the bird? How does the angle of vision Watkins selected for his subject convey a dominant impression about being on the boardwalk?

A *Linnteresting* Professor

Ryan Takeshita

Reflective Memo: When my instructor announced this assignment and told us we'd be profiling a professional within our discipline, I immediately knew I was going to interview Dr. Linn. He is such a genuine, thoughtful, and entertaining individual. For that reason, the interview was chock full of great material to choose from. My biggest challenge was just that though: deciding what to actually use from the interview for the profile. After listening to the audio recordings of the interview, typing out a full manuscript, and then listening to the audio some more, I finally figured out an angle. I decided to combine what he told me that day with themes of his teaching. I hope this piece does him the proper justice he deserves.

A tall, fair-skinned man towers over a crowd of people. His dark brown, fleece-embroidered robe drapes down to his knees. With its large brass buckle glistening in the light, a leather belt neatly wraps itself around his rigid lower abdomen. Beginning at his neck and scaling down to his legs extends a charcoal grey cape that swirls with every movement he makes. To top the entire outfit off, a golden helmet shaped like the tip of a bullet sits firmly over his bronze hair. Two ivory horns extend out of it, divulging the identity of the man: a Viking warrior. Anyone who saw him would truly believe they were looking at an eleventh-century Norseman—if it weren't for the colorful, blue and lime green, worn down Asics on his feet that compromise the rest of the outfit. No, unfortunately it's not a Viking. It's something far better: Cal Poly's very own, one-of-a-kind history professor Dr. Jason Linn, delivering a lecture on the Viking invasions and the Dark Ages.

Coming to class dressed up in a costume related to what he is teaching that day is just one of the many ways in which Dr. Linn is redefining the traditional schooling experience and sharing his passion for history at the same time. In his own quirky yet enlightening way, he has crafted assignments, lectures, and material that truly bring history to life for the students. His unique, colorful teaching style and philosophy take his course beyond what it was designed for. Every class he teaches proves to be not only a testament to why history and other liberal arts are crucial, but they also reinvent what it means to learn. Using history as his vessel, Dr. Linn has earnestly created an exceptional curriculum that truly allows his students—whom he endearingly refers to as his "Padawans"—to learn more than he or she ever thought possible about the past, the world, and themselves (Linn). I fortunately had the opportunity to not only take one of his classes, but also interview him about his methods and mindset.

Most students can attest to the fact that teachers desire just one main thing from them: answers. They're graded on their responses and expected to learn in their quest to come up with them. Yet, Dr. Linn's class turns this seemingly fundamental idea of education upside down. Instead of grading his students on the quality of their answers, he focuses on the quality of their *questions*. Before every lecture, he slaps the whiteboard like a drum to get the class's attention and goes over his self-named "How to Think Tips": eleven open-ended questions that he encourages everyone to keep in mind throughout the lesson. In the middle of his vibrant, pop culture-reference filled presentations, he'll throw up a historical passage for students to ask questions about in an activity he likes to call "Question Quizzes." "I look back on my undergraduate education," he recounts. "I memorized so much, and today it's evaporated. It's not with me anymore" (Linn). Realizing this, Dr. Linn seeks to impart "skills, not knowledge." He sees the good-question-asking ability as "transportable" and applicable in all disciplines and aspects of life.

Dr. Linn practices what he preaches. Not knowing the answers and digging deeper through inquiry remains important to him. In fact, he admits that he enjoys challenging himself by "teaching on the periphery of [his] knowledge [...]. It helps me... see things from the students' perspective a little bit better and my own knowledge expands too" (Linn). On sunny Friday mornings, Dr. Linn welcomes his students to come to his History Book Club to have casual group conversations about historical readings he came across in small, obscure bookstores that he affectionately equates to candy shops. "The great thing about book club is that students teach each other—it's not just the big omniscient professor with all the knowledge," he explains. He adds that he "learns so much from the students" during the meet-ups and enjoys the intellectually-stimulating talks with his bright pupils. Dr. Linn provides a refreshing, alternative college experience that levels him with his students, places them in the educational driver's seat, and produces rewarding results for both parties. He puts it best when he says, "I look at [teaching]... as a team activity—we're in it together." In a lighthearted tone he expands, "I'm expecting to get some things out of this class too. I'm looking to grow intellectually and have fun." In his eyes, his job isn't to impress anybody or show off, as many professors do. Instead, he prefers that he abandon his ego so that he and his class grow together.

Even more significant than Dr. Linn's unconventional perspective on teaching are his quirky, eccentric, charming antics. If his coming to class flaunting the wardrobe of a Viking, monk, or Julius Caesar wasn't evidence enough, he will go to any length to bring history to life for all of his students. Any small story he has to recount will never fail to invoke an Oscar-award-winning-esque performance out of him. Complete with voice changes, acrobatics, projectiles in the form of ungraded papers, and an occasional sprint out of the room, his acting skills for a history professor prove to be unbelievable. If you just so happen to be lucky, you might even catch his belting out a song about Attila the Hun to the thrilled, eager ears of forty-plus students. If asked where all of this comes from, he'll simply smile and reply, "It's just Jason Linn being Jason Linn."

How did this high-energy, whacky teaching style of his develop? Simply put, it's "just [to] keep [the students] awake" (Linn). "If they're bored, they're not going to learn anything; so, feel free to be crazy... If [I've] got their attention, who cares if [I] make a horse's ass out of [myself] or not. It's not about [me]. It's about their learning" (Linn).

This all begs the question: Why does Dr. Linn go to the utmost extremes for his students when it comes to their education? Why does he put on flamboyant outfits and offer a personal, thought-out experience? Why does he want his history students to take so much away from one course? It's partly because in Dr. Linn's eyes, the humanities are dying. Subjects such as history are losing funding across the nation, and their function is becoming less and less apparent in a STEM-valuing world.

In the past decade-and-a-half, the humanities field has been losing popularity among college students. In the years between 2012 and 2014 alone, college students in a humanities major dropped a whopping 8.7 percent and the number continues to plummet (Jaschik). Due to a lack of career opportunities through these degrees and no guarantee that they'll provide a high-paying job after graduation, students have strayed away from humanistic disciplines. This trend is even more prevalent when looking at the student experience here in San Luis Obispo at a polytechnic school. At Cal Poly, only 15.9 percent of the entire undergraduate student body pursues a liberal art major ("Cal Poly"). Among a majority of students here, classes such as English, philosophy, and history simply become nothing more than a single box to check in the General Education area of a degree requirement. With STEM fields seeing a 43 percent growth across universities in 2016, the humanities are in obvious decline (Wright).

Interestingly enough, Dr. Linn once held a similar view in that there was no money to be made in liberal arts. Although he fostered a deep love and interest for history at a young age, he didn't see an economically solid future in the field. He entered "college with the very practical 'I want a well-paying job.'" At the time, he "wanted

LOOK HERE:

For more information about what declining enrollment in the humanities means for universities as a whole, and why humanities majors may have better job prospects than is commonly believed, read the essay from the *Atlantic Monthly*.

to become a commercial airline pilot" (Linn). After taking some complicated aerodynamics classes, he realized that he hated it. During his freshman year of college, he decided to change his sights to something still unrelated to history: politics. At the time, Bill Clinton's impeachment angered him, so he wanted to make positive changes in the political sphere. He grew a deep affection towards Springfield, Illinois, earlier in his life and decided to run for its state legislature by his senior year. While he recalls that the election "gave him something to strive for" during college, he said that it absolutely took a toll on him physically and mentally. Throughout that time, however, he had an escape that helped him maintain his sanity. He says, "I was a little bit like an adulterous husband... I was married to political science, but on the weekends, I would sneak off and do Roman history." As he counted down the days until the election and realized that he was most likely not going to win, he decided that he would pursue post-graduate studies in something he believed to be "safer, easier, and *funner*": ancient history (Linn). When he lost on election day, he really wasn't sad—it felt as if a burden had been lifted off of his shoulders. He was glad to be following through with his true passion of entering past worlds in acts of escapism, imagination, and discovery through history.

Given his career changes, Dr. Linn knows better than anybody the values of both the hard sciences and liberal arts. Ever since he's become a professor, he's been teaching the subject he adores and convincing the world why it needs to stay. He believes that the "humanities are under attack" and that it's "especially true at a polytechnic university... where many students have a very mercenary way of looking at education." He continues that "for someone who teaches GE classes at [Cal Poly San Luis Obispo], [he] really [needs] to sell" history and why it even matters. For this reason, at the end of every lecture he takes a step back in what he calls the Big Picture moment. Drawing on the content just covered, he connects the past to contemporary life in ways one wouldn't be able to see on the surface. Ranging from the philosophical meaning of death to how intolerance in the past relates to the intolerance on our campus today, the closing Big Pictures creatively extract lessons from history in ways that may have never seemed possible to most. Rather than worrying about whether a student retains the names and dates, he cares much more about hopefully conveying "something in that last sentence or two that affects the way they see the world or see themselves." To Dr. Linn, history isn't just antiquarianism, it's the ultimate act of empathy. It's about finding new ways to place ourselves into the shoes of individual people who we will never personally know. It's about digging deeper and unearthing an intellectual gem that you'd never find anywhere else. It's about building up world views and simultaneously breaking them down. It's about life, itself—and so much more. Liberal arts provide perspectives on life that you can't find anywhere else, and Dr. Linn proves it on a daily basis with his curriculum, teaching philosophy, and personality. He is saving the humanities.

In looking to the future and considering the rest of his career, Dr. Linn has one goal: "Teach until I drop dead." As a student whose outlook on life has been positively transformed by him, I hope that he achieves just that. He never really will die, as his legacy lives on in the lives that he's touched. Dr. Linn in his signature Big Picture fashion leaves me with this piece of advice: The journey of education and life may seem like you're traveling on a set of train tracks that you're forced to follow. While this may seem true, don't forget to go off the tracks every now and then to "smell some of the flowers along the side."

Ryan Takeshita is a History major.

Works Cited

Linn, Jason. Personal interview. 8 Feb. 2019.

"Cal Poly Quick Facts." *www.calpoly.edu,* calpolynews.calpoly.edu/quickfacts. html. Accessed 1 July 2019.

Wright, Joshua. "The Rise of STEM Majors and the Decline of Humanities Degrees." *EMSI*, 1 Sep. 2017, www.economicmodeling.com/2017/09/01/ stem-majors-accelerating-every-state-just-humanities-degrees-declining. Accessed 1 July 2019.

Jaschik, Scott. "The Shrinking Humanities Major." *Inside Higher Ed*, 14 Mar. 2016, www.insidehighered.com/news/2016/03/14/study-shows-87-decline-humanities-bachelors-degrees-2-years. Accessed 1 July 2019.

CONSIDER THIS:

- In his interview, Dr. Linn has very specific ideas about what he thinks a university professor should do in the classroom: how that person should act, what kinds of discussions should be led, and so on. How does your vision of an "ideal professor" match up with Dr. Linn's? For you as a learner, what characteristics should an ideal college instructor possess? Compare and contrast Linn's ideas with your own, paying special attention to the differences.

- Takeshita uses his profile to make an argument—that, in spite of declining enrollments in humanities degree programs, a university education in the humanities really matters. Do you agree with that claim? Why or why not? In what way is this argument supported by the profile of Dr. Linn?

Sojourn Grace Collective: A Church, and Yet

Abigail Wilkins

Reflective Memo: For this essay, I was asked to profile a place of refuge. Sojourn Grace Collective stood out to me as both the most important and the most unique place of refuge in my life. As a member of the LGBTQ+ community who is at least spiritual—if not necessarily religious—a church where I am welcomed and celebrated just as I am, and a church where no specific religious beliefs are required, is a very special thing. I find it a deeply needed refuge from a world where my existence is not usually welcomed. For my essay, I conducted interviews with several members of the church, trying to choose people who reflected Sojourn's diversity; the material I gathered in the interviews was amazing, and I had a hard time choosing what to include and what to leave out. I think my peer review group's feedback helped me a lot in making wise decisions about what material belonged in my essay and what was holding it back. Ultimately, I'm pleased with how this essay turned out, and was proud to share it with my class and with people from Sojourn itself.

"Oh! I love this question!" Pastor Kate exclaims, her wide brown eyes lighting up. I've just asked her to choose a metaphor to describe Sojourn Grace Collective, the church she copastors. She thinks for only a few heartbeats before declaring with utter certainty, "A garden. Garden. Absolutely a garden." She elaborates:

> The flower is never bad, right? The soil is missing nutrients; there's not enough water; it needs to move to a different spot where it gets more sun [...]. That is totally the perfect metaphor for our church! It's like a bunch of people who are blossoming constantly, but that also means wilted flowers. Period. Full stop. And that's never going to be blamed on the flower itself, but what it needs more of or less of.

Kate's metaphor rings true. She's one of the originators of this place, after all, and has been leading this group from the very start. She knows her community well. Sojourn Grace Collective is a church, no doubt about it—and yet it is something more. Something different.

Every Sunday at 11 am (or, more likely, 11:15), a group of people gathers in a building rented out from a local Lutheran church. They refer to themselves collectively as Sojourn Grace, Sojourn, or even just Sojo. Chairs from the storage closet are arranged in concentric semicircles, filling the room while the band sets up in the center of the chairs. Coffee, fruit, and donuts reside on folding tables outside. Next to them is another table, this one brightly draped with a cheerful tablecloth; here you can find information and a wholehearted welcome for newcomers. The gentle San Diego sunshine brightens the courtyard that the snack and info tables are set up in, while inside offers a cool, calming relief. At first glance, Sojourn resembles a typical evangelical church—and yet when you look closer, marked differences start to emerge.

"I would say it's very intersectional. There are people from different ethnicities, I would say different beliefs—even within the Christian faith. There are all genders, all sexual orientations, people of all ages and abilities," says Damian Jackson, known as DJ

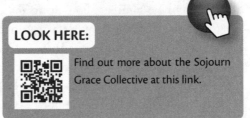

LOOK HERE:

Find out more about the Sojourn Grace Collective at this link.

and a member of the "welcome team" at Sojourn. "I even know some people who go there who aren't Christian, and our church does not make the requirement that 'Oh, you have to believe like we do.'"

Vicky Arteaga, one of the founding members of Sojourn, voices a similar sentiment. "I'd describe Sojourn as a space where people from different backgrounds—spiritually, economically, socially—coincide and build a space where they can share their life together," she says. "It's based on Christianity, but it's open to receive people wherever they are. We have a little bit of everything."

Indeed, Sojourn Grace Collective has no one official creed or set of beliefs. Many of its members do not identify as Christian or believe in a God, per se. Sojourn does specifically profess a belief in love, acceptance, and "practicing wholeness," but little more than that. To many, this lack of definition is one of Sojourn's main draws: there is no pressure to be anything that you aren't already. There is no pressure to be anything other than yourself. Matthew Blake Williams, Sojourn's worship leader, says, "The only reason that I am able to participate in the way that I do is because I am not compelled to believe in a specific doctrine or creed in order to participate fully." He provides an example—he himself does not believe in the physical resurrection of Jesus Christ. "That's something I would not be able to say in 98% of churches in America and still be invited to participate and lead and create and 'churchmake.'" Matthew is careful to emphasize that his personal beliefs are by no means representative of the whole church, pointing out that some people have more "traditional religious views."

It can be difficult to describe Sojourn, in no small part because every person you ask will provide a wildly different answer. Some people emphasize the religious aspect, while others downplay it. Pastor Kate takes the middle ground. For her, sometimes Sojourn is a church, "but that word has a lot of baggage," and so, at other times, to her it is simply a "collective."

Regardless of their particular stance on religion, for many people a big part of Sojourn's appeal is its open, affirmative stance towards the LGBTQ+ community. Every July, Sojourn marches in San Diego's Pride parade. It's a glittery, rainbow-filled day; whole families show up to march as part of the Sojourn contingent, which, by the time the parade starts, ranges in age from babies up to nearly the oldest members of the church. There is face paint and excitement every way you turn. Sojourn hands out rainbow stress balls to those watching the parade as a half dozen children excitedly march at the front, carrying a banner.

All in all, about half of Sojourn's congregation identifies as LGBTQ+. For Matthew, Sojourn is his "last chance" at church. DJ appreciates Sojourn as a community where his son won't be judged for having a gay dad. Vicky describes it as one of few churches in the San Diego area where she and her wife are welcome. "You know, some people say, 'You're gay? You cannot be a Christian.' Well, guess what? You can," she says with a decisive nod, exhibiting her endearing spunk. Her statement is perfectly representative of Sojourn's stance; LGBTQ+ people are not only welcome at Sojourn but celebrated for who they are. "I feel very comfortable and confident […] that Sojourn is putting its money where its mouth is. It's not just paying lip service to those things, it actually is living them out," Matthew says.

Sojourn provides a safe place for people with other identities as well. Many people at Sojourn have been hurt by Christianity, and Sojourn is a healing space for them.

Growing up in an evangelical home, the Bible was used as a measuring stick for everything Amber Wortz did. She either measured up and was a "good person"—or didn't, and wasn't. Every week, after church she felt worse than she did when she arrived. The sermons left her feeling unworthy, like she didn't measure up and needed to "fix" herself. "But I do not feel like that at Sojo," she says. At Sojourn, Amber doesn't feel that she is judged for her performance of what the Bible says anymore; instead, she is reminded every week that she is a "work in progress," that she's "on a journey," and that she is trying her best. "When I leave, I feel free," Amber says, "and that makes me feel good. It makes me feel like I don't hate myself."

Stories like Amber's, stories of being hurt by the Church, are all too common among the members of Sojourn Grace Collective. But for people like Amber, Sojourn is a space to heal, a place where you can be yourself without judgement, even on a bad day. "I can now take everything that hurt me in the past, say it out loud, be angry about it, and no one's going to get mad at me," Kate explains. "No one's ever going to try and shush me or make me quieter or smaller." This is another common reason why Sojourn is so meaningful to people. Emotional authenticity is welcomed and encouraged at Sojourn.

This spirit of welcoming and openness permeates Sojourn, even down to the name of the church. Kate says that she and the rest of the original Sojourn team "poured a lot of thought and heart" into it. Each part of the name is meant to symbolize an important value of the church and serve as a reminder for the leaders of their main goals. The name Sojourn flies in the face of more traditional interpretations of Christianity. In many churches, having "faith" means never doubting or questioning. "Which means that you end up stagnant," says Kate. "You're not growing. Nothing changes." The word Sojourn, meaning "a temporary stay," is meant as a reminder that life is a journey, that every person is on their own journey, and that change happens every day, in every way. "And that's good!" Kate emphasizes. The name is also a nod to Sojourner Truth and her work for abolition and women's rights. The second part of the name, Grace, is meant as a reminder that true grace is for everyone, regardless of who they are or what they believe. That true grace has no strings attached. "It ceases being grace the second there's qualifiers put on it," Kate says. Finally, Collective represents the way Sojourn rejects hierarchy. No one person is in charge. Everyone has a say at Sojourn, and their thoughts are welcome. "This is probably the biggest value of ours," Kate explains. "That's what makes it a community."

Community is an apt descriptor for Sojourn. If you show up on a typical Sunday morning, you'll be welcomed by more people than you have fingers on your hands. It is a joyful welcome, a deep welcome, and truly meant, whether it's your first time at Sojourn or you've been here since day one. For many people, stepping into that sunny courtyard comes to feel like coming home. A handful of excited five-year-olds swarm past in an intense game of tag, and DJ clasps your hand in welcome. Inside, Matthew is just starting the first song. Coffee is waiting.

Sojourn is a church, and yet it is so much more than simply that. At Sojourn, your potential for growth and your inherent worthiness as you are can coexist. Sojourn is a refuge, a safe space, a collective, a family. Above all else, Sojourn is a home.

Abigail Wilkins is a Graphic Communication major.

Works Cited

Arteaga, Vicky. Personal interview. 31 Jan. 2019.

Christensen-Martin, Kate. Personal interview. 2 Feb. 2019.

—. Personal interview. 12 Feb. 2019.

Jackson, Damien. Personal interview. 1 Feb. 2019.

Williams, Matthew Blake. Personal interview. 2 Feb. 2019.

Wortz, Amber. Personal interview. 4 Feb. 2019.

Profiling a Person, Place, Event, or Trend

CONSIDER THIS:

- In this essay, the author makes a special point of asking Pastor Kate to choose a metaphor that describes the Sojourn Grace Collective. Why do you think she made this rhetorical choice? What effect does the metaphor the pastor chooses have on the overall piece?

- Notice the definitional work this essay does on several terms commonly used by communities of faith. What are these terms and how do the interviewees' use of the terms, as they define them, point to an implicit argument? What is that argument?

Living in Eden

Alex Cushing

You travel to the north end of campus: past the market and onto Via Carta. It's a steep road, but you push on with one goal in mind. After passing the baseball fields and horse stables, you reach the Environmental Horticulture Science facility. There will be several small signs pointing to your destination. From the welcome gate, follow the signs through the Poly Plant Shop and greenhouse. Take a slight left turn and you will find a trail. After trekking up a pebbled path, you've found it. With the sign masked by weeping pine trees, you've found the Leaning Pine Arboretum.

Most students have never heard of the Leaning Pine Arboretum or even the word *arboretum*. Even fewer have visited. This could be due to its relative obscurity, bizarre location, or lack of advertisement. I didn't know what an arboretum was when I first arrived. However,

LOOK HERE:

 For more information on the Leaning Pine Arboretum, including its location so you can see it yourself, follow this QR code.

after seeing it briefly mentioned in the *Mustang News*, I immediately became intrigued. I simply had to know what this place was. So, I followed the steps described above, albeit getting a little lost along the way. After needing help from staff members, I finally arrived at the Arboretum. In my search to find its deeper significance, I will learn from the highest authority: Chris Wassenburg, who knows the area like the back of his hand. Having served as Arboretum manager since 1997, he carries an exceptional depth of knowledge and experience.

Although the *Merriam-Webster* definition of an arboretum is "a place where trees, shrubs, and herbaceous plants are cultivated for scientific and educational purposes," Wassenburg describes the area as much more than that: a garden of trees, palms, ferns, cycads, and flowers. Due to the wide variety of plants, it should officially be called a "botanical garden" according to Wassenburg, "but the name 'Leaning Pine Arboretum' sounds better than 'Leaning Pine Botanical Garden' so we stuck with it."

As the manager, Wassenburg determines which plants should be displayed, hires student caretakers, ensures safe gardening practicing, leads group tours, and occasionally writes online advertising articles. Despite having these responsibilities, teaching takes up the majority of Wassenburg's time as he lectures for the arboriculture and horticulture classes. Everything he does reflects the central mission of the Arboretum: having students learn. During my interview with Wassenburg, I began to realize what made the Arboretum so special: the fact that everyone had their own unique reasons for falling in love with the place. It is a breathtaking area where all three tiers of society—students, administration, and community—can learn together about sustainability and inclusivity through its wealth of educational resources and careful attention to detail.

To me and the rest of the student body, the Arboretum offers an invitation to stunning scenery and a passage to contemplative isolation. Upon first entering, a wave of floral decadence and sensations await. Every time I walk up that pebbled path, I cherish the crunch of dirt under my shoe while a western sandpiper calls out searching for a mate. A fountain in the distance provides a calming, bubbling ambiance where I can simply take in the sights. I don't feel any obligation to look at my phone or worry about schoolwork; I am simply here and in the moment.

Even when people stroll by, I can barely pick up a sound. After hiking past the welcome sign, I reach the Australian Garden which is home to native plants having what it takes to survive the harsh climate. I see the detailed label next to every plant and tree: the scientific name, common name, and family. *Adenanthos cuneatus*—Coastal Jug Flower—Proteaceae. These labels repeat plant after plant, adding up to a couple hundred throughout the area. As I make my way through the various gardens, I always find a new shrub or flower that had not been there before, a true embodiment of a living garden. Due to the sheer size, I am never able to complete my tour of the entire area. For other students, though, the Arboretum serves as a second home and a "living laboratory" as described by Wassenburg in an article entitled "Leaning Pine Arboretum." Biology and botany majors will visit weekly to conduct lab experiments including plant testing and soil sampling to see how the climate has affected seedling growth. Without the Arboretum, students would lose valuable access to hands-on research opportunities.

For Cal Poly, the Arboretum is a mission. It serves as a symbol for Cal Poly's attempts to strive for greater diversity and inclusivity on campus. According to The Tribune of San Luis Obispo, in 2017 fifty-five percent of students considered themselves white, more than any other California State University (Clark). The school has even spent $243,000 in hiring a consultant of diversity "to help the university become a more inclusive campus" (Wilson). However, it should have simply looked internally to inspire diversity and equity within students. Boasting over 169 kinds of trees from five Mediterranean regions across five acres of greenery, the garden embodies the diversity that the school simply does not have yet. This should stand as a shining example of inclusiveness that should be expected from the administration. Hopefully, efforts such as these will ensure the student body has a future solid and diverse foundation.

The Arboretum even serves a key educational function in our local community. Wassenburg notes the patio deck and chairs were community service projects by student and resident volunteers. The garden is carefully divided into five geographical zones (Australian, Californian, Chilean, Mediterranean, and South African) that all have a Mediterranean climate similar to that of central California. Each location is labeled and carefully detailed so visitors can visualize a typical garden of the specified region. Even plant selection is a careful process as the Arboretum serves as the "next generation" of plant collection. Workers purposely choose plants that thrive in the aforementioned Mediterranean regions to display in the garden. This way, people who visit know that the available plants are approved to not only be aesthetically pleasing but also physically durable. Because of this, residents can learn about which trees and flowers would be best suited to grow in their own garden. In the professional concentration, landscape architects similarly tour through the garden to find the perfect plant for clients. With new plants arriving every month, anyone who loves gardening or simply observing nature in action should have every reason to keep coming.

"Beautiful. Home." Wassenburg uses these words to describe the Leaning Pine Arboretum, and similar phrases would come to mind for anyone else who has visited. Once you step into the calming, welcoming environment, you immediately feel like you are in an entirely new world and all you can see around you is the stunning beauty. The Arboretum is important because it provides an illustration of successful harmony between varying cultures, backgrounds, and interests. In one short walk, you can see so many plants happily coexisting and wonder why this can't be the case for the rest of the school. Even in my short interview, I was surprised at the number of people who would visit and wave hello to Wassenburg, showing the tight-knit bond of the arboriculture community. All of a sudden, I realized that maybe this place isn't so small and unknown after all. The Leaning Pine Arboretum is truly the ultimate "well-kept secret," and once you have discovered it for yourself, you will want to keep it that way (Loomis and Bashey).

Alex Cushing is a Materials Engineering major.

Works Cited

"Arboretum." *Merriam-Webster*, www.merriam-webster.com/dictionary/arboretum. Accessed 12 Feb. 2019.

Clark, Lucas. "Cal Poly Is the Whitest Public University in California—by a Lot." *The Tribune*, 20 Apr. 2018, www.sanluisobispo.com/news/local/education/article209195019.html. Accessed 1 July 2019.

Loomis, Kyle, and Sophia Bashey. "Leaning Pine Arboretum: Cal Poly's 'Well-Kept Secret'." *Mustang News*, 25 Jan. 2012, https://mustangnews.net/leaning-pine-arboretum-cal-polys-well-kept-secret/. Accessed 1 July 2019.

Wassenburg, Chris. "Leaning Pine Arboretum." *Pacific Horticulture Society*, June 2014, www.pacifichorticulture.org/articles/leaning-pine-arboretum. Accessed 1 July 2019.

Wassenburg, Chris. Personal interview. 8 Feb. 2019.

Wilson, Nick. "Cal Poly Investing $243,000 on Diversity Consultant to Help Campus Become More Inclusive." *The Tribune*, 26 Jan. 2019, www.sanluisobispo.com/news/local/education/article225054390.html. Accessed 1 July 2019.

CONSIDER THIS:

- How does Cushing give us a sense of what the Leaning Pine Arboretum is like, even if we haven't been there? Go back to the text and locate at least three different techniques that Cushing uses to establish the setting for readers. Then, think about other techniques that weren't used in this essay. How else could a sense of place be established?

- In this essay, Cushing draws parallels between the biological diversity of the arboretum and Cal Poly's goal of establishing diversity and inclusion on campus amongst the student body. What do you think about his comparison? Examine the wording. What are the limitations of a comparison like this, and why do we need to be especially careful when we talk of diversity and inclusion?

- Introductions are tricky: you need to grab the reader's attention, and, at the same time, introduce the topic of your essay. Cushing begins his essay by describing the labyrinthine path that leads to the arboretum from the main part of campus. What do you think about this introduction? With a classmate, brainstorm alternative ways to open this essay and compare the advantages and disadvantages of each.

Understanding the Abandoned: An Educator's Immersive Approach

Mackenzie Croxdale

Reflective Memo: *I was not delighted by the results of this piece, but I'm also proud for some of its aspects. After my interview with my profile subject, Dr. Ryan Alaniz, I felt moved by his words, stories, thoughts, and evident drive within him that he could exhibit in such a humble manner. There were many quotes that I wished to have integrated, but I sacrificed using them for the length of my essay. I was pleased with my use of descriptive language for his surroundings and body language—which perhaps filled in some of the gaps for my lack of quotes or stories. I wanted to provoke more emotion in readers by weaving in more stories from his workplace, but I also had to touch on his thoughts on and experiences in the local prison system. I also found it difficult trying to format the order of my paragraphs. My original layout had started with his earliest connections to inmates, then ending with his more recent and relevant time spent at the California Men's Colony. My peers helped me refrain from this structure as there was confusion on the focal point of my essay: his time and passion for his work at the Men's Colony. Overall, I am happy that I could exhibit some sort of reflection for his work. I want people to know who Alaniz is and why our indirect ties to the Men's Colony are important.*

It's seven A.M. in San Luis Obispo, California. The sun has barely met with the horizon, and the sound of students dragging their feet in slippers or sandals mixes with the wind's echo. Ten minutes pass, and a small classroom in Building 38 embraces Cal Poly students into its old desks. Dr. Ryan Alaniz recites his ritual greeting to the class, as the sets of baggy eyes glare back: "Good morning future leaders of the world." What is meant to be a heartening call for his students' determination may reveal the disproportion of privilege within the community; Alaniz teaches another group of students besides those at Cal Poly, for whom his saying is unfit, and better left unsaid. These students are never expected to be the "future leaders of the world." Some will not "see the sun rise or set" ever again. These students are incarcerated at the California Men's Colony, where Alaniz teaches sociology. A maze of concrete walls lead into a skimmed notion of who Alaniz is, or what he calls his office. Although it's located on Cal Poly's campus, the grayness outside is similar to how he portrays the Men's Colony. Yet inside, the room is small and quaint, covered in art and cultural symbolism. The room screams sociology without question.

Hanging on the ceiling is a string of vibrant, paper flags and an overgrown plant, whose limbs

LOOK HERE:

Find out more about the Second Chance Pell Grant Program that Dr. Alaniz helps to facilitate at the Men's Colony.

fall on several levels of a metal bookshelf. Sunlight briefly pierced through the window, so shadows of leaves could dance on the surface of his desk. Folders and jarred foods squeeze between countless textbooks and novels. The aura of the joyous and quirky office space reflects the drive for his work, and a long list of past jobs and volunteer work can confirm it. The wide variety of experiences offer a taste of his diverse career identity: a janitor, a tender to agricultural fields, a smoothie-chef, a kayak instructor, a youth minister, an orphanage volunteer, and the most prominent—an educator. "Every day is a new opportunity to affect the people around us," he says, emphasizing the last few words, "And potentially affect a broader network of people through our work: to inspire, to encourage, and support others." There's an inner intensity that wears off on his students and peers, and it's strengthened by his enthusiasm to save the world. His latest focus has shifted to prisoners and their hidden ties to the community.

Dr. Ryan Alaniz in his captivating workspace
by Mackenzie Croxdale

Alaniz's ambition and experience in the field led him to the Men's Colony. He was consequently in the right place, at the right time; President Barack Obama and his administration launched the Pell Grant program in 2015. After multiple revisions, sixty-seven schools across the country were permitted to provide classes for prisoners, with hopes that they can attain an associate degree in communications or sociology (Ali). Cuesta College was then linked to their looming neighbor, the California Men's Colony. The challenging circumstances of the position thrilled Alaniz's sense to support others. He appreciated the rewards gained through his previous work at prisons, in himself and the incarcerated, so he sought to continue his efforts. His work began with the Men's Colony prisoners in the fall of 2018.

He describes the prison by starting with the physical environment, which can allude to its atmosphere. There are three oak trees beyond the razor wires, a specific and eerie observation. The guard towers hence pose as a substitute for their lacking. He paints a grim picture of the prison: how the amount of concrete buries any hint of beauty; the intimidating, twenty-foot wall dividing society; and the vigilant surveillance, patrolling every inch of surface. The scenery stands as a constant reminder of the prison's enforced rigidity and the internal caution in people's interactions. "…it's like this omnipotent eye, that no matter what you're doing there's cameras and correctional officers watching you." He stressed the change in prisoners' demeanor once the classroom fills and the doors close. Banter and conversation flood the room, contrary to Alaniz's disconnected classroom dynamics at Cal Poly. Students will often express to him that they momentarily lose sight of their incarceration. However, there's still restraint in his classroom at the Men's Colony, needed to maintain his ties to the prison. A guard stands in the corner listening to the conversations and class content, assuring it doesn't discuss inflammatory issues.

Alaniz first stemmed his connection to the criminal justice system 7 years ago. He was on the Board of Directors for San Luis Obispo's non-profit organization, Restorative Partners. The group started classes for inmates at the county jail for recreation or rehabilitation (Restorative Partners). The classes teach skills and qualities that inmates can apply to their future careers or utilize as a route of therapy. "[Prisoners] start to think of themselves not as bad people, but as a good sewer, or a good artist," he says, "[It's] reframing who they think they are…as somebody who can be a positive impact on society." He intensifies focus on this belief about prisoners' revised view of themselves through his class "Incarceration and Society," an upper division sociology course offered at Cal Poly. He took initiative to weave Cal Poly's slogan, "Learn by Doing," into the class by connecting with San Luis Obispo's county jail, deriving from his prior connection with Restorative Partners. Prisoners of low-level crimes reside here, so the degree of confinement is different compared to that of the Men's Colony. Eight students are paired with eight inmates to sit and convene during each field-trip, while they occupy an open space that supports their fluid conversations. The visit lasts for an hour and a half, as students tour the prison and conversate with guards after their introduction to the inmates. *[Editor's note: Alaniz further explains, "after an initial tour of the jail and conversation with the sergeant, students then spend the remaining eight weeks in class with inmates."]* Alaniz believes that anyone receiving a criminal justice degree should first visit a prison, an absent factor in the current, overall education system—but an important feature of "Learn by Doing." There's a facet of transparency that he wants to bring into the equation. The tone of his voice bared his sentiment on the issue, stating "It's like Mother Teresa's saying, 'a lot of people talk about the poor, but few people talk to the poor.'"

Since engaging with the Men's Colony, Alaniz is driven to further integrate "Learn by Doing" in the sociology department; he is in the process of gathering stories from his incarcerated students, to then develop their accounts into his own sociology textbook. "I want to lay out their stories, and then pepper in the concepts and theories as they're relevant to helping us understand the story." He's using hand gestures to accentuate his point, then continuing, "I think that their life provides valuable examples for explaining or understanding sociology, since many of these folks have suffered the worst of our society, leading them in turn to create suffering." It's a contemplative twist on the typical approach for a textbook; he delivers the required material to his students in an interesting manner, but does so while shedding light on the societal patterns of incarceration. Inmates can be humanized, and their stories will be heard. He must wait an agonizing three to six months for approval from the state, so he resumes his formation of bonds with inmates to fortify their stories.

His influence is taken beyond the classroom as well. Families of prisoners live unique lives without the extra pair of hands the inmate would provide. Roles are strained—more than they were before—and the deprivation of resources is a threatening force. The California project "Get on the Bus" relieves this gap, by granting children and relatives the ability to visit their incarcerated mothers on Mother's Day (C.D.C.R.). Alaniz recognized the high numbers of male prisons throughout the central coast, so he and Sister Theresa Harpin coordinated a local bus trip for families on Father's Day in 2006. The Get on the Bus program has since continued, providing bus trips to male prisons across the state of California. Families are rejoiced, relationships are mended, and new memories are made. It can affect children's lives greatly with the revival of their parent figure, and the trending cycle of recidivism, or re-incarnation, can be halted.

The Game of Life, but the 'Authentic Version'
by Mackenzie Croxdal

Alaniz dissects the local prison system as more than an unjust institution, though; he applies it to the student body of Cal Poly, and how they and other occupants of San Luis Obispo must recognize its relativism to their lives. Few students are aware of the Men's Colony, a six-minute drive from the edge of campus. When there is recognition, students may distance themselves from the prison's negative connotation. Prisoners are quickly labeled as deviant and responsible for their decisions in broader society, carrying a weighted burden after their incarceration while continuing to be disregarded. Alaniz mentions this trend of ignorance in regard to a phrase by James Bradford from 1621, "But for the grace of God, go I." [Bradford] was walking past the gallows of people who had just been hung and were dead. Alaniz illustrates how the old saying can challenge the social hierarchy that students are immersed in, recognizing that "it's just minor details in our lives that have led us to where we are today."

He acknowledges the privilege that he grew up with. If the successful students at Cal Poly had the same, severe background as most inmates across the country, then they too would presumably be incarcerated: "Many of us are just a step away. Have I broken laws, similar to laws that they've broken? Yes." He explains what allows the general population to live freely depends on upbringing.

Profiling a Person, Place, Event, or Trend

What follows is the subsequent opportunities and advantages. It's comparable to the board game LIFE, as an individual's outcome as a contributor to society relies on chance.

Dire circumstances ensue for people with pasts of trauma, poverty, and violence. They are often forced to commit crimes for basic and essential resources—money, food, clothes, transportation, anything to sustain a heartbeat. This, or they're repeating actions from their past, ingrain in their way of living. Alaniz stresses these facts and patterns seen throughout history for prisoners and sees the inequity in public thought that abolishes them from over-all society.

Hopefully, reform may change a prisoner's chances at becoming a "future leader of the world." Alaniz's contributions support such a change, building a needed bridge between Cal Poly and the Men's Colony. "I worked really hard and have a good life. But they work hard too. And they've made a mistake," he says, and pauses as he lowers his eyes, "For us to lock them up and throw away the key is fundamentally unfair, because we are often no better than them."

Mackenzie Croxdale is an Animal Science major.

Works Cited

"About Restorative Partners." *Restorative Partners: A Safer Community Where Everyone Belongs*, Restorativepartners.org. Accessed 1 July 2019.

Alaniz, Ryan. Personal interview. 7 Feb. 2019.

Ali, Diana. "Pell Grants for Prisoners: Considerations in the New Administration." NASPA: Student Affairs Administrators in Higher Education, www.naspa.org. Accessed 1 July 2019.

CDCR. "Get on the Bus Program." *California Department of Corrections and Rehabilitation*, State of California Government, 2019, www.insidecdcr.ca.gov. Accessed 1 July 2019.

CONSIDER THIS:

- What is the value of the detailed description of Dr. Alaniz's office space? What do you think the author is trying to convey about the professor with this rich description?

- Dr. Alaniz did not take a traditional path to teaching in academia. How do you think the different parts of his professional journey helped him arrive at where he is today?

- What is the implicit argument being made by both the author and Dr. Alaniz in this essay?

A Farmer, A WAVE, and a Navy Wife

Holly Masterson

William Dickie, a North Dakotan farmer from the depression era, was not blessed with a house full of boys to help run the farm and eventually take over the business. There were no strong, strapping lads to milk the cows or mend the fences, and there were no clever gentlemen to understand finances and production numbers. Instead, there were four capable, intelligent girls that would fill the masculine void in the Dickie family line. And little did he know, that was all he would need.

Marjorie Joyce Dickie was born to Olive and William Dickie on a cold rainy night in Cavalier, North Dakota in 1922. There was no doctor because, as she put it in her memoirs, "[She] was anxious to see this big beautiful world and could not wait for [them]" (Connell 5). Her ambitious, resilient attitude would help her through the rest of her life. A life that not many other women or men would have had the strength to succeed in as she did.

Since she was the firstborn child, little Margie had a lot to do on the farm. As she grew up milking cows, repairing machinery, shoveling manure, and cleaning horse stalls, she rarely had time to make friends. From her teens, she vividly remembers when she would finish barn chores in the morning and not have enough time to clean up before school; "it was embarrassing to go to school with manure on our overshoes, especially when I went to high school. There never seemed time to clean them, as barn chores were a must before school every morning" (Connell). Getting to her high school was no simple task either. The country school her younger siblings attended was in the complete opposite direction of her high school. To solve this problem her family formed a carpool group with other families. In the spring, however, she would be taken to school by her father in a cart pulled by a horse to avoid getting stuck in the muddy potholes.

Upon graduating, Margie didn't have much of an idea on what she wanted for her life. She worked hard on her grandmother's farm to earn money through the end of high school, but she wasn't sure that's what she wanted. Her parents scraped up enough money for her to attend college, but after a year she decided it wasn't for her either. She eventually was certified to teach and taught at a nearby country school. The attack on Pearl Harbor happened the year she began teaching. As boys were drafted into World War II, things began to slow down in Cavalier. "It was a very lonely time for young women" (Connell) she explained tenderly, and at that time she often thought about what she could do to help the war effort. Joining the service as a woman, however, was a seriously controversial topic. Many men believed that if women joined the forces, they would tragically lose their femininity; and if that happened, who would be left to breed their children? Things were different in the Dickie Household. Margie always lightens up as she remembers when her father drove her home one night and asked if she'd thought about joining the service; "Dad had no boys to serve as he had done in World War I, so he was giving me that chance by letting me know he would support me if I was interested" (Connell 21). She was shocked at the nonchalance from her father, but excited at the notion of serving her country.

Army catalogs from WAC (Women's Army Core), WAVES (Women Accepted for Voluntary Emergency Service), and Women in the Coast Guard were all around the house as she struggled to decide. She ended up applying to the WAVES and was sworn in at the train station in Grand Forks

LOOK HERE:

For more information on how women served in World War II, including in WAVES, take a look at this website.

before travelling all the way to New York for boot camp. On the train, she met a sweet girl her age named Charlotte (Todd) Thompson. She was tall with a kind face, wavy blonde hair, and often would use Swedish phrases like "uff da." Margie would never fully understand the meaning, but "decided it had to be used when something was awful or distasteful" (Connell 21). They decided they liked each other immediately and have stayed good friends ever since.

The training was strenuous with lots of marching; "We marched to the mess hall and to exercise and classes where we learned about ships and Navy ways and terms," (Connell 22) she contemplatively wrote in her memoirs. Once the training was finally over, they were able to make three decisions on where to go from boot camp. She and Todd both put the Navy Training Hospital as their first choice and were granted it. In fact, from that point on they would be assigned in the same places as their first station in Idaho, to their last station in Hawaii. They also both passed tests to be upgraded in rank to "Pharmacist Mate Third Class." At their first station, Margie can recall stepping off of the train in her crisp blue uniform, the red cross on her shoulder displayed brightly with pride. Her first assignment was in the surgical ward. She remembers that many of the patients "begged for backrubs, mostly to get the undivided attention of us Corps WAVES" (Connell). This was a rough job and they were making constant rounds taking blood pressure and administering medication. She remembers seeing men that were horribly deformed, and near the end of the war they received prisoners of war from Japan that were depressed and changed from their time overseas. The day didn't end at sundown either; if their barracks were not in ship-shape every night, they were revoked their rights to liberty, which is what they would call their Sunday holidays.

Margie and Todd stayed together throughout their time in the Navy. After the atomic bomb was dropped on Hiroshima and the peace treaty was signed, WAVES were asked whether they wanted to stay on with the service for longer or return to their family. Now that the war was over, they decided it was time to part because they felt that they had fulfilled their purpose. Margie remembers wondering why we had resorted to such horrifying means to end the war, but she was relieved to go home to her family. Saying goodbye to Todd was very difficult, but it was certainly not the end of their friendship.

Margie remains wistful when she speaks about her return home from the service. She recalls waving to people on the coastline of San Francisco while a band played "San Francisco Here I Come" to welcome the veterans home. She is humble and doesn't say much about the results of her service except that she was proud to have served her country.

After leaving the Navy, Margie ended up rekindling her relationship with a boy from high school who happened to be an Aviation Machinist in the Navy. Within two months they were engaged and as she became Mrs. George Duane Connell, she transitioned from being a Navy WAVE to a Navy wife. They were happily married for sixty-eight years until Duane's death in 2015.

Many people don't understand the hardships of being a family in the service. Duane was constantly being re-stationed around the country and eventually outside of it, too. She had no idea what to expect before they were married but knew it would be difficult. In fact, between their engagement and wedding, Duane was away in San Diego. They still wrote to each other as often as they could and knew they wanted to stay together. Fast forward to their married years, and Margie would end up moving from place to place, driving a massive trailer with their furniture, living pregnant with a toddler in the Philippines, and waiting nearly a full year before seeing her husband right after their first child was born. The salary wasn't quite big enough to support a family either, as she explains: "I made my own and Karen's dresses during the lean years which helped stretch the Navy paycheck" (Connell). Despite all this, you would never know she struggled. In fact, as she writes at the beginning of her memoirs: "I have been blessed with many gifts and miracles on my life's journey and I humbly give thanks and praise to God" (Connell 4).

Her grip is strong, and her white curls are tight. She has the back of a dancer, straight as a board—and even at 97 years old, she is a better driver than many people I know. She keeps her lessons from her stern father on appropriateness and strict discipline. Alongside these tenacious traits, is a bountiful supply of kindness, faith, and generosity. Her warm eyes smile at you behind their glasses as she asks about your day and how you are doing. She remembers every detail of your life and makes sure to ask you about them. This is how I've always seen my great aunt Margie. Her fierce yet gentle composure is a direct result of the life she's led and her Christian faith through it all.

My great aunt grew up a Christian and held her values throughout her life. As she moved around and saw the difficult experiences of other people she says, "my thinking was changed and broadened as I realized how all people were God's people and our neighbors no matter where on this earth we lived" (Connell 53). Throughout her life she's had no choice but to be strong as a farmer, WWII nurse, and Navy wife. She is humble and she won't open up much about how difficult her life was, but strong faith is often a sign of hardship.

Many Americans fail to remember the faces of the women that healed wounds, flew planes, and worked long hours during the wars. They are still only considered a small part of our history despite all that they accomplished. Women in the service during World War I and World War II, wives of soldiers who worked hard to bring them home, and those that took over work when it was needed without childcare or even an equal salary; these are the women that helped create a better future for their daughters and granddaughters. A better future filled with opportunities and equality in the eyes of the law. My great aunt Margie serves as an example of one of these women and she'll always be a role model for myself as I strive to be strong in my faith and fierce in the way I live my life.

Holly Masterson is an Animal Science major.

Works Cited

Connell, Margie J. *My Blessings*. 2008. Print.

Connell, Margie J. Phone interview. 2 Feb. 2019.

CONSIDER THIS:

- This profile covers a lot of ground—nearly all of the major events of Margie's life. What are the differences between presenting a broad view when profiling a person (covering a significant amount of time and events) and taking a narrower approach to profiling a person (focusing on a shorter period of time and fewer events)? If Masterson were to revise the essay to give it greater focus, on which parts of Margie's life story do you think she should concentrate? Why?

- Did Masterson strike the appropriate balance between *telling us* about Margie's life story and *showing us* what she was like at different moments in time? Is anything missing from this portrait? Is anything unclear or imprecise?

- In what way can the story of a person—a profile—give us a glimpse of history and its conflicts and struggles? What can we learn from this essay about the role of women in the early to mid-twentieth century?

Journey to the West

May Thiri Kyaw

Reflective Memo: *When we were first given this assignment, I was at a loss. I have never heard of a profile essay before, much less written one. I also had no idea who to interview. But then Professor Nishanta came into mind. I met him during our first dorm meeting where he came to introduce himself as our faculty advisor. I remembered him telling us he was from Sri Lanka and how enthusiastic and expressive he was with everything. I had no idea what to expect when I first contacted him, but after the interview, I knew I had chosen the right person. He had so much to say and had so many interesting stories to share. Through that one interview, he taught me so much about living life with optimism and not letting little things get in the way of being happy. It is my hope that, through my writing, the readers will be able to learn from Nishi's unique experience and perspective, as well as gain a better insight on multilingualism.*

The fluorescent lights beamed white and blasts of air escaped the air-conditioners as shoppers rolled their carts down through one aisle after another. But what was an everyday sight for the average American was a whole new cultural experience for Professor Nishanta Rajakaruna, also known as Nishi, who was still, as he put it, "fresh off the boat." Never having gone shopping before during his life in Sri Lanka, he admitted he would have been completely lost were it not for the help of his university advisor.

As they rolled down their cart aisle after aisle, picking up all the dorm essentials, they came upon the ice cream section. Cool wind blasted Nishi's face as his advisor opened the fridge and pointed to a Ben and Jerry's Cherry Garcia, exclaiming, "You have to try this!" Nishi reached for a pint of the ice cream but froze midway when he saw the $1.89 price tag. Gears turned in his head as he translated this number into rupees, the Sri Lankan currency. His eyes widened and his jaw dropped as he realized this was equivalent to a week's salary of his parents. Not wanting to say anything to his advisor, he added it to his cart. On that first night, he opened it up and restricted himself to just one spoon of the ice cream. Despite wanting more, his guilt stopped him in his tracks. On the second night, he upgraded to a couple spoons after seeing his roommate use a whole pint of ice cream to make root beer float. By the third night, however, he found himself eating straight out of the container. "And that," he proclaimed, as he took a bite of his pizza, "was how quickly I became American."

Now that he was 8322 miles away from home, in a small town in Maine, he learned that he had to "drop the things that were restricting him" if he truly wanted to fit into this new culture. He had let the price of the ice cream keep him from enjoying it the first time around, but fortunately he soon realized that if he continued, he would never be able to enjoy any of the opportunities presented to him. He knew he had to let go of some things "so that [he] could be who [he] wanted to be."

This was the story of Professor Nishanta's very first eye-opening encounter in his first year in the United States. Born in Sri Lanka, Professor Nishanta, who also goes by Nishi, is currently a professor in the Biological Sciences department as well as a faculty advisor of the yakʔitʸutʸu dorms. Brought up being taught multiple languages, Nishanta revealed that he actually used to speak four languages in total. Sinhalese was Nishi's first language.

When he moved to Japan at the age of 3 for his father's graduate research and lived there for three years, he quickly learned Japanese and became fluent in the language. His nickname, Nishi, he tells us, is actually a Japanese word meaning "west." Then when he came back to Sri Lanka, he learned English and Tamil, another language used on the island that is predominantly spoken by South Indians in school.

"Growing up," he says, "I never thought of leaving Sri Lanka." But when civil war broke out in his country and universities were shut down, he had no other choice. With the help of an individual who was a retired engineer who helped Sri Lankan students get into US colleges with scholarships, he was able to attend the College of the Atlantic with a full ride as the very first foreign student at that university.

He recalled that having been in a setting where he was the only international student did not make the transition harder for him, contrary to what one might believe. Because he did not have the option of interacting with other international students, he "was forced to integrate" and he believed that made his transition into the new culture much faster. As an international student myself, his words left a strong impression on me. His words motivated me to immerse myself more into the culture I am now in instead of hanging on to every bit of the one I have left behind.

LOOK HERE:

Check out this *Mustang News* article about "The Professor Next Door."

As the topic shifted over to the lack of diversity here in Cal Poly and how this affects minorities going here, he states that, as foreigners, we should begin to think about the bright side of being a minority in an isolated setting like this. He believes "it works well for us" and that we have a bigger role to play "as an ambassador of another country." Instead of complaining about "the lack of this and that," we, as a community, "have to start celebrating what we have" and try to "figure out the best way to make it work rather than pushing things forcefully."

When asked if he had ever faced prejudice due to his different language background, he immediately shook his head no, saying, "I don't have a single story of ever feeling discriminated against." Although people had a hard time understanding him when he first came to the US due to his heavier accent, it had never been used against him. Nishi proudly says with a wide smile, "I only have a positive story to tell."

Being in a culture where "people seem to want to celebrate diversity," Nishi feels has worked well for him. He admits, however, that he has had to work harder and plan further ahead than his American peers when it comes to things like applying for jobs and internships due to his status as an immigrant. But when asked if he ever felt even slightly resentful of all this, he exclaims, "No, not at all! I loved it!" He says that it "made [him] always ahead of the curve."

Despite all his positive experiences, he acknowledges the struggles other immigrants have faced during their time here and says, "Maybe I've just been lucky by being at the right place at the right time." Whatever the reason, he truly feels he has "had a wonderful life across 28 years in North America."

Rather than just luck, a large part of his positive experience seems to be a result of his overall optimistic energy that radiates happiness to those around him. Both during and after the interview, student after student passed by, calling out, "Hey, Professor Nishi!" with a grin on their faces and Nishi would always wave back excitedly. It was obvious from these exchanges that he was someone they were genuinely comfortable around.

While people generally tend to dwell on negative experiences and let those hinder them from moving forward, Professor Nishanta takes a different path, only focusing on the bright side of things. He has been able to fit in everywhere he goes. "Now, the problem for me," he admits, "is not knowing where home is." Although he has moved some many times and is happy wherever he goes, he feels like something is missing in his life. While his peers settle down into jobs, he is still continuously looking. "I am not rooted anywhere," he explains. "I move constantly, and I always question what I'm looking for." As he takes the last bite of his pizza, he says, "So I think that's a quest I'm going to be on for the rest of my life."

May Thiri Kyaw is a Civil Engineering major.

Work Cited

Rajakaruna, Nishanta. Personal interview. 10 Oct. 2018.

CONSIDER THIS:

- This profile introduces readers to a way of being in the world that they may or may not have ever thought of. What aspects of Dr. Nishanta's journey do you relate to? Which part(s) of the profile surprise you?

- What do you think the story about the ice cream illustrates about Dr. Nishanta's character? What message about Dr. Nishanta do you think the writer intended to convey by including this story?

- What part(s) of this profile make you wish you knew more about this professor? Why? What follow-up questions might you have asked to deepen your knowledge about him?

The Ultimate Experience

John Lazo

As I approach the practice fields about ten minutes early, I feel a little nervous about the impending tryout process. I hope I can show the captains all my skill and ability. I arrive at the field and set down my bag full of gear. Eventually, I decide I should take a second to analyze the moment and write my observations in a note on my iPhone. Immediately, I fixate on the blue hues that are filling the evening sky and foreshadowing the darkness. It's 7:20 PM on a cool, crisp evening highlighted by the smells of fresh cut grass. Little by little, players start filing into the practice fields, and the small murmur of voices transforms into the perpetual sounds of greetings, conversation, and laughs. The edge of the hill above the fields turns into a maze of bags, cleats, water bottles, jerseys, and discs. Players start to warm up, and the sounds of frisbees gripping the air and cutting through the sky as they are tossed among pairs begin to rival the incessant chatter. After several minutes, one of the captains yells "SLOCORE, bring it in!" The tryout officially begins.

LOOK HERE:

SLOCORE is just one example of a Cal Poly campus club. For more information on clubs you could join to make connections with your classmates, or just to have fun, follow this QR code.

Cal Poly's Ultimate Frisbee club was founded in 1978, ten years after Joel Silver created the sport at a high school in Maplewood, New Jersey ("About SLOCORE"). SLOCORE stands for "San Luis Obispo Comrades of Radical Energy" and has served as a popular club on campus for students dating back to its inception in the late 1970s. The club consists of an A-team, in which players compete at the highest collegiate level, and a B-team, in which players learn and develop their skills. Currently, there are over eighty students involved in the club, a vast majority of whom are studying math and science-based majors such as engineering. Recently SLOCORE has risen in terms of national prominence as they finished tied 9th at Nationals in 2017 and tied 17th in 2016 ("About SLOCORE"). In general, Cal Poly's SLOCORE Ultimate Frisbee team aims to establish a competitive but welcoming environment, making it a phenomenal outlet for students to get involved on campus and develop an appreciation for the importance of community and friendship.

The sport of Ultimate consists of seven players per team on the field at once. The objective of the game is to throw the disc among teammates (who are unable to run with it) until it crosses the opposing team's end zone. Once this occurs, the team receives a point. If the throw fails to be completed between teammates, a turnover results, and the defending team now takes control of the disc and attempts to score in the opposite direction. A point lasts as long as it takes for one of the teams to score. In general, a predetermined point total marks the winner of the game. Often times this will be the team that is first to fifteen points, but it can vary. Ultimate is rather unique because it is self-officiated, meaning that the players on the field call their own fouls and penalties. Some tournaments do have an observer who will offer their opinion on a call, but the final decision still remains in the hands of the players.

A few nights after the tryout, I wait to interview Morgan Sommer, a third-year student who has been on the team since his freshman year. He arrives within a few minutes and eventually we head towards the back of the library to a set of red cloth couches. Sommer remarks how he often studies here and that he feels comfortable in the area. We take a seat and as I open up the "Voice Memos" app on my iPhone, he navigates to a photo I sent him containing the interview questions. I press the red button at the bottom of the app and numbers start racing across the screen. The recording starts as we settle in for an interesting conversation.

SLOCORE has been such an attractive club on campus for so many years due to the sense of community that quickly develops between teammates. Sommer underscores the three-day-a-week practice schedule, a variety of out-of-school events, and several pre-season tournaments as the reasons for its prominence, while underlining the club's intent to provide "an atmosphere that's competitive, fun, and social." SLOCORE's goals fall in line with *USA Ultimate's* focus on fun, character, and community ("What is Ultimate?"). As such, these foundational aspects of the game, and the hope of establishing a sense of community early in my college experience are precisely why I was seeking to join the club.

In order for SLOCORE to maintain its popularity on campus, to reach out to new members, and to market the club, it uses the club showcase, word of mouth, and social media. Specifically, SLOCORE's YouTube videos are a unique focal point for growing the club. Incoming students may stumble upon the team's collection of videos, which feature highlights from tournaments packed with ridiculous throws, stellar defense, and incredible diving catches. These videos serve as a way to draw interest to the club and attract talented members to the team. Additionally, the club hosts a yearly tournament early in the season at which community members, Cal Poly alumni, and current students gather together for a day of fun, friendly Ultimate. The tournament enhances the sport's significance in the community and encourages young players to continue to play the sport and strive to be better.

After some discussion, Sommer and I stumble on one of the most exciting developments in the upcoming season. Due to an incredibly strong rookie class, this year's roster is loaded with as much diverse talent as ever and full of "awesome recruits." Sommer notes that qualifying for Nationals is the "number one" goal, but, beyond that, the team aspires to play deep into Nationals in May. It all depends on how the team chemistry develops over the next several months and how well the rookies can perform. In Sommer's eyes, the rookies are the "defining factor [...] because they bring the energy," but it's "up to the upperclassmen to direct that energy" by offering tips and tricks on the field, encouraging good sportsmanship, and establishing a sense of family. The rookies' importance can't be overstated as the differences from high school to collegiate Ultimate can be a challenging transition since the players are "bigger, stronger, faster" and the "overall talent is higher." Sommer describes collegiate Ultimate as a "new level of seriousness" at which players play with a "bigger name on their shirt." Overall, SLOCORE hopes their prioritization of "individual development" and "team culture" helps integrate the rookies and rewards the team once the season kicks off in January. Sommer sees these as vital components in an effort to "do a lot of winning" at tournaments against some of the best college Ultimate teams in the U.S.

At this point, Sommer and I have ventured into some interesting conversation. We decide to delve into a new topic, and I ask him about the state of Ultimate and the direction of the sport as a whole. He pauses, and then after a few moments Sommer comments on the current conversation surrounding the game: Will it be in the Olympics anytime soon? When will it be televised regularly? Will it become part of the NCAA? Sommer brushes aside the potential for the sport to become part of the NCAA anytime soon, but "would like to see it in the Olympics." He notes the sport's relatively strong international presence, allowing it to "transition perfectly" to an Olympic sport. Currently, Ultimate is played in over 80 countries, and an International Club Championship is held every year at which the best players from a variety of countries compete at the highest level ("What is Ultimate"). Furthermore, there does seem to be a marketable audience of viewers, as Sommer finds himself "tuning in" to the live streamed games to enjoy the action. As it stands now, USA Ultimate's Facebook live streams consistently engage several thousand viewers. Meanwhile, thousands more watch the games on YouTube or, occasionally, ESPN 2. As a matter of fact, I also find myself keeping track of various games, watching highlights and learning about some of the sport's best players. Although the sport is still small and consists of a tight-knit community, Sommer believes that as it continues to grow, there will be more people who can play an integral role in the future of the sport. For example, there will be more qualified coaches and people who have the required knowledge to commentate a game. Fortunately, the data provides hope for a small, but passionate community of Ultimate players to see their sport gain relevance, as USA Ultimate has over 50,000 active members and experienced a "94.8% growth in active membership from 2007 to 2015" (Lazar, et al.).

The sport of Ultimate is meaningful to a person for a variety of reasons. Sommer chuckles as I mention a few of the reasons why I love the sport: team dynamic, competition, and health. Oddly enough, these are three of Sommer's favorite aspects of the sport as well and "almost in that order." Sommer reiterates the importance of the team dynamic and says "you gotta like the guys you play with." He believes that the club does a great job of building a strong team environment where "everyone's looking out for each other and everyone wants to hang out with each other." I immediately nod my head in agreement. Throughout the course of last week's tryouts, I felt that no matter the situation, everybody was welcoming, friendly, and willing to give tips. Sommer goes on to say, "I love the competitive aspect of it," while recollecting a spirited game against Stanford in which he remembers simply thinking "this is fun" as he re-envisions dozens of fans viewing from the sideline, the pressure to make every throw and cut count, and the cheers and reactions to all the action on the field. Finally, Sommer comments on how the game keeps him physically fit and the fact that he's more likely to go to the gym, in part, because he doesn't want to let his team down. Interestingly, our mutual love for the health benefits of the sport is also outlined by *USA Ultimate* as one of the principal reasons many people love to play the sport ("What is Ultimate").

The final question I ask is for Sommer's favorite memory during his tenure in the club. He ponders for a moment and settles on something. Sommer prefaces the memory, stating how it's easy to get bogged down by not playing much as a freshman on a team. He recounts an instance where one of his teammates asked him when he's going to sky someone (out-jump another player for the disc). They put him in on the next point. Then, he tells me, "someone throws something lobby and I skied the pile."

His teammates "rush the field" and show their support, making him feel like "a million bucks."

Right there: that's the epitome of Ultimate.

John Lazo is an Environmental Engineering major.

Works Cited

"About SLOCORE." *SLOCORE*, slocore.com/aboutslocore. Accessed 15 Oct. 2018.

"History of Ultimate." *World Flying Disc Federation*, wfdf.org/history-stats/history-of-ultimate. Accessed 15 Oct. 2018.

Lazar, Damien J, et al. "Concussion Prevalence in Competitive Ultimate Frisbee Players." *Orthopaedic Journal of Sports Medicine*, vol. 6, no. 3, 2018.

Sommer, Morgan. Personal interview. 22 Oct. 2018.

"What is Ultimate?" *USA Ultimate*, www.usaultimate.org/about/ultimate/. Accessed 20 Oct. 2018.

CONSIDER THIS:

- One of the challenges of writing about a sport like Ultimate Frisbee is communicating a passion for the sport to a large audience of readers, many of whom may not be familiar with Ultimate. To what extent does Lazo accomplish the difficult task of making connections with a diverse group of readers?

- Effectively organizing and transitioning between points of information is always a challenge when a writer uses an interview to create a profile of a topic. In this essay, Lazo presents the information he gathered by organizing the profile around the interview questions he asked. Did that choice engage you as a reader? If not, what other organizational approaches could Lazo have taken?

How do writers communicate with their audiences? How do they respond to complicated rhetorical situations? What strategies do writers deploy to persuade readers, viewers, and/or listeners?

Rhetorical analysis is a critical reading skill that helps us identify the strategies writers use to communicate with their audiences. By identifying a text's intended audience, its rhetorical appeals (ethos, pathos, and logos), its style, the arrangement of its argument, the timing of its message (kairos), and the medium or mode of delivery, we can understand and articulate how a text has been designed to inform, convince, or persuade.

Constructed Perspective
by Laura Nelson

CONSIDER THIS:

The image on this page was drawn by Architecture major Laura Nelson. Do you recognize this place on campus? Why do you think Nelson elected to recreate this corner of the university in black and white? What mood or message does the image convey? And, notice the title Nelson assigned to her piece. Consider what argument(s) she is making both through her artistic work and the title she gave it.

Catching Fire

Alex Cushing

Reflective Memo: *For this rhetorical analysis piece, I wanted to choose an image that struck home with me and the audience. I wanted to choose an image that would shock the world and leave a lasting impact. I had to dig around a little bit, but I finally found a picture whose story was worth sharing. Although it took hours of researching, writing, and reviewing, I am proud to say the work paid off.*

I have spent the past three years participating in Model United Nations, a club where students (called delegates) represent countries or parties involved in global conflicts and work together to create policy solutions. When going into meetings, delegates must compile background research to identify their motives, wants, and needs. My most powerful delegate experience was when I served as a real-life "leader" of the Venezuelan resistance movement, Jose Vactor Salazar Balza. The Venezuelan crisis started in 2013 after the death of locally celebrated figure Hugo Chavez (Trejos). Chavez' death left a power vacuum and consequently, the country immediately took a turn for the worse. The economy plummeted, hunger and poverty increased, and crime rates rose. The successive President, Nicolas Maduro, crossed the line when he tried to rewrite the constitution in order to grant himself more power in 2017 (Katz).

Demonstrators took to the streets to protest, with the biggest demonstration happening in the nation's capital, Caracas. During one incident, Salazar and other protesters tried to destroy a police motorbike when the bike exploded (Katz). Salazar caught on fire and sprinted down an alley, screaming for help. At this moment, photographer Ronaldo Schemidt snapped an image that emerged as the definitive symbol of the Venezuelan resistance.

The image, called "Venezuela Crisis," was so shocking and impactful that Schemidt won the World Press Photo of the Year in 2018, an achievement that awards excellence in visual creativity of a journalistically important event (see Figure 1). Through the central subject and subtle surroundings, Schemidt uses pathos and symbolism to capture the state of a country in total disarray. This snapshot motivates the audience of informed people to continue supporting the resistance movement and promote drastic change.

The most visually striking aspect of the photo is the central subject, Salazar. His simple outfit is composed of khakis, a plain white shirt, and a gas mask. The viewer then sees that Salazar is literally on fire—something one would only imagine in movies. The scene almost looks fake; his clothes seem on the verge of bursting into flames yet are strangely intact. Schemidt enhances the image by purposefully darkening the background around Salazar. By making the flames serve as the only source of light, the viewer is forced to focus solely on the center of the image.

Schemidt's photograph sends a message without any prior knowledge needed. The viewer has an immediate emotional reaction when seeing Salazar. So many questions form, such as why is this man on fire and how did he even get in this situation in the first place? The way the flames envelop his body also creates a haunting image. When the viewer sees Salazar on fire, they experience a variety of emotions including horror, shock, confusion, and even awe. The image also conveys an impending sense of doom as Salazar's clothes have yet to ignite. Despite this, the viewer can do nothing but stare at what unfolds in front of them. Because Salazar is running, Schemidt utilizes dynamic elements in the photograph that create a sense of urgency.

Figure 1. "Venezuela Crisis" by Ronaldo Schemidt

RONALDO SCHEMIDT/AFP/Getty Images

Had Salazar been stationary, the emotional effect would be tempered. The viewer would have simply assumed the fire was set deliberately. However, by capturing Salazar running, the viewer becomes directly engaged and wants to know if he is actually okay. By employing dynamic motion and a spotlight on the central subject, Schemidt excites the viewer and makes him or her fully invested in the depicted situation.

Schemidt uses subtle symbols in the photograph's background as a desperate plea for help. Looking into the scenery, the viewer can see that the photo took place in a broken-down area laced with graffiti and discolored red bricks. The only semblance of structure the viewer can identify is a gun with the word "*paz*" exiting the barrel. Everything is left in ruins. This bleak imagery symbolizes the country of Venezuela breaking down with Salazar representing the people and their desperate situation.

Having been born in Venezuela, Schemidt has a personal connection to this image. In an interview with *Time* magazine, Schemidt said "For me the picture represents the state of the country. The arrest of the people who were pushed out on the streets to protest. It's a humanitarian crisis" (Katz). The "humanitarian crisis" Schemidt speaks of can be seen indirectly in the image. Because Salazar is masked, he could represent any local Venezuelan. Salazar's discomfort from being ablaze parallels how Venezuelans feel about the political state of the country. As Salazar begs to put out the flames, the citizens beg to end the country-wide crisis.

The gun adds another notable element, as "*paz*" means "peace" in English. Schemidt chose to include the object to illustrate the contradiction of the government preaching peace while using violence to quell the masses. Beyond all the spectacle and emotion that arises from the man on fire, Schemidt utilizes symbolism to repeatedly convey the idea of a country that is, in his own words, "burning" ("'Burning Man' Image"). Amazingly, Salazar survived the incident with only first- and second-degree burns (Gibbs). His survival serves as an extended metaphor for the strength of the resistance. Because Salazar is still alive and actively protesting, so should the rest of the country.

In the photograph "Venezuela Crisis," Schemidt utilizes a perfect combination of pathos and symbolism to enhance the *kairos* of the photograph. Had this image been taken while Venezuela's economy was prospering, its impact would not have been as widespread. However, the picture's timing coincides perfectly with the country's collapse. Venezuela's economy severely plummeted the moment Maduro became President. Over the past three years, the Gross Domestic Product per capita has decreased, unemployment has increased, and inflation has risen an astounding 1,000% ("The World Factbook: Venezuela"). Because of the dire economic, political, and social situation, viewers can connect with the image on more than one level.

Overall, I believe Schemidt does a convincing job of getting his message across: Venezuela is having a national breakdown; the country needs anyone and everyone to lend a helping hand. By highlighting the man on fire, the viewer's sympathies lie with Salazar and the country of Venezuela that he represents. The surroundings further highlight tensions between the government and its citizens that might not be obvious at first glance. Schemidt is able to use the burning man symbol to appeal to the viewer's emotions and get them riled up and angry at a system that is harming everyday people. He identifies the culprit as the Venezuelan government and makes a highly effective political statement that incites all of us to extinguish these flames.

Alex Cushing is a Materials Engineering major.

Works Cited

"'Burning Man' Image Wins AFP Top Prize at World Press Photo." *The Straits Times*, 3 Apr. 2018, www.straitstimes.com/world/europe/burning-man-image-wins-afp-top-prize-at-world-press-photo. Accessed 1 July 2019.

Gibbs, Stephen. "Rise up and Overthrow Maduro, Opposition Urges Army Leaders." *The Sunday Times*, The Sunday Times, 5 May 2017, www.thetimes.co.uk/article/rise-up-and-overthrow-maduro-opposition-urges-army-leaders-0w2xsrwbx. Accessed 1 July 2019.

Katz, Andrew. "Caracas: Harrowing Photos of Protester on Fire in Venezuela." *Time,* Time, 4 May 2017, time.com/4766400/venezuela-caracas-protester-fire/. Accessed 1 July 2019.

"The World Factbook: Venezuela." Central Intelligence Agency, Central Intelligence Agency, 1 Feb. 2018, www.cia.gov/library/publications/the-world-factbook/geos/ve.html. Accessed 1 July 2019.

Trejos, Amanda. "Why Is Venezuelan President Nicolás Maduro so Controversial?" *USA Today*, Gannett Satellite Information Network, 23 Aug. 2017, www.usatoday.com/story/news/world/2017/08/23/nicolas-maduro-venezeula-president/5 73363001/. Accessed 1 July 2019.

CONSIDER THIS:

- Cushing's path to finding and analyzing this image came through his involvement in a club he participated in, the Model United Nations. What clubs have you participated in and how have they led you to questions, research, and analysis in your academic work?

- Cushing claims that anyone viewing this image gets an immediate, even visceral sense of the Venezuelan crisis. Do you agree? Why or why not? What was your initial reaction to the image?

Blue Brides

Meha Sharma

It's a joyous occasion: A girl says a fond farewell to her parents as she looks excited at the prospect of embarking on the thrilling adventure that is married life. That girl is not 15-year-old Maya from Nepal; she is not 12-year-old Thea from Norway; nor is she 13-year-old Mariama from Niger, all of whom have already had their wedding days—joylessly ("7 Short Child Marriage Stories"). Nor is that girl one of the 650 million child brides from around the world who were married before they could even reach 18 years of age (Cappa). Child marriage has profound negative effects, pushing girls into roles they are not prepared for and limiting their freedom. Child marriage is not just a problem; it's a man-made pandemic made with the unfortunate blend of the so-called tradition, unawareness, poverty, gender inequality, and insecurity ("Why Does Child Marriage Happen?"). According to United Nations Children's Fund (UNICEF), "the term 'child marriage' is used to refer to both formal marriages and informal unions in which a girl or boy lives with a partner as if married before the age of 18" ("Child Marriage"). Each year, 12 million girls are married before the age of 18; that is 23 girls every minute—nearly 1 every 2 seconds ("An Information Sheet").

Figure 1. Sinclair, Stephanie. "Child Bride: Nepal." 6 April 2015.

Trying to bring the issue of child marriage to the forefront is Stephanie Sinclair with her photographs and gallery shows. Sinclair's photograph shows a young girl in traditional Nepalese bride dress. The red-clad girl is in half profile at the center, highlighted by the contrasting dark background. She is dressed such that only her face can be seen; has red powder at the start of her hairline and some on her forehead; her expression is dejected. With her red nose, chewed lips and sad downcast eyes, she can be the personification of the word "misery." At a cursory glance this photograph is just that, but nothing about this picture is simple. Every pixel is a blend of metaphor and symbolism, and with the clever use of irony, Sinclair successfully underlines to the viewer the gravity—both literally and metaphorically—of child marriage.

LOOK HERE:

Sharma's essay is a rhetorical analysis of a photo of a child bride.

The photograph is the life story of every child bride.

The vast, engulfing darkness rising behind the girl, threatening to envelop her is the personification of evil, the practice of child marriage. The dark, uncertain background embodies every child bride's life—her past, present, and future. It symbolizes their past, their unfinished childhood. Like an unfinished sculpture, they have yet to form themselves from the mass of clay life presents; but this evil is already eating up whatever form they have amassed to date. The dark background gives the room a subdued air, this symbolizes the present: the current state of misery the child must feel. Shackled to a person who she doesn't even know, the child bride forever marks this sorrowful day of her marriage as the moment after which all her presents will belong to some other person, never more hers. The darkness also symbolizes the obscure, lackluster, unhappiness-filled future of the girl. This is further expanded on by the organization Girls Not Brides, a global partnership of more than one thousand civil society organizations committed to ending child marriage and enabling girls to fulfill their potential. Their website states:

When a young girl becomes a bride, the consequences are lifelong—for the girl, for her family and for her nation. Child marriage denies girls their rights and their childhood…frequently resulting in profound physical, psychological and emotional consequences…limiting millions of girls from fulfilling their potential and leading happy, safe and productive lives ("An Information Sheet").

This disgusting practice sucks the vitality in the child brides.

Red has lots of references around the world. It's the color of blood and health, of love and passion, of warning and danger. Red also embodies the response situations like child marriage deserve—anger. In the girl's culture, red stands for prowess which is ironic as she is the one with the least power in this situation. The brutality signified is highlighted by the fact that this little bride is wrapped up in red clothes all the way to her neck. This is an apt symbol of her condition, of how she is bound in a dangerous situation with no chance to escape; even her face is dominated by this color.

Sindoor—the red powder on her forehead—is applied by the groom on the bride. It can be considered as an insignia of marital state just like an engagement ring in the western culture. In short, it too is a mark of possession. According to Hindu astrology, Mesha Rashi, or the House of Aries, is on the forehead. The Lord of Mesha is Mars, and his color is red; thus, when applied on the forehead, it is a sign of good fortune (Pathak). By a quirk of fate, the way the red powder is spread across the crown of her head gives the impression of injury. The injury that is being caused by the society and by her parents who are supposed to be her protectors. This sardonic seal is stressed by her downcast face. Her profile, bowed, is indicative of the upcoming immense familial obligation that was placed on her slight shoulders. It is a sign of subjugation, her unhappy acceptance of the finality of her loss of childhood, her acquiescence of the fact that there is no getting out of her predicament. According to Elyse A. Jennings of the Harvard Center for Population and Development Studies, "In general, marriage in Nepal occurs at early ages and is universal" (Jennings). In the photo, the girl's sorrow is underlined by her expressions.

The location of her expressive face is in general, centrally located. The downcast tear-filled eyes, red nose, and chewed lips all accentuate the fact that she must have been crying on her what should have been one of the happiest days of her life. Geometrically, the epicenter of the photograph is at her lips. The gnawed lips are significant as they betray her emotions: anxiety, stress, the uncertainty of future, the struggle she must have gone through, and the effort to not cry out loud, another sign of subjugation. Her unhappiness is also a sign of her innocence. Children, generally, have a case of hero-worship for their parents; they can do no harm. Her marriage was probably arranged by her parents ("Most Child Marriages"), and her unhappiness over this decision could be a potential source of guilt. Shouldn't she be happy because parents always want the best for them? In this case, the question just begs to be asked: which "them"? The parents or the children?

Sinclair's photograph is a warning—a call of action to every person around the world.

A universal misconception is that child marriage is the issue faced by under-developed or developing countries, particularly in the Middle East and South Eastern Asia. Mabel van Oranje, the widow of the prince of Netherlands, who has pledged to end child marriage by 2030, addresses this misapprehension:

People sometimes approach the subject with prejudices [...] They think, 'Oh, this must be a Middle East problem,' or, 'This is all about India.' Child

Analyzing Rhetorically

marriage is happening all over the world, in all cultures and in all religions (qtd. in Hawksley).

Similarly, Girls Not Brides states: "Child marriage is a truly global problem that cuts across countries, cultures, religions and ethnicities. Child brides can be found in every region in the world, from the Middle East to Latin America, South Asia to Europe" ("Child Marriage Around the World")

Highest Three		
1	Albania	27.20%
2	Turkey	23 %
3	Kyrgyzstan	19.10 %

Lowest Three		
1	Kazakhstan	0.90%
2	Ukraine	2.20%
3	Serbia	5.90%

Figure 2. Rates of officially registered marriages involving girls aged 15–19.

From data reported by UNFPA.
https://eeca.unfpa.org/sites/default/files/pub-pdf/Child%20Marriage_27072015_web.pdf

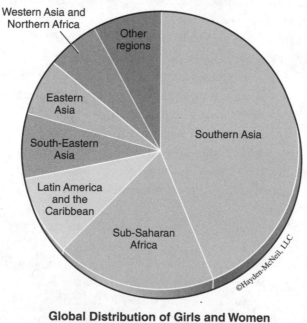

**Global Distribution of Girls and Women
Married Before Age 18 (2017)**

Figure 3. (Cappa)

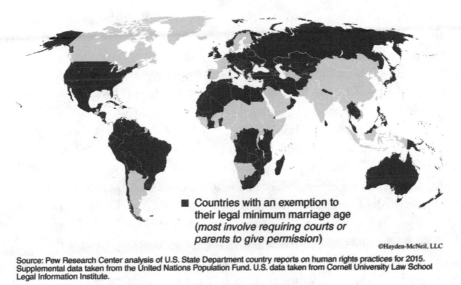

Countries with an exemption to their legal minimum marriage age (*most involve requiring courts or parents to give permission*)

©Hayden-McNeil, LLC

Source: Pew Research Center analysis of U.S. State Department country reports on human rights practices for 2015. Supplemental data taken from the United Nations Population Fund. U.S. data taken from Cornell University Law School Legal Information Institute.

Figure 4. Countries where child marriage is legal.

In Niger, 77% of women between the ages of 20 and 49 were married before age 18, and more than half of these girls' husbands are at least 10 years older than them. In both Chad and the Democratic Republic of Congo, 68% of girls are married by age 18 and in Mali 55%. In Guatemala, 14 is the legal minimum marriageable age with parental consent, while Yemen is one of those countries who have yet to set a legal minimum (Selby). The United States, which is considered one of the most developed countries, in fact, has no federal law against child marriage: state legislatures set the minimum age of marriage in the states. While the minimum age in most states is 18, there are exceptions in every state that allow those younger than that to marry, and laws in 25 states do not set a minimum age below which a child cannot marry ("United States—Child Marriage Around the World"). According to data collected from 41 states, more than 200,000 minors were married in the U.S. between 2000 and 2015 (Ferguson).

On a positive note, the global rate of child marriages is decreasing, with several countries seeing significant reductions in recent years. According to UNICEF, "the proportion of women who were married as children decreased by 15% in the last decade, from 1 in 4 to approximately 1 in 5" ("25 Million Child Marriages Prevented"). Growing up in a country that fights daily battles against child marriage, I have seen it gradually fall firsthand. India has the highest absolute numbers of child marriage, and over the past decade has seen one of the largest declines in child marriage rate—from nearly 50% to 27% ("India—Child Marriage Around the World"). I have seen people's mindset change: I remember being 6 and hearing my mother convince our maid that her 16-year-old daughter was too young to marry; I remember her stressing the importance of education;

I remember her winning and agreeing to foot the bill of the girl's education. Today, that girl is a mother herself, and is adamant that her daughters will marry whenever they want, and they will study however long they want.

The efforts of millions of people are paying off, like a Turkish photographer who stopped a man from marrying a 15-year-old girl (Wang et al.) or the 8000-mile-long human chain protest against child marriage in India ("Millions of Indians"). Another medium that is helping bring this change about is photojournalism. Stephanie Sinclair, the photographer whose work I am analyzing in this essay, is an American photojournalist who focuses on gender and human-rights issues such as child marriage and self-immolation. As per the International Women's Media Foundation, "the ongoing capstone of Ms. Sinclair's career is her 15-year series, Too Young to Wed, which examines the deeply troubling practice of early, forced and child marriage as it appears in a variety of cultures around the world today." She is also the Too Young to Wed's Founding Executive Director, a nonprofit organization whose mission is "to protect girls' rights and end child marriage" (International Women's Media Foundation).

On Sinclair's return visit in 2015 to Kagati village, Nepal, she saw, once again, the couple who she had met when they were just 14 and 16 years old, as they were being married. This couple is one of those millions personally impacted by child marriage but whose children will not marry young. They will study and have a better life than the couple themselves had. Sinclair has been engaged in efforts to improve the situation of girls from around the world for more than a decade. She first visited this village in 2007, when the girl from the couple mentioned before and the girl in the photograph got married. The change in the mindset of the couple is proof that the battle against child marriage might be long but is not in vain. Photojournalism is but one of the ways to cure child marriage through awareness. Like all pandemics, child marriage, too, can be eradicated. We just need to work for it. Together.

Meha Sharma is a Computer Engineering major.

Works Cited

"7 Short Child Marriage Stories." *Plan International.org*, plan-international.org/7-child-marriage-stories. Accessed 25 Jan. 2019.

"25 Million Child Marriages Prevented in Last Decade Due to Accelerated Progress, According to New UNICEF Estimates." *UNICEF*, 6 Mar. 2018, www.unicef.org/press-releases/25-million-child-marriages-prevented-last-decade-due-accelerated-progress-according. Accessed 1 July 2019.

"An Information Sheet: Child Marriage around the World." *Girls Not Brides*, 23 Nov. 2016, www.girlsnotbrides.org/wp-content/uploads/2017/01/Child-marriage-around-the-world-Nov-2016.pdf. Accessed 1 July 2019.

Cappa, Claudia. "UNICEF Global Estimates of Child Marriage 2018." *Girls Not Brides*, 15 Mar. 2018, www.girlsnotbrides.org/resource-centre/unicef-data-on-child-marriage-2018/. Accessed 1 July 2019.

"Child Marriage around the World." *Girls Not Brides*, www.girlsnotbrides.org/where-does-it-happen/. Accessed 25 Jan. 2019.

"Child Marriage." *UNICEF Data*, Mar. 2018, data.unicef.org/topic/child-protection/child-marriage/. Accessed 25 Jan. 2019.

Jennings, Elyse A. "Family Composition and Marital Dissolution in Rural Nepal, 1945–2008." *Population Studies*, vol. 71, no.2, 2017, pp. 229–248.

Ferguson, Sarah. "What You Need to Know About Child Marriage in the U.S." *UNICEF USA*, 29 Oct. 2018, www.unicefusa.org/stories/what-you-need-know-about-child-marriage-us/35059. Accessed 1 July 2019.

Hawksley, Rupert. "Girls Not Brides: Meet the Woman Who Has Pledged to End Child Marriage by 2030." *The National*, 10 Jan. 2019, www.thenational.ae/lifestyle/girls-not-brides-meet-the-woman-who-has-pledged-to-end-child-marriage-by-2030-1.811697. Accessed 1 July 2019.

"India—Child Marriage Around The World." *Girls Not Brides*, www.girlsnotbrides.org/child-marriage/india/. Accessed 25 Jan. 2019.

International Women's Media Foundation. "Stephanie Sinclair." *IWMF.org*, www.iwmf.org/community/stephanic-sinclair/. Accessed 25 Jan. 2019.

"Millions of Indians Form Giant Human Chain to Protest against Child Marriage." *Their World*, 22 Jan. 2018, theirworld.org/news/millions-form-giant-human-chain-protest-child-marriage-bihar-india. Accessed 1 July 2019.

"Most Child Marriages in 2017 Arranged by Parents: Study." *The Hindu*, 17 Dec. 2018, www.thehindu.com/news/national/tamil-nadu/most-child-marriages-in-2017-arranged-by-parents-study/article25767225.ece#!. Accessed 1 July 2019.

Pathak, Prateek. "Why Indian Women Put Sindoor in Their Maang." *Speakingtree.in*, 22 Apr. 2014, www.speakingtree.in/allslides/why-indian-women-put-sindoor-in-their-maang. Accessed 1 July 2019.

Selby, Daniele. "Child Marriage: Everything You Need to Know." *Global Citizen*, 21 Feb. 2018, www.globalcitizen.org/en/content/child-marriage-brides-india-niger-syria/. Accessed 1 July 2019.

Sinclair, Stephanie. *Child Brides-Nepal."* *Stephanie Sinclair Studio*, 6 Apr. 2015, stephaniesinclair.photoshelter.com/gallery-image/Child-Brides-Nepal/ G0000PnUjNfNAJFg/I0000HPBelp34FIg. Accessed 25 Jan. 2019.

"United States—Child Marriage Around The World." *Girls Not Brides*, www. girlsnotbrides.org/child-marriage/united-states/. Accessed 25 Jan. 2019.

Wang, Chengfen, et al. "Turkish Photographer Praised for His Shot to Stop Child Marriage." *Reuters*, 11 July 2018, www.reuters.com/article/us-turkey-wedding-girl/turkish-photographer-praised-for-his-shot-to-stop-child-marriage-idUSKBN1K12GO. Accessed 1 July 2019.

"Why Does Child Marriage Happen?" *Girls Not Brides.org*, www.girlsnotbrides. org/why-does-it-happen/. Accessed 25 Jan. 2019.

CONSIDER THIS:

- For analysis to be meaningful, it has to add to what we can already see, giving us explanation or interpretation. At the same time, for the analysis to be convincing, it needs to be closely tied to the source. Compare the internet image of the photo *Child Brides-Nepal* (see the "Look Here" link) with paragraphs 2 to 5 in Sharma's essay. Do you agree with all of her analysis? Is there anything you would modify or challenge?

- Sharma's essay seems to have two purposes: to analyze a photo of a child bride in Nepal and to convince readers of the harms of child marriage. Does Sharma successfully accomplish both of these goals, or does her analysis sometimes get in the way of the argument, and, vice-versa, does the argument on child marriage ever pull focus away from the analysis of the image?

- Sharma has developed an impressive list of Works Cited sources for this essay. Look carefully at the sources she cites, looking them up online if possible. Are all the sources credible? Which sources are stronger than others? Which are weaker? Which might have potential biases? Is all the research needed, or would the essay have been stronger without some of the sources?

Blaming the Victim Is a Crime

Stephanie Botto

In many regions of India, women and girls wouldn't dare leave shelter without necessities like mace and a taser. Mothers give up work to personally care for their child, fearing that a caretaker will take advantage of her little one. At the end of a long day, women debate whether or not to splurge on a car ride home, fearing that alternatively, walking may be a matter of life or death. According to *The Guardian*, "The National Crime Records Bureau (NCRB) data observes that a woman is raped every six hours in India," and rape is merely one of the many forms of sexual assault that occur too frequently (Thekaekara). There is no algorithm that leads to assault, and thus no algorithm to avoid it, but somehow accountability seems to always be attributed to the victim. Victim-blaming is a continuous and toxic cycle that understates and disregards the harmful effects of assault on the victim, thus normalizing the crime and continuously "adding fuel to the fire." In her set of posters titled, "The Good Victim Starter Pack," 21-year-old graphic artist, Shreya Arora, aims to prompt a conversation on the issue of female victim-blaming in India. She successfully achieves this goal by using satire and symbolism within the medium she chose to use, and both are enhanced by her awareness of *kairos* regarding this social problem.

Shreya Arora's set of posters can be described as pages from a 60's to 70's magazine. This includes a cover poster and four other posters with an advertisement and article, one of which uses the illustration from the cover. The cover page, intended to be the most enticing, includes the magazine's title, a headline, overarching phrases, the title of the Exclusive article, and a curious watercolor-pencil illustration in the background.

The magazine title, "LOGUE," is a play on words, referring to the popular fashion and lifestyle magazine, *Vogue*. Even with the choice of title, Arora uses satire to emphasize her message. *Vogue*'s target audience is predominantly young, female, white-collar adults looking to read advice on fashion, culture, lifestyle, and stereotypically, how to attract men. Arora makes fun of the magazine, in that her underlying message strictly opposes that of *Vogue*'s, in which women are encouraged to fawn over men and be flirtatious in order to gain attention.

The topic at hand here is also extremely serious, but Arora emphasizes the absurdity of victim-blaming by incorporating it into a magazine that is a fairly brainless read. Arora also uses satire in

LOOK HERE:

See the cover poster described in this essay, as well as the rest of the posters from Shreya Arora's set titled "The Good Victim Starter Pack."

the article headlines because the underlying message is again, quite heavy. She makes light of the issue by providing a headline catered to the audience of a fashion magazine titled, "The Good Victim Starter Pack: This Season's Hottest Fashion Tips to Avoid Victim Blaming." Right below the headline is an exclusive titled, "Why Getting Sexually Assaulted Is Your Fault," in which Arora uses satire because the underlying message is the opposite of what the text actually reads. Satire is a powerful tool that can elicit a range of emotions such as humor, or potentially shock, fear, and anger. Appealing to emotions is a deliberate way of forcing the viewer to consider the trigger to this reaction.

Arora's intent in using satire, and subsequently, pathos, is to illuminate the issue. By focusing on the issue, the process of reasoning and actually going about forming a solution will flow more easily, and in addition, the emotions we feel provide a cause and motivation to embark on this quest. It suddenly may become more apparent as to how society in India may right the wrongs involving normalized assault and blaming the victim. Simply raising awareness of this pressing issue could be the onset to a potentially empowering movement of change.

In addition to satire, Arora uses symbolism to draw attention to the crimes against women occurring customarily in India. The first thing you may notice in the cover page is the drawing of the young, innocent, and submissive-looking girl. Her head is slightly tilted, her lips are curved up, she is wearing a sari with a striped shirt, and her wrists are chained together. Her head being slightly tilted and lips slightly curved up resembles that of a girl who's acting "ladylike," dumbfounded by a man, or passively concerned, possibly pondering how her wrists got chained together. In this illustration of the girl, Arora begins to clarify the context and magazine audience by dressing the girl in what appears to be a sari—a cloth traditionally worn by Indian women—and giving her handcuffs that resemble bangles, which is the type of jewelry worn by married women in Indian culture. Without explicitly stating it, these symbols tell us that the magazine headline, "How to Be a Good Victim," is directed towards young Indian woman.

The bangles, being an indication of marriage and sexuality, are chained together, symbolizing how Indian women can feel like a prisoner of their marriage or the men they encounter, and are often left puzzled as to how they always end up being the one chained up. In addition, the poster using the illustration from the cover page includes an article titled, "Wear Your Bangles the Sanskaari way." The subsequent texts states to "Live your life bound by the ideals of a 'sanskaari ladki'—ideals dictated to you by patriarchy, the male gaze, and sometimes your own families…" By living like a cultured, well-mannered woman, it should be impossible to be at fault in the case of sexual assault, however, "they probably will blame in on you anyway" (Arora). Being the victim of assault and crime, in addition to being blamed for such, is seemingly inescapable for women in India.

The chained bangles represent this crucial injustice that females in India struggle to resolve when they are told that being submissive and "behaving" according to the ideals of a "sanskaari ladki" is the safest option. According to *The Conversation*, "India's National Crime Records Bureau reported 338,954 crimes against women—including 38,947 rapes—in 2016… up from 309,546 reported incidents of violence against women in 2013" (Bellinger). The climbing rates of crimes against women, combined with women's lack of empowerment to intervene, shows that victim-blaming in India is a massive issue and will only continue to worsen if its citizens aren't aware and willing to seek out solutions to help win back justice for the female victims.

Symbolism also exists within the closed red lips and striped shirt. Nowadays, red lips can often be a reference to the "Red My Lips" Organization, an "international nonprofit organization designed to raise visibility and awareness about the realities and prevalence of sexual violence, while combating rape myths and victim-blaming" ("Red My Lips"). In addition, most view red lipstick as a symbol of sexuality or even danger. By combining common knowledge about red lipstick and the connotation of the color, the red lips that Arora illustrates here can be viewed as a silent symbol. The girl may be indicating that she feels trapped in this box of sexuality by which males in India force women to be defined. In addition to the red lips, there's something to be said about the striped shirt paired with the traditional sari. A horizontally-striped shirt can be a complementary symbol to the chained bangles, in that they both portray the imprisonment sensed by the women being inevitably blamed for the normalized male-on-female assault in India. Arora's use of symbolism in the cover page illustration helps viewers understand the overall context of the message for the posters, since Arora chose to emphasize the issue victim-blaming by using satire within the posters and her choice of medium.

The medium Arora chose to use adds significance to the message being that she chose to create a parody of a lifestyle magazine and chose to date this magazine back to the 60s to 70s. In an interview with *VagaBomb*, Shreya Arora says that "the posters are designed to look similar to the sexist ones in the 60s and 70s," and the textual ads and phrases promote a "good victim," or a woman that doesn't speak up and accepts all responsibility for rape (Madhavi Pothukuchi). On the front cover underneath "LOGUE," there are two phrases to consider, with the bolded one reading "Kya Kahenge." The English translation of this Hindi "What Will They Think." The context of this phrase can be further explained by a popular 1983 Bollywood Indian film titled "Log Kya Kahenge," which documents the widespread ignominy for Indian women who attempt to challenge the way in which the society expects them to act, especially towards men. The "they" in the phrase refers to the men, and in Indian society, women must always consider what *they* will think about the way she behaves. Even in the case of assault, women are taught to protect the man's satisfaction. This rule of thumb, which one might assume to be expired in 2018, continues to persist today in India, which is why Arora follows "Kya Kahenge" with the phrase, "Not As Long Ago As You'd Hoped." Many would feel that it's safe to assume that the ads and message relayed in this magazine are dated and merely representing a time in which they were relevant, but the sad truth is that the message is more significant and relevant today than it has ever been. By including this phrase, Arora is responding to the shock that her viewers might experience once they realize that victim-blaming is not an issue of the past, as many may have "hoped."

Shreya Arora's awareness of "the opportune moment," or *kairos*, adds to the strength of her message because the issue of victim-blaming holds relevancy, and relevancy leverages the urgency for change and awareness that people will perceive when viewing these posters. In the interview with *VagaBomb*, Arora mentions where her inspiration in creating the magazine is mainly derived from. Having grown up in Mumbai, Arora felt particularly disturbed when she heard foreign students discussing their fear in traveling to India during an exchange program to France, due to the soaring rate of crimes, especially against women (Madhavi Pothukuchi). Despite this era of newfound awareness for victim-blaming and the #metoo movement encouraging victims to speak out, many regions of India maintain the patriarchal mindset that loads all encumbrance of a crime, especially a sexual crime, on the victim. Victim-blaming preserves rape culture, empowering criminals of assault while destroying the minds and lifestyles of the victims. According to an article on *Bloomberg*, government data show that in India "crimes against women surged 83 percent from 2007 to 2016... resulting in 39 crimes every hour" (Chaudhary, Pandya, Rai). The most disheartening fact is that even if a woman wanted to report an assault, there are 37 million more men than women in "Two-thirds of the country live in villages that follow feudal, caste and gender hierarchies" (Chaudhary, Pandya, Rai). This means that the majority of women don't make formal reports in the case of harassment, thus perpetrators march on unpunished, making it more difficult "to draw international comparisons" (Chaudhary, Pandya, Rai). Many people, especially outside of India, may not know about the extremities of assault in India because there is really no accurate record of harassment cases that exists. Those in America may wish to believe that sexual assault and victim-blaming is becoming less of an issue due to heightened awareness in the US, but in India, this issue is only becoming more and more severe. The juxtaposition between America's rising efforts to solve victim-blaming and India's miniscule efforts creates a dangerous gap of ignorance. Arora realizes that now is the opportune time to close this gap and illuminate the severity of this unreported issue in India before the gap becomes so large that assault and victim-blaming becomes irrelevant and impossible to prove. If people are aware of the problem in India, especially those from other countries, people can incorporate anti-victim-blaming programs into Indian society and begin to promote a movement to change.

On a lower level, Arora's message to everyone, including those living in India, is to simply try to understand the issue, act with caution, and always consider the unfortunate, yet common outcome. When people perceive the urgency of the issue, as Arora hopes that her viewers will, people will be compelled to begin to fill in the gap of ignorance. The widespread and combined effort could result in a life-changing campaign for the victims of harassment in India.

Through her use of satire, symbolism, and sense of *kairos* within the art and text of her magazine posters, Shreya Arora successfully raises awareness of victim-blaming in India and the urgency for a movement of change to transpire. Through satire and symbolism, Arora aims to evoke intense emotion and concern in the viewers, while her awareness of *kairos* aims to highlight the severity of the issue today more than ever, and thus prompting a conversation regarding the necessary solutions for victim-blaming in India. Especially in India, more content like this needs to be on display because only then will people be forced to grasp the issue of victim-blaming and make a change to help sufferers gain the justice they've waited far too long for.

Stephanie Botto is a Graphic Communication major.

Works Cited

Bellinger, Nisha. "India Has a Sexual Assault Problem That Only Women Can Fix." *The Conversation,* The Conversation, 19 Sept. 2018, www.theconversation.com/india-has-a-sexual-assault-problem-that-only-women-can-fix-101366. Accessed 1 July 2019.

Chaudhary, Archana, et al. "Sexual Violence Is Holding Back the Rise of India." *Bloomberg.com*, Bloomberg, 28 May 2018, www.bloomberg.com/news/features/2018-05-28/sexual-violence-is-holding-back-the-rise-of-india. Accessed 1 July 2019.

Madhavi Pothukuchi, Srishti. "This Young Graphic Artist's Posters on Victim Blaming Is What the Country Needs to See Right Now." *VagaBomb*, 25 May 2018, www.vagabomb.com/This-Young-Graphic-Artists-Posters-about-Victim-Blaming-They-Need-to-Be-Seen-by-All/. Accessed 1 July 2019.

Red My Lips, "Who Are We." *Red My Lips*, 3 Oct. 2018, www.redmylips.org/. Accessed 1 July 2019.

Thekaekara, Mari Marcel. "Sexual Violence Is the New Normal in India—and Pornography Is to Blame." *The Guardian*, Guardian News and Media, 9 Aug. 2018, www.theguardian.com/commentisfree/2018/aug/09/sexual-violence-india-rape-pornography. Accessed 1 July 2019.

"Logue" cover artwork by Shreya Arora. Reprinted with permission of the artist.

CONSIDER THIS:

- The subject of this essay is politically and emotionally intense. How does the author organize the essay to create a balance between logos and pathos, i.e., logic and emotion? Why is it important that she does?

- The author makes several claims about the artist's effective use of satire in her work. How do you feel about the use of satire for a subject so important? Is it effective? Why or why not?

- What do you understand about *kairos* after reading this analysis? How does attention to *kairos* strengthen an analysis or persuasive text?

A Snapshot of Living in the Syrian Civil War

Joshua Schipper

Reflective Memo: *The Syrian Civil War is the first conflict for which I can remember how it started. The main reason I chose to cover this event was because I was curious as to how a country could endure warfare for years upon years, even 7–8 years in the future. The photograph I found was especially striking, as it reflected how war could almost become normal. Developing this piece served as a reminder of how much we still have to overcome in this world.*

ABDULMONAM EASSA/AFP/Getty Images

Figure 1. A snapshot of the Syrian Civil War

When news of the Syrian Civil War broke out on televisions across the globe, I was still in elementary school. Seven years later, there is a new U.S. president in office, a satellite has reached Pluto, and I am now a college student. The Syrian Civil War still rages on and more intensely than ever. Years after the Syrian government said they would "crush the rebels," the war situation devolved into a multi-faction mess between tens of groups fighting each other for their own interests ("Why"). Over eleven million Syrians have fled the nation, escaping to neighboring countries and to Europe, in what has been called a "crisis" since 2015 (Dockery). However, despite the constant air strikes, guerilla warfare in the streets, and even chemical attacks by Syrian President Assad against his own civilians, many have not left the country. Whether by personal choice or necessity, the ones who remained have had to carve out a life in midst of the rubble and dangers of the war. The people of Syria have adapted as well as anyone to the hostile conditions, but even past the ten thousandth day of death and destruction, the active repression of the military and the constant conflict keep citizens locked in the danger zone of battlefields and attacks. The image taken by Abdulmonam Eassa depicts the resiliency of Syrians, but also the toll the country's state has taken on them by placing a Syrian mother and child in the foreground against the ghostly grey background of destroyed streets (see Figure 1).

Perhaps the most visually jarring part of the photo is how casually the mother seems to be walking along the bombarded avenue. She appears to be strolling through a devastated road, in a manner like celebrities walking through cosmopolitan centrals like New York City or San Francisco. Whereas the whole background is dusty and ruined, she seems untouched by the devastation. Her clothes are well-maintained and look new, serving as a sign of resiliency against the dispiriting war. Her hijab and sunglasses hide any emotion, giving the impression she is unaffected by the gaunt sights in front of her. The child also stands out as unharmed; however, it is easy to see how deeply affected the child's emotions are. The kid gazes out forward, seemingly dazed by the stripped and collapsing shells of the buildings around her, buildings which she may not be old enough to have ever seen intact. The emotion of shock and uncertainty on the child becomes a strong metaphor for how emotionally scarring the war experience has been for Syrians and how long and difficult any attempts to recover will be.

For an older audience who may have seen Syria when it was untouched by war, the location provides more emotional weight to the image. Specifically, the photograph was taken in Eastern Ghouta, now one of the last rebel strongholds in the Syrian capital of Damascus. Before the war, Damascus was a safe center of Middle-East culture and a popular destination with a great deal of historical importance. Even though Assad still rules from the ruined city, the conflict has reduced it and many others to a shell of its former glory. Many age-old monuments have been obliterated, some purposefully by extremist groups like ISIS that have arisen from the chaos of the region (Domonoske). Due to this destruction, people unfamiliar with pre-war Syria will only recognize the land as a warzone, shown in images like Eassa's, and not as the cultural capital it once was.

LOOK HERE:

The documentary *White Helmets*, available on Netflix, chronicles the activities of emergency first-responders in Aleppo, a rebel-occupied area of Syria.

The photograph embodies the loss and continuing struggle of Syria's people in the face of terrorists and the actions of its own government. The woman's completely black outfit matches the somber mood, as it would be appropriate to wear to a funeral. Symbolically, it works as a muted token of mourning for the loss of over 470,000 people, the one million injured, and the many millions more forced to abandon their homes and survive as refugees (Marks). This disproportionate impact on civilians in the war is emphasized by the photograph as the woman and child are featured in the center, with no government support or officers seen anywhere to aid in recovery. Another fitting coincidence within the image is the cloudy weather of the snapshot. In addition to keeping the image monotone and melancholic, it well represents the ongoing storm of the war. Like the overcast sky, there has been no break of peace in this struggle.

Now, in late 2018, the war in Syria may be finally reaching its end. Russian and Iranian military aid have turned the tide in Assad's favor, allowing the regime to recapture territory (Sparrow). Unfortunately, the situation might not be the break in the clouds Syria's people desperately need. The war itself was started by anti-government protests in Daraa, which were violently crack-downed by the regime (Marks). This escalated into the current conflict, and now nearing victory, the Syrian government is possibly even more stifling than ever before. Assad's regime consistently misuses humanitarian aid meant for the suffering citizens to fund its own war effort and agenda (Sparrow). It is due to Assad's regime that Eassa's photograph will remain relevant to Syria's future until the bloodshed ends. For now, the fighting continues, but Syria's future remains uncertain under a government which has used chemical weapons against its own citizens many times, even as recently as this April (Hubbard). Like the grey landscape in the image, there aren't many pockets of color or hope coming for Syria anytime soon.

The situation for a Syrian trapped within the war-torn nation remains as bleak as ever, and while some physical rebuilding will likely follow the inevitable end of the war, little if any progress towards making internal amends or improving the human rights within the country is expected to take place. The other nations in the world did little to directly aid this trialed people, often only taking much action when the refugees started to flood their nations, a symptom of the root problem. With Russia and Iran backing Syria, there is little chance any other power will do much to alleviate the situation. This is a troubling precedent, a failure for the maintenance of human rights on the international level. When another government decides to order a wave of brutality on their own people, who will respond? Will there be another seven-year war, killing off hundreds of thousands more? Probably.

Joshua Schipper is an Environmental Engineering major.

Works Cited

Dockery, Wesley. "A Chronology of the Refugee Crisis in Europe." *InfoMigrants*, 5 Sept. 2017, www.infomigrants.net/. Accessed 1 July 2019.

Domonoske, Camila. "ISIS Destroys Ancient Theater, Tetrapylon In Palmyra, Syria Says." *NPR*, 20 Jan. 2017, www.npr.org/sections/thetwo-way/2017/01/20/510732864/isis-destroys-ancient-theater-tetrapylon-in-palmyra-syria-says. Accessed 1 July 2019.

Eassa, Abdulmonam. "Picture of the Day: 25 March, 2018." *The Telegraph*, 25 Mar. 2018, www.telegraph.co.uk/news/2018/03/25/pictures-day-25march-2018/. Accessed 1 July 2019.

Hubbard, Ben. "Dozens Suffocate in Syria as Government Is Accused of Chemical Attack." *The New York Times*, 8 Apr. 2018, www.nytimes.com/2018/04/08/world/middleeast/syria-chemical-attack-ghouta.html. Accessed 1 July 2019.

Marks, Julie. "Why Is There a Civil War in Syria?" *History.com*, A&E Television Networks, 14 Sept. 2018, www.history.com/news/syria-civil-war-assad-rebels. Accessed 1 July 2019.

Sparrow, Annie. "How UN Humanitarian Aid Has Propped Up Assad." *Foreign Affairs*, Foreign Affairs Magazine, 27 Sept. 2018, www.foreignaffairs.com/articles/syria/2018-09-20/how-un-humanitarian-aid-has-propped-assad. Accessed 1 July 2019.

"Why Is There a War in Syria?" *BBC News*, 7 Sept. 2018, www.bbc.com/news/. Accessed 1 July 2019.

CONSIDER THIS:

- According to the well-known proverb, "a picture is worth a thousand words." Why is an image—like the one analyzed in this essay—able to capture the horrors of war in a way that text alone could not? What is a photo able to do that words on the page wouldn't? By the same token, what does Schipper's analysis of the photo (his text) add to the image that isn't apparent by simply viewing the image on its own?

- How do the different parts of the essay—the analysis of the photo, and the discussion about the war in Syria as a whole—work together, or were there any places where, as a reader, you felt like the focus shifted? If so, where did you notice these focus shifts? If, by contrast, you felt like the essay did form a solid, coherent whole, how did Schipper maintain that coherency—how did he tie everything together?

Engaging in Public Rhetoric and Argumentation

Which issues do you care most about?
How can you use your rhetorical skills to effect change in the world?

Public rhetoric almost always addresses thorny issues that consist of many different positions and competing points of view. The authors featured in this section develop complex arguments about issues they care about, issues they want to better understand. They don't neglect the perspectives of readers who may not fully agree with them. Instead, they try to accommodate multiple ways of thinking about a topic, using rhetorical strategies to bring order to often unruly public debates.

Bodily Movement
by Laura Nelson

Engaging in Public Rhetoric and Argumentation

CONSIDER THIS:

- Much like complicated public issues, Nelson's collage might initially overwhelm you. The more time you spend examining it, however, the more you begin to see an underlying sense of order. Take some time to consider its composition: the background and foreground elements; figures that appear to be rising and/or falling; right-side up and upside down; the use of color versus the black-and-white text. What meanings can you draw from the juxtaposition of these contrasting elements?

- Part of writing a good argument depends on your ability to put sources in conversation with each other. Some of Nelson's background text refers to "The Clapback," a senior project by English major Amelia Meyerhoff. Visit her website, www.the-clapback.com, and consider how Nelson's collage might be in conversation with Meyerhoff's project.

The OG Feminist: Queen Elizabeth I

Leanna McMahon

Reflective Memo: During winter break, my mother and I argued over whether Queen Elizabeth would be classified as a feminist today after religiously reading about her (for the new movie), so I knew what to write about from the start. However, it was difficult in the readings for me to find when the author would be providing historical truths versus their opinion, and also pinpointing the ideal of feminism in old novels. Once I figured out the research portion of this paper, all of the other portions flowed easily. I think a strong point in this essay is my counterargument against Anne Somerset's opinion because I think all of the evidence I brought up previously backed my statement about Elizabeth being a strong woman.

Queen Elizabeth I is known for being one of the greatest monarchs who has ever lived. During her reign from 1558–1603, known as the Golden Ages, peace and progression prospered, though human rights did not. Although Queen Elizabeth represents an ideal leader for women's rights advocacy, because of the time period and the court's patriarchal power, her abilities to create greater gender equality were limited. In spite of the fact that Elizabeth publicly spoke against the foundations of feminism, she still behaved like a feminist through her personal and private lifestyles.

Queen Elizabeth's private life insinuated a change for women, by virtue of her being educated, unmarried, and a ruler of men. England in the 1500s allowed women the right to education, though that right only targeted a select few. Luckily, Elizabeth was born into privilege and could afford "to be educated at home by private tutors" because women "were not allowed to go to school or university" (Sharnette). These patriarchal laws prohibited most women their right to education, further oppressing them into an unequal gendered society. Educated women were rare, so the very fact that the people were ruled by a woman who was educated was something new and gave hope to many of the English women.

Another contributor to Queen Elizabeth's identification was that she never married; Elizabeth holds the reputation of the Virgin Queen. Women had an obligation to marry, because they were considered burdens in their households if they chose to stay. The concept of dowries symbolized that the woman's family had to pay the groom for the encumbrance of taking her in. These social rules subjected women to inferiority, but Queen Elizabeth stood against it. In one of her famous addresses to the father of a suitor she said, "I would rather be a beggar and single than a queen and married" (Tudor). The strength of her conviction over being unmarried turned her into a role model for many English women. Though Elizabeth was a revolutionary exemplar of women's rights, it is important to note that she could only avoid most traditional laws because of her being

royalty; most women could not escape the traditional laws that bound them to motherhood and illiteracy. It would take much longer for the English population to accept changes for women at the commoners' level, but Queen Elizabeth did influence the beginning of that change.

Queen Elizabeth's private life as well as her public triumphs during her problematic reign proved herself as a strong woman and a strong monarch. By illustrating that women can be both a fearless leader and womanly, Elizabeth perfectly embodied feminism. Queen Elizabeth dealt with many complications during her reign, but found solutions specifically with the rising poor, the Spanish Armada, and how she would transition England into the Reformation period. During her rule, her population nearly doubled, thus doubling the number of vagrants (see Figure 1). To cure this problem, she initiated the poor laws which provided vagrants with "local support in the form of food, money, clothing..." (Stock 183). This helped boost England's economy by giving the majority a means to get into the middle class. Queen Elizabeth also defeated Spain, the most powerful country in the world, when the Spanish Armada, a total of 130 ships, attacked England in 1588. A woman's rule defeated the Spanish Armada. This victory symbolized not only the beginning of England's notorious reputation for having the greatest naval power, but also that all religious affiliations, Protestantism and Catholicism, would be accepted in England. This was significantly important because Queen Mary, Elizabeth's half-sister and predecessor, chose Catholicism, which led to her demise and widely known hatred. By Queen Elizabeth adopting a more open and cautious approach she maintained the love of her people, while proving herself a strong woman monarch in the eyes of the public. The Queen's motherly yet conquering approach of caring for the people of her country, demonstrated that being a woman and an amazing monarch are not at odds, but rather complementary positions.

Decade:	Population:
1541	2.7 Million
1569	3.2 Million
1599	4.0 Million

Figure 1. From Elizabeth's birth in 1533 through her death in 1603, the population of England nearly doubled (Hanson).

Where does the debate exist? Although Elizabeth embodied feminism in both her public and private actions, her public speeches sharply contrast with the ideals of feminism.

Elizabeth verbally contributed to stereotypes of women so that she could be accepted as a monarch by the court and church, not because she actually believed in them. Queen Elizabeth was a smart ruler, a ruler who knew she already posed as a threat to men

LOOK HERE:

The British Library's online exhibit contains the original manuscript of Elizabeth's "Speech to the Troops at Tilbury."

and therefore had to degrade herself as a woman in order to maintain her crown. One specific example of her strategically stereotyping women is in her famous speech at Tilbury, after defeating the Spanish Armada. Elizabeth in front of her army said, "I know I have the body of a weak and feeble woman; But I have the heart and stomach of a king" (Tudor). This speech was in front of thousands of soldiers, all men, who had just fought for her country. She needed to state that there was some masculine aspect to her so as to not offend her soldiers who would be listening to the commands of a woman. By degrading herself and her gender, she dignified the soldiers, whose support she needed to maintain. Another example is in her published prayers, one of which stated, "Thou hast done me so special and so rare a mercy, that being a woman by my nature weak, timid, and delicate, as are all women..." (Mudd 107). This stereotypical comment demonstrated just how much Elizabeth had to abide by the church's patriarchal ideas and expectations of her prayers, because she was never weak or timid. A queen so strong and so educated would never degrade her accomplishments without purpose. Elizabeth acknowledged that people had access to her prayers, therefore had to write the publications for the only people who could read them: the men of her country. By publicly degrading her gender, Elizabeth could maintain her crown and from that position encourage women to advance in society. In the novel *Elizabeth I*, the author Anne Somerset states that "Elizabeth, herself, was no feminist" to which I would have to disagree (59). Elizabeth believed in the right to equal access (in education and resources) and believed women should have the right to choices (marrying or not). Elizabeth had no choice in stereotyping women; it was a thought-out strategy that allowed her to rule and let all of her people thrive regardless of religious affiliation or gender. A feminist is someone who believes in "political, economic, and social equality of the sexes," and in this case I believe Queen Elizabeth's actions spoke much louder than her words ("Feminism").

Queen Elizabeth will always be known as an amazing monarch because she repaired the relationship between the crown and the people, while at the same time improving their quality of life. She had to choose which issues better helped the population and could maintain her position as ruler. Due to the patriarchal powers at the time, she was rendered helpless in the quest for women's liberation, though that did not stop her from being a strong advocate. By studying the premeditated strategies Elizabeth took to advance women in their quest for equality, women today can appreciate the struggles of their predecessors. Queen Elizabeth broke one of the very first glass ceilings for women, so if she could do it in a time period that was against her, why can't you?

Leanna McMahon is a Business Administration major.

Works Cited

"Feminism." *The Merriam-Webster Dictionary*, merriam-webster.com, 26 June 2019.

Hanson, Marilee. "Tudor Population Figures & Facts." *English History*, 8 Feb. 2015, englishhistory.net. Accessed 16 Feb 2019.

Mudd, Lindsay Jill. *God's Exceptional Queen: Elizabeth I's Representation of Herself as the Virgin Queen*. Louisville University Press, 2011.

Sharnette, Heather. "Elizabethan Women: Women in Tudor History." *Elizabeth I*, elizabethi.org. Accessed 16 Feb. 2019.

Somerset, Anne. *Elizabeth: I*. New York, Anchor Books, 1991.

Stock, Jennifer York. "Daily Life in the Elizabethan Era." *Elizabethan World Reference Library*, vol. 1, no. 1, 2007, pp. 181–194.

Tudor, Elizabeth. "Speech to the Troops at Tilbury." 9 Aug. 1588, *The British Library*, bl.uk. Accessed 27 June 2019.

CONSIDER THIS:

- Typically, histories of feminism begin with the first-wave feminists who fought for women's suffrage in the 19th century, and, as a concept, "feminism" didn't exist in Elizabethan England. Does McMahon convince you that Queen Elizabeth's rhetorical tactics and political leadership make her an early feminist?

- McMahon's argument takes a sharp turn after the fourth paragraph, when she asks, "Where does the debate exist?" Why does she ask this question at this point in the essay?

- Consider McMahon's use of Elizabeth's "Speech to the Troops at Tilbury." McMahon uses the speech to help her argue that Elizabeth used stereotypes about women strategically. How does McMahon's analysis of a primary source document establish the ethical and logical appeals of her argument? How is this different from, say, citing an article from the internet or from a library research database?

Blinded by the Bubble

Jaxon Silva

Reflective Memo: This essay was definitely an interesting one. I found that when researching this, it was simultaneously too niche and not niche enough. I think that was generally because of this topic lying on the cross-section of three pretty separate fields of study: Journalism, Technology, and Politics. Still I really feel after researching this that this is an issue that is not discussed widely enough, and also some disquieting notions that maybe people truly want to have a bubble. Regardless, it came together more piece-meal than straightforward, which I think gave me a greater way to consider the structure of it all. Still, I am afraid that it is a bit unfocused, as it is not an easy topic to explain, as I believe it requires a bit of a logical process to get where I want to prove, and I must prove every step along the way to prove the overall argument.

Secretly there is something watching you, with every move you make, every search on Google, and every like on Facebook. Quietly in the shadows of HTML jargon, it collects the digital breadcrumbs you leave behind, learns everything about you, and sells it to the highest bidder. But the people behind this aren't hackers or some sort of crazy cyber-stalker, they are the companies you trust every day when you go online.

This wasn't always the case. The internet was initially promised to bring freedom, as the ultimate and final place where the collective knowledge of humanity would be stored. A superhighway of information. However, today that is not the case. Due to the excessive monetization of the internet, it fails to meet its original purpose as a free, open source of information to all. Companies such as Facebook and Google, using practices to target users by exploiting the data they generate, create echo chambers for virulent and dangerous mistruths to accumulate. All the while, factual sources and content hide behind paywalls and subscription services to only deliver the truth to those who can afford to have it.

However, the most prevalent aspect of how the internet has changed is how much we are tracked these days online, our choice or not. Every day we are bombarded by messages on websites telling us that they are tracking our movements. Mainly through cookies, which Indiana University's IT Support Center defines as "messages that web servers pass to your web browser when you visit Internet sites" (UITS). Generally, these signals consist of tracking almost everything you do online. From where you visit online to how long you are on the website. Where you are, how fast you are moving, what you search for. Almost everything and anything connected to the internet is collected by companies like Google and Acxiom, and sold to determine what ads you see every day online.

Not only that, but every search, like, and click is used to determine what you see every day online. Companies know essentially everything about your digital self, which is generally an extension of our real selves.

By knowing everything about our digital selves, companies can then shape our worldview. In 2009, Google began tweaking its search engine. Instead of showing the most visited websites first, they began to use the data that we generate to tailor search results toward what an algorithm thought we would like to see, and the effects were immediate. Following the Deepwater Horizon oil spill, Eli Pariser writes, "[i]n the spring of 2010, I asked two friends to search for the term 'BP'…. One of my friends saw investment information about BP. The other saw news" (Pariser 2). Google, by doing this, exemplified an alarming trend that is occurring over much of the internet. As algorithms and code are used to show more of what we want to see, they essentially create our own digital bubble for us to live in, proving us right when we are wrong and never showing us what we need to see. One can see this in social media sites like Facebook, which actively tailors results over what you like and what you don't. While from an efficiency standpoint it's effective, the fact is that if one wants to find the truth of a matter, they must put a concerted effort towards finding evidence against one's own beliefs and prejudices. And if one wants to get the truth, one has to pay for it, as most major news outlets have paywalls, ads before videos, or ads covering most of their webpages. The University of Oxford's Reuters Institute of Journalism found in a study that "whereas higher social grade individuals and lower social grade individuals use the same number of sources offline on average, lower social grade individuals use significantly fewer online sources on average" (Kalogeropoulos and Nielsen 1). The current state of affairs can lead people to becoming radicalized and thereby commit terrifying crimes and atrocities.

One terrifying example was on December 3, 2017 when, as the Asheville *Courier-Tribune* reported, a man named Edgar Welch entered a Washington DC pizzeria, "fired three shots from an AR-15, then surrendered peacefully after finding no evidence of child sex slaves in the restaurant" (Douglas and Washburn). This man believed that a child sex-ring existed and was centered in this restaurant. After reading much online about this false conspiracy theory, he went to go investigate it himself. He was surrounded by so much false information proving himself correct that he nearly killed others. But this is not the only example of how the echo chambers created online lead to misinformation. Back in 2013, following the horrendous Boston Marathon bombing, there was a well-televised and publicized manhunt for the suspects in the bombing. Following along online were citizen journalists, who managed to get an innocent man harassed and nearly arrested for a crime he didn't commit. They believed that this man was the bomber, and a huge chunk of the online community believed them. However,

because everyone was so wrapped up in their own digital worlds, no one received the information that maybe these citizen journalists' methods were not perfect, or that the evidence didn't add up.

This is coupled with an already dying news sphere, as local news sources are either going into bankruptcy or being bought out by major corporations like Gannett Co., which owns eighty-one daily newspapers as part of the USA Today network. This is

LOOK HERE:

View a *This Week Tonight* segment about Sinclair Broadcast Group's influence on local TV news broadcasts.

also seen in television, most notably television news stations, as seen in Sinclair Broadcast group's ownership of over 173 local television stations, as reported by the *Washington Post* (Rosenberg). Why are these news sources dying or being swallowed up? Mainly because of the filters the internet has, which can more efficiently and effectively tell users what they want to hear more than any newspaper, magazine, or television news can. As found in research by Harvard University's Shorenstein Center for Media, Politics, and Public Policy, "the decline of local newspapers has contributed to the nationalization of American politics: as local newspapers close, Americans rely more heavily on available national news or partisan heuristics to make political decisions" (Darr et. al. 1007). Today, the filters in place by social media companies and search engines have led to entire online worlds and media based on certain ideological or political beliefs, such as the widely followed alt-right cybersphere, where websites such as Breitbart, less credible news sources like InfoWars, and social media enclaves like Reddit's /r/the_donald propagate and spread these falsehoods even further to the point that they become active discussion points. News sources seeing the trends at play, have merely adapted their strategies. It is no small wonder why both Fox News and CNN have gotten more partisan in recent years, as their viewer-base has gotten more partisan due to the effects of the filters in place. One can see this in the 2016 election, where articles about Hillary Clinton being terminally ill after being filmed coughing, or the "Pizzagate" conspiracy mentioned above, flooded the internet, eventually being discussed on the evening news to the point that they took on an air of credibility.

Naturally, people may question my arguments, as they may argue that the internet can't be free in our economy, and that personalized search results and social media help the internet more than they cause harm. However, I'm not saying that they must be removed, so much as renovated. The EU recently passed the General Data Protection Regulation (GDPR) which gives people more control over their personal data, stating that "[t]he protection of natural persons in

relation to the processing of personal data is a fundamental right" (Rinehart and Edwards). The US could easily model a bill after the GDPR, and would bring little to no harm to the tech companies while delivering huge protections for consumers. We can have data to give us better results, but when it comes to news and analysis, we also need to be shown ideas, events, and evidence outside of our own bubble of data so that we may gain a clear picture of the issues our world faces every day, and right now we do not receive that privilege. Why not have search engines both try to optimize what you are looking for and try to add an element of serendipity to the search. To try to actively disprove their assumptions about who you are by throwing information at you that you wouldn't have otherwise seen?

Plenty of information can and probably should be monetized. It's because of Apple Music that I'm able to get thousands of songs for a fraction of what I would have to pay if I bought them all at a record store or on iTunes. Sure, watching ads on YouTube, hearing them on Spotify, or seeing them the next time you scroll through Instagram are all annoying, but these aren't propagating mistruths, and for the most part they aren't tailored to your individual preferences. Search engines can be tailored to show users information that they normally wouldn't see in their own filter bubble, as Microsoft did with an experiment with Bing in 2013, which found that, while 81% of Republicans and 76% of Democrats "click on items from one of the most polarized outlets of their own view, they rarely clicked on polarized outlets of the other side (4 and 6% respectively), suggesting a filter bubble in action. The researchers then modified the Bing search engine's results page… [and] they observed a change of 25% toward the center" (Bozdag and van den Hoven 257). It is only when companies use the data we generate to tailor what we see to create our very own echo chambers that it becomes a problem. If we are only seeing what proves us right then we will only learn a confirmation bias towards our own prejudices, for civil discourse and personal growth do not come from being right, they come from being proven wrong.

This does not have to be a problem. It is time for us to pressure our lawmakers to create laws that are similar to the GDPR. Recently, California passed a law that reinstated Net Neutrality, flying in the face of the FCC's decision to repeal Net Neutrality protections, which proves that the internet can be taken back. However, even on a personal level, we must support browsers like Firefox, which supports data privacy, or websites like Knowhere, which is trying to support truth in an economy of irrationality. We must learn to post less and learn more. We need to look beyond what is presented in front of ourselves and to find what the truth is, regardless of what side we stand for. What made the internet of the 1990s interesting was that one still had to go out and search for what they were looking for. In the end, it was the hunt, not the eventual destination that made it special, as you would never know what you would learn along the way. Instead of relying on automated search features and automatically-generated posts and articles, it was serendipity and understanding that guided us, not a filter that only proved ourselves right.

Jaxon Silva is a Civil Engineering major.

Works Cited

Bozdag, Engin and Jeroen van den Hoven. "Breaking the Filter Bubble: Democracy and Design." *Ethics and Information Technology*, vol. 17, no. 4, 2015, pp. 249–265, *SpringerLink*, doi.org/10.1007/s10676-015-9380-y

Darr, Joshua P., Matthew P. Hitt, and Johanna L Dunaway. "Newspaper Closures Polarize Voting Behavior." *Journal of Communication*, vol. 68, no. 6, pp. 1007–1028, *Oxford Academic*, doi.org/10.1093/joc/jqy051

Douglas, William, and Mark Washburn. "Religious Zeal Drives N.C. Man in 'Pizzagate'." *The Courier-Tribune* [Asheboro, NC], 6 Dec. 2016, courier-tribune.com. Accessed 27 June 2019.

Kalogeropoulos, Antonis and Rasmus Kleis Nielsen. "Social Inequalities in News Consumption." *Reuters Institute for the Study of Journalism,* Oct. 2018 Factsheet, https://reutersinstitute.politics.ox.ac.uk. Accessed 27 June 2019.

Pariser, Eli. *The Filter Bubble: What the Internet Is Hiding from You*, New York, Viking, 2012.

Rinehart, Will and Allison Edwards. "Explaining the EU's General Data Protection Plan." *American Action Forum*, 22 May 2018, americanactionforum.org. Accessed 27 June 2019.

Rosenberg, Eli. "Trump Says Sinclair Is 'Far Superior' to CNN: What We Know about the Media Giant." *The Washington Post*, 3 Apr. 2018, washingtonpost.com. Accessed 27 June 2019.

UITS Support Center. "What Are Cookies?" *Indiana University IT Knowledge Base*, kb.iu.edu. Accessed 27 June 2019.

CONSIDER THIS:

- Silva cites a wide array of precise examples of the different positions that technology and media companies have taken towards user-generated data: Google, Facebook, Acxiom, Apple, Microsoft, Knowhere, Firefox, and others. How do all of these examples help position Silva as a writer aware of the complexity of the issues surrounding data privacy?

- In his sixth paragraph, Silva moves away from his main argument about how user data is being tracked to filter online content to make a brief digression about the shrinking influence of traditional local news sources. How does this digression connect to his larger argument?

- In his last three paragraphs, Silva discusses opposing arguments to help him do three specific things: 1) clarify what he is *not* trying to argue; 2) accommodate an opposing argument by agreeing with it; and 3) challenge an underlying assumption that data privacy issues are an inevitable problem of monetizing the internet. Can you pinpoint exactly where he makes these three moves and explain how each of them helps his argument?

Voter Registration

Kayla Cheyno

Reflective Memo: *The topic of this essay was very interesting for me to research. I did not know much about voter registration when I started this essay. I wanted to pick a topic that directly affected myself. Since I just had registered to vote a few months prior I thought that it would be an interesting topic to research. The most challenging part was finding reliable sources to back up what I wanted to argue in my essay. Overall, this piece helped me understand how I and others can be affected by voter registration.*

Have you been through the long, strenuous process of U.S. voter registration? Voting has the power to prevent the government from making serious decisions that are not in the people's best interest. It is a constitutional right that allows every citizen to be able to cast a ballot on election day. In previous years, women and minorities were not always given this right. However, that has all changed and now every citizen possesses the right to vote, so why do so many people still not vote in the elections? Citizens must register to vote in every state but North Dakota. The registration process varies from state to state; however, many have deadlines and other restrictions that can potentially prevent U.S. citizens from exercising their right. Registration is implemented and maintained by the federal and state government, and it benefits registered voters and political parties. Voter registration causes the U.S. to have low voter turnout and unequal representation, which affects low income and minority voters directly by restricting their right to vote.

This system of control was first created in order to limit the voting rights of many minorities. During the nineteenth century, many registration laws and voting regulations were put in place, such as literacy tests and poll taxes specifically limiting African-American participation in elections (Stone 522). This began a trend of using voter registration to restrict certain types of voters. Many African-Americans during this time period could not pass the literacy test or afford to pay poll taxes that were required to be eligible to register. This was the start of the flawed system. The government and many politicians began to use the voter registration process to manipulate and control the popular vote, violating many people's constitutional rights.

Even without the threat of literacy tests and poll taxes, governments still find ways to limit many people's right to vote. Many of the states in the U.S. have different rules and regulations for voter registration. This system of control can also be caused by the state's individual laws. Many of the states "do have the power under the Constitution to set voter qualifications, thereby defining the group of

persons with this base entitlement to vote on election day" (James 1623). The procedures set to limit who can vote may not be as obvious anymore, but they can still be effective. They could be as simple as putting fewer places to register in areas with a population that does not follow the popular political opinions of the current government. They could potentially make it significantly harder for people to register because of long lines and not being able to travel further distances. The manipulation that both the federal and state government use to limit certain types of people from being able to vote has caused and continued this problematic system of control over time.

Voter registration laws are made by each state individually. The federal government gives the states the freedom to make many of their own registration procedures. The "majority of states continue to maintain registration deadlines of up to fifty days before an election and authorize restrictive practices such as inconvenient registration sites" (Quinlivan 2364). While citizens see problems in their state's voter registration system, many election and government officials do not. A study that examined a Chicago election in 1920 found that "while most citizens and organizational leaders interviewed believed that there were serious problems about the convenience and complexity of registering, more than 75 percent of local election officials did not see such problems" (Stone 525). Election officials continue to ignore problems that they see as insignificant, and citizens feel as if those in power do not want them to exercise their right to vote so that they can maintain an unequal system.

Both state governments and political parties benefit from voter registration. State governments claim that voter registration is beneficial because "fraud prevention is a compelling state interest. States do have an interest in assuring that only persons meeting the residency, age, competency and citizenship qualifications vote, and do so only once" (James 1633). If the state were using registration for this sole purpose, it could benefit everyone. However, the reality is that many citizens do not have the opportunity to vote because the registration system is flawed. What many people do not see is that "political parties take on much of the registration work. Their incentives are skewed, and as a result the electorate can become skewed. That's because the political parties' goal is not to register people. Their goal is to register their people" (Gerken). The voter registration process makes it easier for political parties to reach out only to voters who support their party. Even before campaigning, trying to register people who support your party can help in the long run. It can be a huge benefit to the political parties if they reach out and put in the effort to get their supporters to register and eventually vote for them in the next election.

If voting is a fundamental constitutional right, every person should have the opportunity to vote. Since many residents are not registered, they cannot easily exercise this right. In *The University of Pennsylvania Law Review*, Quinlivan points out that "roughly 35-40% of eligible Americans are not registered to vote" (2363). If registration became more easily accessible, the U.S. would experience a higher voter turnout, creating more accurate elections. Looking specifically at California, "[t]he state's wealthiest counties have the highest voter registration rates…. The lowest registration rates are in the counties with the highest poverty levels…. Ultimately, these disparities in registration leave wealthier and more educated populations with significantly more representation in the state's electorate" (Romero and Fox 14–15). Voter registration gives the upper class an advantage in elections. It does not allow for equal opportunity between people with different financial statuses. Many people in poverty-stricken areas cannot afford to take time off work to go to their nearest registration place. People not being able to vote because their lack of an opportunity to register can create serious political problems and unequal representation in government.

Most states make the registration process long and inconvenient. A person has to be motivated and informed of the process in order to be registered in time for the next election. They will have to "ascertain (at a minimum) where and when to obtain the registration form, how to fill it in, whether supporting documents are needed, what the deadline is, and whether a declaration of party affiliation is required" (Stone 522). Once a citizen is registered, problems can occur with their registration information. As many as "one in eight registrations in the United States is either invalid or contains significant inaccuracies. Nearly two million dead people are on the rolls, 2.75 million people are registered in more than one state, and 12 million voter records contains incorrect addresses" (Gerken). Even when someone has taken the time to register, they still might not cast a ballot because of technical issues with their registration. An MIT study showed that 2.2 million voters could not vote on election day because of problems with the registration system (Gerken). The government turns away people who not only made the effort to register but who also took the time to show up and attempt to vote on election day.

Voter registration issues can negatively affect all citizens; however, it mostly affects minority groups. Many minority groups struggle when trying to register to vote because of the different laws and restrictions. In many states "black, Hispanic and Asian citizens are statistically more likely to be unregistered than white citizens" (Jacobson) because of poverty and the fact that political parties neglect to advertise voter registration to them. Political parties often choose to not focus on minorities because they do not make up a large portion of the voting population in many places, instead targeting upper-class white citizens when

advertising registration. In many minority communities, there are "monetary costs of lost wages or lost income while taking the time to register, costs of inconvenience due to the time a voter must spend to get registered and to vote, and the information costs of finding out how to register. These costs are borne more heavily by those with less education, with less income or with minority status" (Stone 523). Even if they are informed of how and where to register, many people in these situations cannot afford to take time off from work or to pay for transportation in order to register. These citizens are denied their constitutional rights simply because they do not have the same access to the resources that upper-class white people have.

The negative implications of voter registration also affect many citizens who are not easily motivated or aware of elections before they happen. The deadlines set for voter registration often "prevent those citizens whose interest in an election peaks as the election day approaches from casting a ballot… Compounding this problem is the

LOOK HERE:

If you are a U.S. citizen and a resident of California, you can register to vote through the CA Secretary of State's online voter registration system (you can even pre-register if you're under 18).

fact that registration is often limited to a single central location in a country" (Quinlivan 2372–2373). If people become interested late in an election campaign, it may be past the deadline for them to register. Not only do many states make the deadline to register fifty or more days in advance to the election, but they often make people travel far just to vote. If and when the less-motivated voter makes it to their polling place, they may find "too few poll workers or voting machines or polling books to process voters quickly. Registration problems put more pressure on the system than it can bear. Little wonder there were people voting after midnight in 2012" (Gerken). On top of having to register early and travel many miles to their polling place, voters may have to wait in lines for hours as well.

The U.S. has a very different voting process than most other democratic countries. In many other democracies "voting is a collective responsibility in which both the government and the individual citizens are involved in ensuring universal participation in the political process…The United States is the only western nation that continues to follow the 'obsolete' English practice of placing the entire burden of registration upon the individual" (Quinlivan 2376). The U.S. expects its citizens to do all of the work in order to vote. They make it harder on them through voter registration when they should be trying to improve the voting process in order to have a higher voter turnout. In other democracies it is a group effort, which makes citizens feel as if their government truly wants them

to vote. It makes people feel more obligated to vote because their government is encouraging them by automatically registering them. Automatic voter registration is a system that would automatically register citizens to vote once they become of the voting age and are eligible, unless they decide to opt out. The U.S. voter registration system does not create this sense of urgency and obligation to the country, but it could if we implemented automatic voter registration.

Voter registration has become a huge problem because it overall restricts U.S. citizens' constitutional right to vote. It is maintained by the U.S. government because it can be manipulated to benefit different parties' political views. Low-income and minority groups overall suffer the worst consequences of voter registration. Even citizens who register may have trouble voting because there are so many technical flaws in the system. All of this put together results in minority voters not getting the chance to vote just because of voter registration. The only way to eliminate this problem and motivate more people to vote is to implement automatic voter registration. Citizens should not be expected to put in all of the time and effort into being eligible to vote. Our democracy needs to take responsibility and change the way we vote in order to create equal opportunity for all citizens.

Kayla Cheyno is an English major.

Work Cited

Gerken, Heather K. "Make It Easy: The Case for Automatic Registration." *Democracy Journal*, 1 July 2016, democracyjournal.org. Accessed 27 June 2019.

Jacobson, Louis. "Think Automatic Voter Registration Just Benefits Democrats? Not Necessarily." *Governing Magazine: State and Local Government News for America's Leaders*, 5 Oct. 2017, governing.com. Accessed 27 June 2019.

James, Deborah S. "Voter Registration: A Restriction on the Fundamental Right to Vote." *The Yale Law Journal*, vol. 96, no. 7, June 1987, pp. 1615–1640, *JSTOR*, doi:10.2307/796496.

Quinlivan, Mark Thomas. "One Person, One Vote Revisited: The Impending Necessity of Judicial Intervention in the Realm of Voter Registration." *The University of Pennsylvania Law Review*, vol. 137, no. 6, June 1989, pp. 2361–2395, *JSTOR*, doi: 10.2307/3312220

Romero, Mindy, and Johnathan Fox. "California's Voter Registration Rates." *Boom: A Journal of California*, vol. 2, no. 4, Winter 2012, pp. 14–17, doi: 10.1525/boom.2012.2.4.14

Stone, Mary N. "Voter Registration: Context and Results." *The Urban Lawyer*, vol. 17, no. 3, Summer 1985, pp. 519–528, *JSTOR*, www.jstor.org/stable/pdf/27893313.pdfrefreqid=excelsior%3Ad076f463d79919864d4dc90d70c19b26.

CONSIDER THIS:

- Note how Cheyno often integrates multiple sources into a single paragraph, and she also often uses the same source in multiple ways throughout her argument. Choose one source that she uses extensively, and explain exactly how she used it. How many times did she cite it? What specific points did it help her to make? How did she integrate it with another source in the same paragraph so that both sources could help her make a larger point?

- Cheyno's argument does not call excessive attention to its own claim and reasoning. Rather, she often leaves it to the reader to infer her line of reasoning as her discussion develops from paragraph to paragraph. What's the effect of this writing technique for conveying her argument? Can you still identify her basic claim and her main reasons?

- Where does Cheyno's argument accommodate an opposing viewpoint? How does she respond to her opposition?

Comfort v. Necessity

Bryanna Gay

"The Crisis That Is Cal Poly," read the signs.

Silent protesters gathered on Dexter Lawn with signs exclaiming the truth about racism and sexual assault prevalent on California Polytechnic State University's campus. Open House was supposed to be a time for current Mustangs to inform me, a prospective student, about the positive attributes of the top-ranking university. Instead, the students, who felt silenced by Cal Poly, gathered to express their support for targeted students of the Black community. Protesters of the recent Black face incident resisted President Armstrong's claim that the incident was "protected by free speech, and freedom of expression" (Leslie). As members of the Black Student Union and their allies made their way to the lawn, confusion and a small tinge of hesitation sparked within me. Based on the signs, literally and figuratively, this was not the school I worked so hard to get into. I explained to one of the protesters how passionate I am about social justice and how I did not think I could make this place my home. She then told me something I will never forget. "If you want to make a change in this world, go where you're needed, not where you're comfortable." In that moment, I knew I would accept Cal Poly's offer of admission.

Students normally choose their college based on the things they admire about it, but I chose Cal Poly for the things I did not. After learning more about the widespread racism on campus, I no longer thought about the inclusive environment and bustling city around Seattle University. SU was my dream school, but going there would keep me in a stagnant state with like-minded people. In order to make change, I must step out of my comfort zone. I knew Cal Poly would be an amazing place to speak my mind and continue my activism. I decided that joining the Black Student Union would be my first step. I have always been passionate about civil rights and I think it's important to embrace cultures different from my own; White and Mexican. I also want to show my support for the changes BSU is trying to make on Cal Poly's campus.

Laughter and smiles filled the room as I walked into my first BSU meeting. Ambitious Black scholars enjoyed a space where they built a community here on campus. Everyone was very welcoming, but seeing no one who looks like you can be intimidating and create a feeling of insecurity. *Is this how Black students feel every day when entering Cal Poly's predominantly white campus?* This thought reinforced how important it is for underrepresented students to build a community. A community that promotes, embraces and appreciates Black culture. Having people who understand your struggles and overcome them with you is a

major factor to future success. The BSU is a safe space for many students all over the country, but before this organization flourished, Black students had minimal representation or support on college campuses.

Racial inequality has always been an issue in America, but tensions were extremely high in the mid 20th century due to the issue of college access. During the Civil Rights Movement, many universities fought against integration. Americans who supported white supremacy believed their race and culture was superior, so educated Black students were seen as a threat. Black students were forced to focus on overcoming the obstacles of discrimination and racism while pursuing higher education. Black Student Unions were quickly formed at universities to give Black students a common place to fight against the racist regime in America.

The first BSU was founded at San Francisco State University in 1966 (Whiting). Two Black men, Jimmy Garrett and Jerry Varnado, who were eager to make progress at universities across America, created the term Black Student Union. Later, a conference in California informed other universities of the new term and its use became widespread. Their goal was to create a "college advocacy group that would work towards civil rights everywhere" (Whiting). Black Student Unions have the common goal of creating a support system for Black students' academic success as well as personal success.

The BSU at California Polytechnic State University, San Luis Obispo, was founded in the Fall of 1968. This group was formed both in an "effort to expand equality for African American students on campus and to expand curriculum to reflect the increasingly diverse student body at Cal Poly" (Manning 102). Cal Poly was established in 1901. This is fifty-three years before *Brown vs. Board of Education of Topeka*, the Supreme Court case that would prohibit universities from denying students based on their race. Black students made up about 1 percent of the total student body, but the BSU was still very active in making changes on campus. Some requests from the members included segregated housing, to have a safe place for Black students, and an African American studies major. Robert E. Kennedy, Cal Poly's president at the time, refused both. He believed segregated housing would make the university look "discriminatory against Blacks" and "did not see the value in a degree in Black studies" (Manning). Although Kennedy denied many suggestions, the BSU persisted and continues to work with the administration to better the lives of Black students. Richard Jenkins, in a letter to the editor of *Mustang Daily*, stated that the Black Student Union "never [came] to the administration with clenched fists, but with creative and productive ideas to improve race relations at Cal Poly" (Manning 103).

From 2008 to 2014, Cal Poly did not have a BSU due to the lack of staff to run the program. According to Malcolm S. Mills, the "lack of Black faculty and staff at Cal Poly does not allow Black men to [have] successful models when it comes to navigating life at Cal Poly" (Mills 4). When interviewing Steve Ross, the coordinator of the Black Student Union and Black Academic Excellence Center, he told me about the importance of the resources these organizations provide. Steve was hired to promote Black student success at Cal Poly and created the Black Academic Excellence Center. Black students graduate at a significantly lower rate than White students due to the "hostile campus climate, lack of social support, and difficulty navigating a space not designed to support or accommodate Black students" (Mills 14). These programs advocate inclusivity and diversity while providing Black students with free resources such as study rooms, books, scantrons and supplies. The cross-cultural coordinators also plan multicultural events in order to get minorities and underrepresented groups to embrace and share their stories with others.

LOOK HERE:

An April 2019 article in *Mustang News* reflects on Cal Poly's campus climate one year after the Lambda Chi Alpha incident.

The BSU is not only a social club that works to advocate Black culture on campus, but when social unrest arises, members are quick to collaborate and stand up for what they believe in. In the spring of 2018, a fraternity named Lambda Chi Alpha had a "gangster"-themed party where participants dressed as gang members and thugs, appropriating many cultures that are minorities here on campus. This made national news because one of the brothers wore blackface, an extremely racist tactic used by actors in the mid-19th century to stereotype and demean Black people in plays. Due to the fact that this is not the first racist hate crime on Cal Poly's campus, the BSU decided to take matters into their own hands (Clark). Students from numerous multicultural groups joined together to protest and show their support for the Black student population. "By using freedom of speech to promote hate, you silence those you target," said a protester, during my Open House, who was rebutting the popular belief that this action was protected under freedom of speech. The nonviolent protesting tactics used by Cal Poly students resembled those used by peaceful leaders during the Civil Rights Movement. Instead of studying for exams and focusing on their studies like most college students, Black students and their allies were forced to dedicate their time to protesting racism. Thankfully, support systems were in place to provide counseling and a passionate community of people ready to share their experiences.

Engaging in Public Rhetoric and Argumentation

More clubs and groups at Cal Poly that support Black student success include The National Society of Black Engineers (NSBE) and Black Faculty Staff Association (BFSA). NSBE is an academic support program that helps to increase the graduation rate of underrepresented students in the Engineering department. Black students are often represented by and work with the BFSA. This program collaborates with Black students, helping them feel more welcome and included on Cal Poly's campus. Making a more inclusive environment allows for all students to feel equal and valued.

Many people have doubted me and my mission to make Cal Poly a better place. Joining BSU and meeting so many passionate students gives me strength and hope for the future. This experience has humbled me. The strength that the Black community has is incredibly inspiring. It is unfair that we have to fight against racism when everyone is truly equal. The color of one's skin should never bring up a feeling of hostility or hatred. Cal Poly has a lot of changes to make, but with the help of organizations like BSU, we are sure to overcome any challenge. This community is dedicated to enhancing the lives of Black students and teaching acceptance. This is the most effective way to strengthen the relations amongst students at Cal Poly. Fighting for what you believe in when the odds are against you is a hard task, but it is a challenge we accept. I am needed here. I have found comfort in my commitment.

Bryanna Gay is a Communication Studies major.

Works Cited

Clark, Lucas. "Nearly 1,000 Cal Poly Students Call for Support, Action at Public Forum with School President." *The Tribune [San Luis Obispo]*, 12 Apr. 2018, sanluisobispo.com. Accessed 8 Oct. 2018.

Leslie, Kaytlyn. "Blackface Is Free Speech, so Student Likely Won't Be Expelled, Cal Poly President Says." *The Tribune [San Luis Obispo]*, 12 Apr. 2018, archived at archive.org. www.sanluisobispo.com/news/local/education/article208728619.html. Accessed 10 Oct. 2018.

Manning, Megan. "The Civil Rights Movement at Cal Poly." *The Forum: Journal of History*, vol. 5, no. 1, 2013, digitalcommons.calpoly.edu. Accessed 9 Oct. 2018.

Mills, Malcolm S. "Struggling to Survive: Addressing the Graduation Rate of Cal Poly's Black Men." *DigitalCommons @ Cal Poly*, digitalcommons.calpoly.edu. Accessed 10 Oct. 2018.

Whiting, Sam. "The Black Student Union at SFSU Started It All." *SFGate*, 1 Feb. 2010, sfgate.com. Accessed 10 Oct. 2018.

CONSIDER THIS:

- Gay opens her argument with an extended personal narrative. How does her personal story serve the purpose of establishing all three rhetorical appeals for her argument: *ethos, pathos,* and *logos*? How does her story provide evidence for her argument? How does it establish her credibility as a writer? How does it emotionally connect you to her and to the issue?

- All of Gay's sources are intensely local: Cal Poly's Digital Commons, the SLO *Tribune,* and the *San Francisco Chronicle's* website *SFGate.com.* Yet her argument speaks to a larger national conversation about racism and institutional racism. How does she manage to connect the campus to the larger national context?

- Gay's argument focuses on the history of Cal Poly's Black Student Union. The BSU is just one of many campus organizations working to make Cal Poly a diverse and inclusive place. Research other campus organizations related to diversity and inclusivity whose presence and history on campus might make for an interesting research topic and argument.

Cal Poly Needs More Composting

Sarah Bates

Reflective Memo: *While developing this piece, I went back and forth between many topics before I realized that by choosing a specific topic, like one that affects a college campus, I could really advocate for change instead of just a change of perspective. Composting is a great thing to implement for many reasons, and once I made the decision to write about this topic, I was able to throw myself into it.*

Dear President Armstrong,

We can do better than "when in doubt recycle." We can do better than 90% in 2016 and 86% in 2017 waste diversion based on facilities rather than campus population. We can do better than letting our compost be contaminated. We are Cal Poly, and I think we can do better. As of 2019, we have one year left until the CSU-wide 2020 Sustainability Policies are supposed to be met, but Zero Waste cannot stop there. I think that in order for our campus to remain on a sustainable track, waste facilities, with the presidential push, need to place compost bins in every residence hall on campus alongside trash cans and recycle bins.

The waste management on campus can be difficult to fully understand, as many of the statements made public about Cal Poly's waste are ambiguous or do not focus on the general populations' waste habits. In May of 2014, The California State University adopted the Sustainability Policies in order to ensure that their affiliated campuses were leaders of environmentalism while also sparking innovation statewide to help tackle the goals. While we must advocate for every policy they have laid out, the Zero Waste policies are particularly important because universities provide housing for thousands of students per year that each generate an average of 4.7 pounds of waste per day ("Waste Disposal"). According to the CSU Sustainability Policy Assessment, "The Sustainability Policy directs campuses to reduce their solid waste disposal rate by fifty percent by 2016 and 80 percent by 2020… eight out of twenty-three campuses had achieved the 2016 goal" ("Sustainability"). While Cal Poly is a campus that has surmounted the 2016 goal, and is on track for the 2020 goal, we have only done so based on the inclusion of facilities' waste generation. According to Anastasia Nicole, Cal Poly's Zero Waste Coordinator, "We have really heavy waste streams that are making up for public trash…. Cement is heavy and that gets recycled for construction. And if we were not an agricultural college, we wouldn't have such good diversion rates" (qtd. in Ladin). Though it is important to divert as much waste as possible from all sectors on campus, Cal Poly must work on the waste generation being made campus-wide—specifically in the dorms, since they have already mastered waste diversion from facilities.

Knowing that waste calculations are less directed at student waste generation and more towards big scale facilities' waste generation, it is much easier to understand the need for dorm-wide compost bins to be easily accessible. According to the Environmental Protection Agency, there are many benefits of composting such as enriching soil, reducing methane emissions from unnatural landfill decomposition, and reducing the need for chemical fertilizers—as the product of composting is used as a natural way to bring nutrients back into soil. Cal Poly, as a school that does make composting efforts and is a largely agricultural school, knows these benefits and has implemented composting for such benefits. We have partnered with Engle and Gray, a company that processes the dining hall's organic waste for use off campus, and we also have our own onsite compost that uses the seven million pounds of CAFES' produced manure to make natural fertilizer in a closed-loop system. Both of these are important steps towards Zero Waste, but we cannot stop there. The next step is providing every residence hall, if not every dorm room, with an area to bring their organic waste to be composted. The system ideally would still be partnered with Engle and Gray, as to least impact monetary funds. We are a university that prides itself on the innovation bred here and the learn by doing principle, so let's lead the movement towards zero waste by not stalemating environmental progress.

While there is no denying dorm-wide composting is an important idea to apply, there are some obvious drawbacks that would need to be addressed. The first problem would be the fiscal reasonability of executing this plan. With an increase in compostable items being collected,

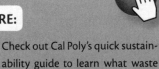

LOOK HERE:

Check out Cal Poly's quick sustainability guide to learn what waste goes in which bin.

there will be an increase in the price to pick up the organics that Engle and Gray set. Currently the rate is around $65 per ton of waste ("Cal Poly"). The other fiscal impact is the price of putting compost bins in the residence halls. However, this is not a huge amount of money required to get the program started. The only continuous rate being paid is the Engle and Gray price of pick up, while the price of buying the bins to put throughout the dorms is a one-time upfront cost that will not have to be paid again unless replacements are needed. Working with the Zero Waste Team/Club and other donors, Cal Poly can easily manage the monetary implications of this program and benefit from the organic fertilizer being produced at Engle and Gray if we direct it back to our campus' agriculture unit or any other landscaping on campus.

The other major setback to dormitory composting is from the abundant contamination of organics seen in other post-consumer compost collections. One example is from The Avenue: the pre-consumer and post-consumer compostable items recently had to be separated so the uncontaminated pre-consumer organics do not become contaminated with the ketchup packet or water bottle ridden post-consumer "organics," (Linthicum). According to Bob Engel, Engle and Gray Vice President, it does not make sense from an economic standpoint to manually remove the contamination. He also states, "The problem is not just happening at Cal Poly... [people] are dealing with this across the country" (qtd. in Linthicum). The problem is that consumers producing multi-material waste (think of a Bishop's Burgers' meal: water bottle, cardboard container, and half of a burger) are not properly educated about what waste goes in which bin. Though this is a serious problem, I have faith that as bright Cal Poly students we can all easily become educated about the proper receptacles of certain waste. The pictures posted around the three bins in the Avenue, are extremely helpful to students as they give a visual description of the proper container to put waste into. This is an easy way to ensure that students effectively compost, recycle, and landfill the appropriate waste by giving exact examples. If the potential compost bins of the residence halls had similar visual aids posted on the outside, as well as more specific descriptions as to what materials to put in the bin, there would be much more student success with waste diversion. We can also promote the idea of landfilling items that we are unsure about, as opposed to "when in doubt recycle," in order to keep the bins uncontaminated and more fiscally feasible to maintain.

We are also already seeing many campuses that are successful with complete, 100% zero waste systems in place. One example of a waste neutral campus is University of California Santa Cruz. UCSC is mandated by the University of California policies, including their version of the CSU Sustainability Policies. In response to these new environmental policies, UCSC began their pilot composting program that started small but grew to cover several parts of their campus—including dining, in preparation, and throughout residence halls ("Progress"). As of the 2017–18 academic school year, UCSC was able to divert almost 400 tons of housing waste from landfills through advanced composting and recycling programs that educated their students on why it is important and how to get involved ("Latest"). If Cal Poly implemented systems like UCSC's, designed to reduce waste through obvious education and direct application, we would be able to make a substantial decrease in our campus' total waste generation and an overall increase in the health of our environment.

In conclusion, I believe the best way to achieve our 2020 Sustainability Policy goals, while also making the most substantial individual impacts on our campus' waste generation, is to bring composting bins into all residence halls.

By making composting as easily available to students as recycling and landfilling, we are ensuring the beauty and health of our small-town home. The closed-loop composting system in partnership with Engle and Gray can strengthen our power as being environmental advocates and truly push to making a whole student population change, rather than complete our goals solely based on facilities' waste management. Let us not stop our progress towards making change, and let us perfect this new system through learning by doing. We can do better than 72% waste diversion: we are Cal Poly.

Sincerely,
Sarah Bates

Sarah Bates is an Anthropology and Geography major.

Works Cited

"Cal Poly Campus Dining's Sustainability Measures." *Cal Poly Corporation*. 22 Apr. 2015. www.calpolycorporation.org. Accessed 27 Feb. 2019.

"Composting at Home." *EPA,* United States Government: Environmental Protection Agency, 16 Oct. 2018. www.epa.gov. Accessed 27 Feb. 2019.

Ladin, Ashley. "Students and Faculty Fail to Keep Up with Cal Poly's 2020 Zero Waste Goal; Facilities Keep Campus on Track." *MustangNews*, 4 Dec. 2018, mustangnews.net. Accessed 27 Feb. 2019.

"Latest Diversion Charts: UCSC Fiscal Year Material Total Comparison—Facility Type." *RecyclingUCSC*, University of California, 2019, recycling. ucsc.edu. Accessed 27 Feb. 2019.

Linthicum, Austin. "Why Cal Poly Waste Can't Be Composted." *MustangNews*, 30 Nov 2016, mustangnews.net. Accessed 27 Feb. 2019.

"Progress Report 2017-2018." *UCSC Campus Sustainability,* University of California, 2019, sustainabilityplan.ucsc.edu. Accessed 27 Feb. 2019.

"Sustainability in The California State University: The First Assessment of the 2014 Sustainability Policy." *CalState*. The California State University, Office of the Chancellor, Feb. 2018, www2.calstate.edu. Accessed 26 Feb. 2019.

"Waste Disposal Rate Inches Up as California Economy Improves."*CA.gov,* State of California, 6 July 2018, www.calrecycle.ca.gov. Accessed 27 Feb. 2019.

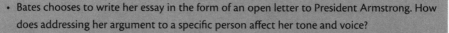
Engaging in Public Rhetoric and Argumentation

CONSIDER THIS:

- Bates chooses to write her essay in the form of an open letter to President Armstrong. How does addressing her argument to a specific person affect her tone and voice?

- With a narrow focus, Bates succeeds in creating an argument specific to Cal Poly. What types of sources does she use to support her topic, and how does move from on-campus issues to those outside of Cal Poly?

- While Bates sets President Armstrong as her main audience, she also consistently addresses her fellow students. How does she account for the diversity of her readers?

Curving Our Enthusiasm:
The Downsides of Grading Curves

Kevin Lee

Reflective Memo: When I began writing this essay, I honestly hoped to find the advantages of grading curves through research. This is because I am in many classes that are graded on the curve. Unfortunately, the more research I did, the less favorable grading curves appeared. I found a lot of very interesting research that was done on grading curves and it was very hard to fit it all into one cohesive essay.

Have you ever felt that you were given an unfair grade that did not accurately reflect your knowledge? Many professors at Cal Poly unfairly assess students by grading on a curve and do not understand the numerous downsides. Grading on a curve is "a method of grading that is based on the belief that letter grades in any given class should be distributed along a bell curve" (Richert). Traditionally, the mean performance is equivalent to around a "C+" letter grade. Since the belief is that the distribution of scores is normally distributed, most students receive a grade in the "B" to "D" range with a small percentage of students achieving "A" or "F" letter grades. Grading on a curve is a common practice in universities in the United States; however, it should not be implemented in courses at Cal Poly because it goes against Cal Poly's explicitly stated academic learning objectives to "demonstrate expertise in a scholarly discipline in relation to the larger world of the arts, sciences, and technology" and to "work productively as individuals and in groups" ("University"). Both of these two objectives are directly impeded by the use of grading curves due to their underlying statistical problems and their psychological impact on students.

The psychological impact of grading on a curve goes against the objective to work in groups and is mainly due to the quotas caused by the fixed percentage cutoffs. Since grading on a curve compares relative performance, there is a fixed number of passing and failing letter grades. Adam Grant, a professor of psychology at the University of Pennsylvania, found that this imposes a mindset on students that creates a "zero-sum world" where people are encouraged to compete against each other and are discouraged from cooperating. This mentality results in a "toxic" atmosphere that teaches the idea that the success of others is tantamount to personal failure (Grant).

That particular mindset is especially harmful to the objective to "work productively as individuals and in groups" since helping others is not rewarded ("University"). Letting peers fall behind increases the probability of getting a passing grade—greatly disincentivizing reaching out to lend a helping hand. The failure of others leads to a sense of security and joy while the success of others

leads to a sense of relative dread and resentment. People respond to incentives; in this case, students are not incentivized to work together. This directly goes against the academic learning objectives of the university.

To better reflect the desired objectives, Cal Poly professors need to implement systems that encourage teamwork and collaboration. For instance, Professor Adam Grant of the University of Pennsylvania finds that the key to accomplishing this is to "make preparing for exams a team effort." Grant describes the optimal environment as "a collaborative culture with a reward system where one person's success benefited someone else." To make this goal a reality, he designs his tests in a manner such that students can pick one question on the exam and write the name of one classmate. If the chosen classmate gets it right, both students get points (Grant). He observes that an effect of the implementation of this alternate policy was that "more students started studying together in small groups, then the groups started pooling their knowledge" (Grant).

The system that Grant uses, as opposed to grading on a curve, is very specific and may have varying results if implemented at Cal Poly; however, the general idea of his study remains. It is possible to create an environment where students are enthusiastic about working in groups and collaborating. People respond to incentives; and in this case, students are in fact incentivized to work together. Grant's system is just one of many possible ways that professors could create a better work environment through incentivizing collaboration. Some professors at Cal Poly have shifted towards a more collaborative environment, but many still maintain the hypercompetitive and toxic environment created by grading on a curve.

This competitive environment is most commonly found in science, technology, engineering, and math (STEM) courses in universities and directly opposes Cal Poly's objective to promote sciences and technology. A recent study on grading curves finds that "there is currently a shortage of

LOOK HERE:

Sal Khan, founder of the Khan Academy, discusses methods for avoiding learning gaps and building subject expertise in this *TEDTalk*.

students graduating with STEM degrees, particularly women and students of color" (Haley). The study proceeds to state that "approximately half of students who begin a STEM major eventually switch out. Many switchers cite the competitiveness, grading **curves**, and weed-out culture of introductory STEM classes as reasons for the switch" (Haley). While this study is based on data from the universities across the nation as a whole, the general relationship between grading curves and STEM classes is still maintained. This shortage of graduating STEM students directly relates to Cal Poly's academic goal to "demonstrate expertise in a scholarly discipline in relation to the larger world of the arts, sciences, and technology" ("University"). The ability to "demonstrate expertise" in science and technology is impeded by the competitive culture caused by grading on a curve ("University"). Since competitiveness and grading curves are main factors for people switching out of STEM majors, it can be reasonably assumed that eliminating grading curves and creating a collaborative environment would increase the proportion of students who continue to pursue science and technology related studies at Cal Poly.

However, some professors overlook the psychological downsides and continue to insist that grading curves are necessary—especially in STEM courses. The main arguments in favor of grading on a curve are that it is seen as fair and also as a solution to grade inflation. Eugene Volokh, a law professor at UCLA, finds that "the absence of a curve is unfair to a class that has an unusually harsh professor." Volokh also goes on to reason that newer professors do not have the experience to know "the distinction between A–s and B+s." Therefore, the only fair way to assign grades is to compare students relative to their peers (Volokh).

The other main reason they ignore the downsides of grading on a curve is to combat grade inflation, which is the trend of rising average grades. This is common in STEM courses as many students are highly motivated and have been weeded out by the college selection process—creating a homogenized group of individuals who tend toward above average performance (Kulick and Wright). The belief is that too many "A" letter grades are being rewarded, shifting the mean grade much above a standard mean grade. To correct for this, it is believed that curves need to be implemented.

However, especially in these situations, a curve should not be implemented. This is due to the way the statistical model of the normal curve does not accurately reflect all situations and luck plays a much greater role than skill. A simulation analysis performed by Kulick and Wright found that "the correlation between ability (as defined in the model) and final test averages is dependent on both the mean and the standard deviation of the level of preparedness [probability of a student getting a question correct]" (13). Put simply, grading on a curve does not work when the distribution of student preparedness is small because random luck becomes too influential in the determination of scores.

An extreme case of this is best illustrated with a group of four hundred monkeys taking a true–false organic chemistry exam. The spread of scores is normally distributed, and some monkeys get "A's"; however, luck plays a much greater role than simply how prepared a monkey was to take the test. This is why "instructors cannot make the claim that just because they have test scores that are normally distributed they must have designed an exam that fairly distinguishes among student abilities" (Kulich and Wright 13).

Engaging in Public Rhetoric and Argumentation

Monkeys may have a low variation of preparedness, but college students have a much higher variation. In many cases, students will be varied enough that their skill will outweigh luck. However, the case where students have the least variation is in the exact same case where curves are most used: STEM courses experiencing grade inflation. Courses where grade inflation occurs are not normally distributed and are skewed to the left due to above average performance. In order to correct this and make the distribution normal, "instructors must make the exams more difficult, more specialized, or even more obscure to ensure that fewer students get high scores" (Kulick and Wright 8). This decreases the mean score but does not affect the standard deviation of student preparedness. Since the students are so tightly packed together, in regard to preparedness, luck plays a bigger role in their grade than how prepared they are for the exam; this is very close to the situation with the monkeys. For that case, there is no correlation between how prepared a student is and what grade they receive (Kulick and Wright 8).

The exact situation where grading on a curve is most commonly implemented is the exact situation where it fails to accurately reflect student ability. A system where luck plays a greater role than preparedness can never be seen as fair and should not be implemented at Cal Poly. The academic objective of demonstrating "expertise in a scholarly discipline" cannot be achieved when grades are disproportionately based on luck rather than actual mastery of concepts ("University"). Even though grading on a curve still works in the case where students are greatly varied in preparedness and no additional artificial difficulty is implemented, the psychological effects of grading on a curve outweigh any potential fairness gained by using a curve-based grading scheme. Students cannot be enthusiastic about learning when trapped in a hypercompetitive environment where luck outweighs skill. It is extremely clear that Cal Poly professors should not grade on a curve in order to ensure that student preparedness comes before luck and to maintain the academic learning objectives explicitly stated by the university.

Kevin Lee is a Mechanical Engineering major.

Works Cited

Grant, Adam. "Why We Should Stop Grading Students on a Curve." *The New York Times*, 10 Sept. 2016, nytimes.com. Accessed 28 June 2019.

Haley, James M. "To Curve or Not to Curve? The Effect of College Science Grading Policies on Implicit Theories of Intelligence, Perceived Classroom Goal Structures, and Self-efficacy."*Dissertation Abstracts International*, vol. 76, no. 8. 2016. *University Microfilms International*.

Kulick, George and Ronald Wright. "The Impact of Grading on a Curve: A Simulation Analysis," *International Journal for the Scholarship of Teaching and Learning*, vol. 2, no. 2, 2008. pp. 1–17. doi.org/10.20429/ijsotl.2008.020205.

Richert, Kit. "Why Grading on the Curve Hurts." *Teachingcom*, teaching.monster.com, accessed 28 June 2019.

"University Learning Objectives." *Academic Programs & Planning, Cal Poly*. Academicprograms.calpoly.edu. Accessed 28 June 2019.

Volokh, Eugene. "In Praise of Grading on a Curve." *The Washington Post*, 9 Feb. 2015, www.washingtonpost.com. Accessed 28 June 2019.

CONSIDER THIS:

- Lee cites two articles from what are considered to be lower-tiered sources. Since the authors of each article demonstrate credibility in the subject matter, how would you categorize these sources?

- Along with his use of varied sources, Lee also uses different types of source introductions. What do you think of the balance Lee strikes with both quote and title/author integrations?

- Lee crafts several transitional statements between both paragraphs and sentences, which helps to keep his audience engaged. How does his choice impact the overall effectiveness of his argument?

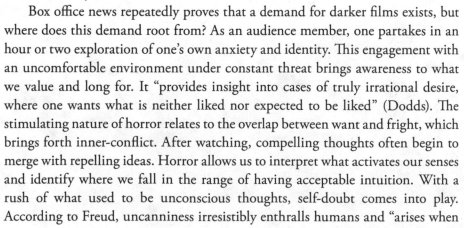

Eyes for the Dark

Stephanie Mullen

Reflective Memo: Shame on me. Shame on me for not liking Friends, Parks and Rec, The Office, *and sitcoms in general. Shame on me for always choosing* Westworld *or* Sharp Objects *over a comedy. Despite the opposition, I am more than proud to share my appreciation for the dark arts. I've learned the most about myself through witnessing the evil shades of human nature. The strangest and most rewarding effect is self-validation. Discomfort and pleasure become less foreign. My heart skips a step, not because of all the low-budget jump scares, but because I genuinely can't believe how people treat each other. And I love it. I cannot explain how refreshing and exhilarating it is to feel vulnerable. After years of exploring fright walks, horror movies, and plays, I wanted to just double-check that I wasn't a psychopath. Research and discussion allowed me to understand more about the genre of horror and its range of responses.*

SEVENTY MINUTES. The mob of eleventh-graders unanimously agree to the seventy-minute wait time after racing to Fright Walk, a limited October attraction at Santa Cruz Beach Boardwalk. They pay, hoping for shrieks and goosebumps. A blend of desire and dread fuels their craving for safe danger. Such absurd juxtapositions drive a huge portion of the entertainment industry as people seek horror whether it's in the shape of film, video games, virtual reality, or live shows. Logically, many would assume that terrorizing only generates fear. Yet, considering the complexity of the brain and cinema, humans display a spectrum of negative and positive responses. Themes within fictional horror intrigue audiences, blurring boundaries around norms, morality, and reality. Hence, the horror genre deserves respect rather than disapproval. Excluding children, horror in entertainment possesses the power to benefit its audience through both the mind and body.

Box office news repeatedly proves that a demand for darker films exists, but where does this demand root from? As an audience member, one partakes in an hour or two exploration of one's own anxiety and identity. This engagement with an uncomfortable environment under constant threat brings awareness to what we value and long for. It "provides insight into cases of truly irrational desire, where one wants what is neither liked nor expected to be liked" (Dodds). The stimulating nature of horror relates to the overlap between want and fright, which brings forth inner-conflict. After watching, compelling thoughts often begin to merge with repelling ideas. Horror allows us to interpret what activates our senses and identify where we fall in the range of having acceptable intuition. With a rush of what used to be unconscious thoughts, self-doubt comes into play. According to Freud, uncanniness irresistibly enthralls humans and "arises when something seems paradoxically both frighteningly alien and strangely familiar, when something or someone reminds us of a repressed, projected or split off aspect of ourselves" (Dodds). Instinctively, one may be intimidated by the complexity of pleasure. Psychoanalysis consistently shows that it's our desires that we fear the most. Yet, many people enjoy the challenge of trying to explain their own amusement. Directors play with this challenge. They have an intricate way of designing cinema that unmasks the vulnerable versions of people, allowing us to accept insecurities.

Considering the physiological effects, experiencing safe terror has the potential to positively affect health. Movies can drive emotion, but well-made horror movies can also prompt physical responses. In a study at the University of Westminster, researchers observed various horror film viewers. The

LOOK HERE:

Film Theory argues for the connected worlds of *IT* and *The Shining*.

participants voluntarily agreed to watch *The Shining*, which "topped the list of the calorie-scorching horror films [...one subject] rid 184 calories: roughly the number of calories a 140-pound adult would burn after 40 minutes of walking" (Heid). Suspending disbelief and engaging in the film allowed the audience to participate in a form of exercise. These participants jumped and shrieked because they felt short-term stress. Short-term stress, also known as eustress, involves a brief production and rush of adrenaline that focuses energy toward an excited state in the body. Eustress also applies to other forms of amusement like haunted houses and video games. "It might be simpler to think of horror movies as a form of 'good stress.' While stress gets a bad rap—and long-term stress is associated with everything from depression to heart attacks—brief bouts of stress have often been linked to improved immune function and activation, says Firdaus Dhabhar, a professor of psychiatry" (qtd. in Heid). Stress also relates to the fight or flight response, which is a temporary increase in short term immune function. Then again, not every viewer naturally feels waves of eustress. A classification of people called high sensation seekers willingly take risks in order to feel sensations through activities: "SS [sensation seeking] has been found to be positively related to the enjoyment of frightening films and scary video games" (Lin). On a biological level, high sensation seekers function better at high levels of cortical arousal, which resides in the sub-cortical limbic system" (Zillmann and Vorderer). Stress allows the body to be more awake and active, refreshing the body. The sense of ease following stress also provides pleasure. The more that people engage with horror, the more knowledgeable they become about their methods of relieving stress.

Dark entertainment also sheds light on oppressed thoughts. People who seek a diversion from normal find an appeal from witnessing such a contrast to everyday routine. Horror films often incorporate the concept of disrupting the status quo. Survival goes to characters who efficiently adapt to new environments and unusual events. Thus, "horror attracts because anomalies command attention and elicit curiosity" (Zillmann and Vorderer). Violations of norms fascinate those who rarely witness it in their everyday lives. Therefore, those people can connect with characters who have rule-breaking tendencies. Many find the concept of madness and destruction to be aesthetically pleasing and novel. Mayhem on screen can serve as a "symbolic catharsis. According to this view, exposure to media violence had potentially therapeutic properties for individuals who were angry and who, because of this emotional state, were inclined to behave aggressively.... They leave the entertainment experience with their pent-up aggressive tendencies purged or cleansed" (Zillmann and Vorderer). By witnessing rather than being involved with danger, people can still interpret and feel stimulated by such threats while being assured about their own safety. In the theater, viewers sit through an intensified state of arousal that amplifies emotion, challenging their mental strength. Therefore, any senses of relief, achievement, or positivity intensifies as well.

The emerging technology of virtual reality introduces a vivid, immersive effect that surpasses film's capabilities. Recent studies revolve around a new survival zombie horror game where a meta-analysis "showed that VR treatments elicited frights similar to real events and was effective in lessening anxiety and phobia when compared to those who were in the controlled conditions (i.e., delayed treatments). Presence and immersion were found to be important theoretical constructs to elicit mediated frights" (Lin). A coping mechanism called self-talking helps reassure the player that they aren't alone or fighting in silence. Players mentioned that they found relief after screaming and swearing to express their discomfort. These explicit reactions also act as a form of protection. Thus, games can serve as practice for the brain to cope with physical and emotional responses to fear. And, "those who are high in SS [sensation-seeking] and neuroticism employ this strategy more often" (Lin). Many also resort to the avoidance method, which acts as a voice in the head, repeating that the experience does not associate with reality. Safe terror acts like a teacher, informing us about the less-explored layers of our minds.

What's more realistic than films, video games, and virtual reality? Live theatre in-the-round.

This fall, Cuesta Community College collaborated with Cal Poly's Professor Philip Valle to create a forty-minute experimental show called *Ghost Ship*. Its advertising specifically permitted ages eighteen and up to purchase tickets since the level of terror didn't suit younger audiences. Valle crafted *Ghost Ship* to progressively raise the stakes. Once the exposition passes, "then the stakes ratchet up. The sound gets louder, the lights get weirder. There's more fog. The story gets more perverse and violent so that by the peak of it, there's nowhere else to go. You're just hurled out of that world because there's nowhere else to go—except something that might get you as a member of the audience" (Valle). Months of research contributed toward an immersive theatre experience. Valle played with defying traditional performance methods by seating the audience on benches inside a Blackbox theatre. Unlike horror films, the actors and audience shared senses, including sound, smell, and even touch. While a ticket guaranteed safety throughout the show, everyone in the room shared the intensity of such high stakes. Valle explains that "the thing that's most terrifying is to be touched because it breaks the fourth wall. That's the final barrier" (Valle). Film can be less powerful in the sense that it can't touch us. It can't bring such a rush, psychologically. Valle's decision to have sailors grab viewers' ankles made his show significantly more memorable. Some audience members laughed after the show ended since they felt so in shock and awe. His production proved to be a success, considering that audience members genuinely felt the same rush of terror as the actors.

While horror can please and relieve, not all people have the mental capacity to benefit from immersing themselves in fear. Children, especially, have a high risk of long-term distress and interruption in behavior if they expose themselves too early. "Mediated fright induced not only an immediate fright reaction but also lingering effects, which could be life-long memories.... Media content affects children's sleep or thoughts" (Lin). Since kids lack a full understanding of how to differentiate reality from fantasy, they may perceive horror movies as real. This belief sticks with their memory after they turn off the TV. Adults, too, who continue to deal with trauma, no matter how extreme, are a vulnerable group. They'd be classified as low sensation seekers and watching horror can worsen their ability to cope with stress. Memories of events that endangered us remain clear and accurate in the future. That prompts us to be ready to act quickly again whenever we come across similar events (Cantor). A term called fear conditioning relates to dangerous aspects of film. "If we experienced intense fear while watching *Jaws,* our implicit fear reactions (e.g., the heart rate increases, blood pressure changes, and muscle tension) became conditioned to the image of the shark, to the notion of swimming" (Cantor). Even after time passes, these stimuli can trigger the same uneasy reactions. Then again, the genre of thrillers and horror stretches across such diverse topics. People have wide access to finding media that doesn't relate to their serious phobia or past trauma. Although overcoming fear takes patience and support, the variety within entertainment has the potential to appeal even to those who still struggle to face their fears.

Watching others suffer relates to the idea of power. Pleasure comes with power. But when one sits in safety as the surrounding environment sits in danger, empathy may also emerge. Strangely enough, one can feel pleasure, power, safety, and empathy while being saturated with uneasy thoughts. Dark fiction allows us to validate and balance all these emotions. This rush of sensations comes when one chooses to suspend disbelief. This rush of sensations is rare. It's exhilarating. And it doesn't deserve to be taken for granted.

Stephanie Mullen is a Food Science major.

Works Cited

Cantor, Joanne. "'I'll Never Have a Clown in My House'—Why Movie Horror Lives On." *Poetics Today*, vol. 25 no. 2, 2004, pp. 283–304. *Project MUSE*.

Dodds, Joseph. "The Monstrous Brain: A Neuropsychoanalytic Aesthetics of Horror?" *PSYART: A Hyperlink Journal for the Psychological Study of the Arts*. 14 Feb. 2011. Psyartjournal.com. Accessed 28 June 2019.

Heid, Markham. "You Asked: Is Watching Scary Movies Good for You?" *Time*, 25 Oct. 2017, time.com. Accessed 28 June 2019.

Lin, Jih-Hsuan Tammy. "Fear in Virtual Reality (VR)." *Computers in Human Behavior*, vol. 72, 2017, pp. 350–361.

Valle, Phillip. Personal interview. 5 Dec. 2018.

Zillmann, Dolf and Peter Vorderer, eds. *Media Entertainment: The Psychology of Its Appeal*. Mahwah NJ, Routledge, 2000. *EBSCOhost*.

CONSIDER THIS:

- In her introduction, Mullen draws her reader into the action of the essay by using brief narrative. How does this help to frame her overall argument?

- Mullen continually thinks about her readers' objections to a somewhat controversial topic. How does she limit the scope of her audience and argument to certain age groups and still keep her reader engaged throughout the essay?

- When looking at the arch of her argument, how well does Mullen structure her essay? How well does she convince her audience that horror is healthy while answering her readers' concerns?

Menstruation Nation: Let's Free the Tampons

Holly Masterson

Introduction:

The oval office, the bog, the privy, the loo, the john; there are so many different ways to say "the bathroom" in our language—probably because we spend such a large portion of our lives in it. The women's restroom in particular is a pivotal location where a plethora of magical events take place. Makeup application, transformations from gym clothes to little black dresses, or long, deep conversations between friends. There is, however, an underbelly to the establishment: a darker "black market" as some may call it. The black market of tampon dealing. Women sneak the product into the bathroom under their jackets or in their purses. If a fellow sister is in an emergency and needs the product, she must either hope she has a quarter to put into the rusty vending machines and say a little prayer that the product is not as old as it looks, or she must call upon a nearby pusher to obtain some. But if it comes down to the worst, she must resort to sitting on the bathroom floor in shame—rolling her own with the toilet paper from one of the stalls. Yes, indeed the women's bathroom is both a magical and a dark place, but it does not have to be this way.

America is a country where the word "capitalism" is floated above us in star-studded lights, but why must we have it apply to every aspect of our lives? Companies monopolize the most private items we need, like medication and even sanitary products. Menstruating women, who consist of nearly half of the population, are sometimes unable to afford these products, or cannot easily access them when they are really needed; this is why feminine hygiene products should be free. First, I will examine and explain the need for liberation of feminine sanitary products; then, I will present arguments against my claim with rebuttals; and finally, I will discuss solutions in order to reach this goal.

The Need:

A study conducted by the Center of American Progress, specifically focused on American women's perspective of financial insecurities, found that "[forty-two] million women, and the 28 million children who depend on them, are living one single incident—a doctor's bill, a late paycheck, or a broken-down car—away from economic ruin" (Shriver). Taking into consideration that on average, women between the ages of twelve and fifty-one experience menstruation, a significant number of women who are in that poverty range are menstruating and thus have a need for sanitary products, which they cannot afford. Should women that close to economic ruin be expected to also pay for the necessary medical products they

require as human beings? Girls Helping Girls Period states that although there are many free food benefits offered to people in the United States through the Supplemental Nutrition Assistance Program (SNAP), feminine hygiene products, toilet paper, and other necessary items are not part of those benefits ("The Facts"). A story by Linda Carroll on Reuters Health news includes a survey on women who cannot afford tampons or pads. They resorted to using rags, toilet paper, or diapers in order to avoid bleeding in public (Carroll). Within the topic of those in poverty, women in correctional facilities similarly struggle in receiving sanitary products due to the fact that these institutions are primarily designed for men. In an article from Harper's Bazaar on the subject of menstruation and hygiene, an inmate is quoted describing her experience in a correctional facility: "Pads are not dispensed as they are supposed to be. We are forced to reuse them, we are forced to beg for what we need, and if an officer is in a bad mood, they are allowed to take what we have and say we are hoarding" (Kosin).

Besides the urgent need for access to sanitary products for those in poverty and correctional facilities, there is also a need quietly persisting in plain sight at the office and in school. Speaking about menstruation in public places like school and work is considered risqué for a majority of the population, but this has resulted in our reluctance to realize the importance of addressing such concerns. Women in the workplace are at a serious disadvantage to men. As someone with endometriosis (pelvic pain resulting from endometrial tissue outside of the uterus), I know the extreme pain that can result from having a monthly period. This pain can prevent someone from working to their best ability or even merely attending work, and it is endured on average for five days, twelve times a year (Stöppler).

An organization called "Free the Tampons" started by Nancy Kramer, shares the stories of women experiencing humiliating circumstances of starting their period in public without having access to sanitary products. They have multiple stories listed on their website including this one by an anonymous woman:

> I was at work at my local YWCA when I felt my period come. I hadn't packed a pad that day because it was about a week before it was meant to start, so I freaked out. At that point I realized that I was in a women's center and there must be a box of pads or tampons somewhere, but I found nothing. It's truly upsetting that my place of work—a women's center—would not have pads or tampons available to us ("Stories").

Along with the workplace, similar horror stories can be heard in schools. The worst part about these situations is that many of the younger girls experiencing them are taught not to mention such things, or that the subject of periods is not allowed to be discussed. They are left humiliated and confused when stories like the one included above happen to them. The stigmatization of menstruation in public places needs to stop before we can move forward from here.

The last order of concern around feminine hygiene is applicable to all and any women menstruating. The price of a period on a whole is significantly more expensive than just paying for pads. Women need to pay for heating pads, birth control, pain medication, and new underwear, along with the typical products like pads and tampons. Considering we need so many supplies to take care of ourselves during this time of the month, the extra cost of tampons and pads are highly unnecessary. An article from Huffington Post by Jessica Kane attempts to average out the price of a period. Women can spend thousands of dollars on Midol alone in their lifetime, along with the coveted tampons landing at almost two thousand dollars (Kane). This is a significant amount of money to pay for a health concern that happens to half of the entire population—not to mention the parents paying for their daughters supplies. I live in a house of three girls and a single mom. You can only imagine how much we spend yearly on our feminine hygiene needs.

Counter-Arguments:

When individuals are presented with the idea of free feminine hygiene products, the first responses are often negative: *Aren't pads like toilet paper? Why should they be free and toilet paper not?* Or, *Men have to pay for razors! Shouldn't they be free too if women get their stuff free?* My rebuttal to the first two questions is that in most cases, specifically in public, toilet paper is available to the public for free. If you go into a restroom, you can be sure that nine times out of ten there will be one stall with paper on the roll. The same thing cannot be said about tampons or pads. If a woman is in public when the "red knight" attacks her, she had better have something on hand because it is not very likely that there will be product available to her. As for the second argument, comparing something like a razor to feminine hygiene products is ineffective because growing out a beard is nothing like sitting in your own bodily fluids. It would also be futile to sum up the cost of a monthly period in merely the cost of pads or tampons considering the list mentioned earlier of what we must purchase along with them.

The next argument against free tampons is that women in the olden times did not use tampons, and so we "modern women" should not see them as a necessity but rather a luxury. Here are some statistics that can help refute this claim: The US National Library of Medicine Archives holds a study relating lack of proper feminine hygiene to infections and diseases. They state in the conclusion: "the results of our study demonstrate a strong association between poor MHM [Menstrual Hygiene Management] practices and two lower RTIs [Reproductive Tract Infections]: BV [Bacterial Vaginosis] and *Candida albicans* infection" (Das 12). Another study in a *Time* article by Jennifer Weiss-Wolf confirms that lack of proper menstrual hygiene in developing countries has been linked to high rates of cervical cancer due to infections caused by use of filthy, unwashed rags. Similar

results are seen in the homeless here in America (Weiss-Wolfe). This is why it is crucial that women have access to the appropriate and advanced medical supplies to protect their reproductive health—just as most people use advanced medicine when they are ill.

Solutions:

Now that we have reached a clear explanation of the needs and reasoning behind why feminine hygiene products should be free, we must take a look at what our solutions might be in eventually making it to that endpoint.

The first step to making a better future for our daughters and granddaughters is to remove the controversial "tampon tax" that persists in our legislature. An NPR article by Ema Sagner explains that the states that exclude health and medical supplies from taxation do not consider tampons to be part of such supplies but instead a luxury product (Sagner). As explained in my counter-argument earlier, tampons and pads should not be considered luxury items, but a necessity. Medicine has developed beyond the unhygienic habits of reusing rags like in developing countries and olden times; no woman should be expected to expose themselves to disease when we are perfectly capable of preventing it.

How, then, do we go about this rather daunting task of convincing the government (which is still overwhelmingly male concentrated) to remove a tax? We can start with Cristina Garcia. Garcia is an American assembly woman with a mission to end the "pink tax." She has put forth Assembly Bill Nine, which "exempts from the sales and use of tax sales on purchases of tampons, sanitary napkins, menstrual cups, and menstrual sponges" (Garcia). Following ambitious, influential women like Garcia, and voting in the next election to put more women in office, is the fundamental action we can take to push forward our needs as women.

Besides the cost of sanitary products, we must also think about the waste. According to the Harper's BAZAAR article mentioned earlier, around twelve billion pads and seven billion tampons end up in landfills yearly (Kosin). There are many wonderful, *reusable* products offered today like menstrual cups and menstrual underwear. These products are safe, healthy, and reduce the wastefulness of disposable pads and tampons. Increasing use of these products would not only help the environment, but also reduce the amount of money we spend on disposable products. With the extra money left over, one could simply donate a little bit to companies like Africa Bag, which puts your donations to giving girls reusable pads in developing countries. The company is completely self-sustainable—using resources only from Africa, teaching African workers to make them, and selling them locally. You can find them at www.africabags.org.

Figure 1. A menstrual cup

The third solution for freeing tampons is a top-secret mission. Turn yourself into a Hemorrhaging Hero and speak with administration every time you see a public restroom without free sanitary products. If you are a little shy to do so yourself, no problem! Nancy Kramer from "Free the Tampons" is happy to help you by speaking to them for you or giving you the courage to do it yourself. In Kramer's TEDTalk, she happily announces the impact of putting free sanitary products in her own office restrooms: "For one year for every one of our female associates, we spend four dollars and fifty-seven cents. I think that's an investment that's worthwhile" (Kramer 5:21).

The final and most important action needed to work towards a less stressful future for women, is to change the stigma around puberty and menstruation. Most of us grew up with sex education involving separation of boys and girls followed by quiet, polite lessons on how our bodies either bleed out of their vaginas or harden their penises. The cringe-inducing imagery used in the previous sentence was purposeful: why should our lessons be quiet and polite on a topic that is so clearly *neither* quiet *nor* polite. Our bodies are *screaming* at us during puberty, so we should address this subject with a little more attention rather than trying to shove it under the table. If we teach it in an obvious, non-embarrassed manner, future generations will treat it in an obvious, non-embarrassed manner. This applies to both men and women. Treating our bodies with the respect they need and deserve is important, and we cannot achieve that if we hide our problems.

Therefore, I propose that from here on out, we treat the subject of puberty and menstruation with the gravity it demands. We cannot stigmatize women for having vaginas, or men for having penises. The best way to enact this is to treat

the topics of periods and puberty with less derogation when discussing them with kids. We need to talk about our bodies in a freeing way with family and close friends.

LOOK HERE:

See student reactions to Cal Poly's initiative to offer free feminine hygiene products on campus.

Conclusion:

In a modern society where medicine is on the top of a shelf at CVS, or written on a prescription card from our Doctors, it's hard to imagine there are still those who struggle to obtain the most basic resources. Whether you are homeless in the city, starting your first job, serving in prison, studying at junior high, or living with a disability, you have a basic human right to your reproductive health. Feminine hygiene products should be free because there are women who cannot afford them and women who do not have easy access to them. After examining and reasoning the arguments for free sanitary products, perhaps the best solution is really all about perception. Eventually, we will reach a better future, which will have a thorough sex education for children all over the world *sans* censorship. Ideally it will be inclusive for people of every background, gender, and sexual orientation. One day we can do it. It's definitely possible, but we need to change our actions now to improve the lives of future generations.

Holly Masterson is an Animal Sciences major.

Works Cited

Carroll, Linda. "Even in the U.S., Poor Women Often Can't Afford Tampons, Pads." *Reuters*, 10 Jan. 2019, www.reuters.com. Accessed 28 June 2019.

Das, Padma, et al. "Menstrual Hygiene Practices, WASH Access and the Risk of Urogenital Infection in Women from Odisha, India" *PloS One,* vol. 10 no. 6, 30 June 2015, pp. 1–16, doi:10.1371/journal.pone.0130777.

"The Facts. Period." *Girls Helping Girls. Period.*, 2015, www.girlshelpinggirlsperiod. org. Accessed 28 June 2019.

Garcia, Cristina. "Assembly Bill 9: Exempts specified feminine hygiene products from the sales and use tax." *California State Board of Equalization,* boe. ca.gov. Accessed June 2019.

Kane, Jessica. "Here's How Much A Woman's Period Will Cost Her Over A Lifetime." *Huffington Post*, 18 May 2015, www.huffpost.com. Accessed 28 June 2019.

Kosin, Julie. "Getting Your Period Is Still Oppressive in the United States." *Harper's BAZAAR*, 9 Oct. 2017, www.harpersbazaar.com. Accessed 28 June 2019.

Kramer, Nancy. "Free the Tampons." *TEDx Columbus,* YouTube, 16 Oct. 2013, www.youtube.com/watch?v=tE_1KjHvuAk. Accessed 28 June 2019.

Sagner, Ema. "More States Move to End 'Tampon Tax' That's Seen as Discriminating Against Women." *NPR*, 25 Mar. 2018, www.npr.org. Accessed 28 June 2019.

Shriver, Maria. "The Shriver Report Executive Summary." *Center for American Progress*, 12 Jan. 2014, www.americanprogress.org. Accessed 28 June 2019.

Stöppler, Melissa Conrad, MD. "Definition of Endometriosis." *MedicineNet*, 12 Apr. 2018, www.medicinenet.com. Accessed 28 June 2019.

"Stories." *Free The Tampons*, FTT Foundation, www.freethetampons.org. Accessed 28 June 2019.

Weiss-Wolf, Jennifer. "America's Very Real Menstrual Crisis." *Time,* 11 Aug. 2015, time.com. Accessed 28 June 2019.

CONSIDER THIS:

- Masterson immediately gains her reader's confidence by using humor in her introduction. How does this choice set up the rest of her argument and frame the overall tone of her essay?

- With the use of headings, Masterson combines the scientific format with the rhetorical situation. How might her argument change with the use of transitional topic sentences instead?

Reasoning, Argumentation, and Writing

What rhetorical choices can you make to persuade your audience?
What kinds of arguments do you find persuasive?
Which issues do you care most about?

The following essays demonstrate a level of persuasion and argumentation more advanced than the work completed in GE A1 classes. These authors are developing a command of deductive and inductive reasoning and have a sharpened awareness of their audience's expectations. Moreover, these authors are working with a wide range of sources to attain a fuller grasp of the topics they explore.

The Stacks
by Alexander Watkins

Reasoning, Argumentation, and Writing

CONSIDER THIS:

- Watkins's photo shows the dunes of Morro Bay, with the smokestacks of the former Morro Bay Power Plant, which closed in 2014. The fate of "The Stacks," as they are known, is the subject of ongoing public debate. Some want to remove the now-abandoned structure, seeing it as a distraction from Morro Bay's natural beauty. Many locals see The Stacks as a reminder of bygone days, which gives them a nostalgia and fondness for the landmark. Others wonder who should be in charge of the situation, the city government or the property's corporate owners. Based on this image, where do you think Watkins stands in this debate? How might this image influence your own stance? Research the situation further online and consider how effective argumentation is needed for negotiating so many different positions.

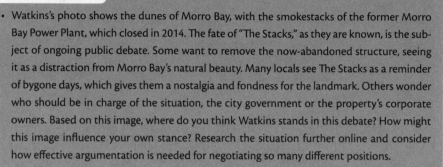

Not in the Loop

Bo Cole

Reflective Memo: In English 145, I wanted to try to write a series of three essays focused around the "Three R's" of waste conservation: Reduce, Reuse, and Recycle. While I am completely on-board for efforts to reduce waste, the current strategies to mitigate our overwhelming waste problem are disappointing considering the strides we've made in other industries. For many of us, The Three R's idea was forced from an early age, and while an effective mnemonic, are only somewhat effective in actually conserving our resources. With this essay, I tried to highlight Reusing specifically, both as a concept and in practice. As it happened, the Loop system had recently been unveiled when I was searching for a topic, and this paper attempts to evaluate the conservation system on a handful of criteria, based on the somewhat sparse information available about it at the time. I enjoyed the research that went into the paper as well as learning more about Loop's vision. Ultimately, I took a stance against the company based on one key flaw of the model in practice, but I believe that the concept is solid and that Loop may become synonymous with "Reusing" in the foreseeable future.

Consensus-building on national and global issues seems to get harder all the time. Just click on cable news. Caffeinated adults, their faces shaded with bronzer and framed by silk ties or pearl earrings, spar over topical issues in 6-minute segments that never end in agreement. Regardless of your politics, one issue for which the path to consensus seems more direct is that making an effort to reduce environmental waste and pollution will have long term benefits for the planet, for living things, and for future generations. The 3 R's of environmental sustainability (Reduce, Reuse, & Recycle) are the toolset we all have, and need to use, in order to achieve the common human goal of taking care of this big blue rock where we all live. We can *reduce* our waste by simply buying less, and thus, having less to throw away. In the US, we can *recycle* materials like glass, paper, and certain plastics right on the curb in front of our house. However, the *reuse* of consumables such as single-use packaging is where our inner eco-warrior gets challenged and needs some help from the marketplace. The beauty of free enterprise is that it rarely misses an opportunity to chase a dollar and a dream, and New Jersey-based TerraCycle is the first player from the US to jump into the reuse game. Later this year, they'll introduce *Loop*, a new zero-waste platform which offers major consumer products in reusable packaging delivered right to your door. Risk-taking and green-hearted—a perfect crossroads of things I respect. However, some initial aspects within Loop's model carry with them a substantial environmental cost that seem to outweigh Loop's pioneering and eco-friendly intentions.

The challenge of Loop's reuse mission is daunting, because…let's be real, alternatives like recycling are easier for the consumer. Most kids in a pre-K class are recycling. Not hard, and—specifically in the United States—not that effective. The Environmental Protection Agency found that of the 78 million tons of containers and packaging collected in the US in 2015, only 41 million tons were recycled (12). Since recycling alone isn't doing the job, reusing packaging—especially for consumable products—is a logical next step forward for keeping excess waste out of landfills. TerraCycle's Loop is taking that next step, and to put the idea in perspective for the consumer, TerraCycle CEO Tom Szaky's elevator pitch for Loop has been, "We're going back to the milkman model of the 1950's" (Roth). When framed like that, the concept sounds nostalgically achievable, and a perfect way for small, local farms or urban-based micro growers to capitalize on an increasing segment of consumers focused on sustainability.

Except, it's more than milk—*way* more than milk. Szaky's vision of the 20th century milkman is grander than the dairy aisle and aims well beyond providing a great deal on locally-sourced figs. Loop will be a full-on e-commerce operation with a sleek website from which you will be able to order

LOOK HERE:

Check out the Loop program here.

products from many well-known brands such as Proctor & Gamble, PepsiCo, and Nestlé—basically, an all-star lineup of consumer goods conglomerates (Makower). Loop's "milkman" (or woman) drives a UPS truck and sports the UPS browns, while delivering your Häagen Dazs and Fresh Scent Tide straight to your front door. This is *not* the Bezos-ian nightmare of hyper-packaging that laughs in the face of resource reduction by sending us shoebox-sized cartons, filled with inflated plastics bags to protect the one pair of socks we ordered. No, this is different. Loop's products are packaged in durable containers made of stainless steel and engineered glass designed to be reused over 100 times, and safely organized in a padded, insulated, and—of course—reusable tote (Danigelis). Once you've polished off that last pint of Mint Chip and your tote is filled with the remnants of an embarrassing "who's who" binge of the entire Frito-Lay crunchy snack line, a judgement-free UPS driver will come and grab that tote and take it to a Loop facility for cleaning and sterilization. From there, the packages are refilled and turned around for the next Loop user (East). With curbside recycling, there is a risk of our Cheez-It boxes ending up in a landfill or our Gatorade bottles washing up on the sands of Kauai's north shore. With Loop's model, though, the beauty is that there are no more Cheez-It boxes or Gatorade bottles to wind up in the garbage or on beaches—an extremely powerful vision for an idyllic future.

The system is designed in a way that demands minimal consumer action but leaves them feeling like a single-handed savior of the planet. I *love* this idea, because basically, we're all lazy. Loop taps into that lazy in a very 21st century way, providing a service you didn't know existed but now must have. The company says Loop products will cost more or less the same as the off-the-shelf version with traditional, disposable packaging. Customers pay a deposit for the container but get it back upon returning the container to Loop (Makower). This model is not too dissimilar from the plastic and aluminum cash refund that exists in California, but Loop is relying on the convenience aspect to make sure the consumer does their part. It's a smarter approach to zero-waste, which has traditionally run into roadblocks by creating more work for the consumer, and thus making the traditional deposit approach more difficult for people to embrace (Taylor). Loop is grocery shopping and hugging the earth all rolled into one and is far easier than either of those two things alone. In terms of satisfying the customer, Loop gets five stars: it perfectly hits our sweet spots of sustainability and convenience, all while not charging absurd prices.

In many ways, we already reuse more than we may think, and Loop wants to make that effort a bit more conscious. Take, for instance, the midnight jonesing for Frosted Flakes we all get. We grab that big, beautiful box and pour those tasty jewels of empty sugar calories into our cereal bowls. After we refill and finish a second round of Flakes, we wash the bowl and use it again when the sugar demons call on us the next time. But once the cereal box is empty? Throw it away, of course! Or a better idea, recycle it! In Loop's model, there's no box at all. Loop just wants to apply the same logic for reusing the cereal bowl to the cereal *container*. Let's face it, there are so many things that could be reused that aren't. We pour dish soap out of the bottle it's packaged in and into ceramic hand pumps that color scheme well with our kitchen décor because that's what the lovely host on HGTV does. Those ugly plastic jugs simply transport the soap from the store to our house and then we "do our part" by recycling them. And that's exactly where Loop comes in: selling the products in aesthetically-pleasing reusable containers to begin with, therefore eliminating the need for unnecessary packaging.

Loop also wants to get out of your kitchen and become more personal. For example, consumer goods giant Unilever, whose family of products relies heavily on single-use packaging, has turned to Loop as a way to promote sustainability through reusable packaging in product lines like—among other things—Axe and Dove deodorant (Makower). This is my personal tipping point: I'm all for reusing things, but everyone has to draw a line somewhere. As much as I want to save the earth, and as cleaned and sterilized as Loop's reused packaging may be, the fact of the matter is that I really don't want to use someone else's deodorant applicator. Maybe that's just me, but I doubt it. Hats off to Unilever and Loop for the gumption and the effort but staying out of my shave kit and focusing on the bigger, easier targets is probably a better place to launch their business from.

Reusing is good for the environment; it prolongs the life of manufactured goods, keeping them from becoming part of the waste stream. Loop's entire ethos is built around reuse. So, by that logic, Loop must be good for the environment too, right? This line of reasoning seems legitimate but isn't necessarily the whole truth. Moving away from the customer-facing aspects of the service, let's focus on how the products arrive at your doorstep. What is often left out during CEO Tom Szaky's press junkets on Loop are the logistical specificities behind the brand in its early stages, when the only US market to be served is the New York area (Sitzer). For as beneficial as Loop can be in leading the way in creating a practical reuse economy, the inconvenient truth is that their on-the-ground logistical strategies are built around a heart that beats on a lifeblood of petroleum—a network of trucks turning blue skies brown. In order for one pint of Häagen Dazs Mint Chip ice cream to get to a New York Loop user, it must travel by truck from the Bakersfield, CA manufacturing facility to a storage facility in Maryland. From there, it's loaded onto another truck which takes the ice cream to a distribution plant in New Jersey to be packed into a tote (Wiener-Bronner). Twenty-seven hundred miles, 12 states, and 4.5 days later, that tote will ultimately land on the doorsteps of New Yorkers who love ice cream and the earth as much as I do. But that's a big journey and a lot of fossil fuel for a pint of ice cream that tastes the same out of a reusable container as it does from a disposable one that can be bought at a 7-11 down the street. Oh, and after the last spoonful has been scooped, that sleek and shiny Mint Chip container hops back on a truck to begin the cross-country return trip to the packaging facility in Bakersfield to be cleaned, refilled, and sent out to the next New Yorker (Wiener-Bronner). While no packaging was disposed of by the consumer, the refrigerated, 18-wheeled, diesel-powered truck on a nationwide trek is nobody's idea of saving the earth. Criticizing a company with a great idea and even better intentions seems wrong on every level, but there is always a trade-off or cost—and I'm not talking dollars and cents. In trying to fix one problem, Loop has added to another. Granted, as Loop grows and expands, the logistical processes will certainly become more efficient; but I feel strongly that, at the very best the initial framework of the service may be a prohibiting factor in its growth, and at worst, can be seen as outright short-sighted. Loop provides for a promising and positive future in theory but has disappointing and damaging practices in play for the short term.

TerraCycle's Loop looks to expand on our reuse, and provides a practical, convenient service that plays into many of our existing habits and lifestyles. With recycling existing as a broken system and reducing now forgotten in the age of American consumerism, reusing may be our planet's last front in the fight against our own waste. While our waste with regard to landfills may kept at a minimum, the additional toll Loop takes on fossil fuel waste is substantial. Loop's ideas are solid, and intentions are pure, but the current means to achieving those two things are flawed. The concepts behind Loop may be some of the first strides toward a sustainable future, though I fear that the enormous carbon footprint left by the system's logistical misstep is a near fatal flaw that Loop may not be able to survive.

Bo Cole is a Business Administration major.

Works Cited

"2015 Fact Sheet." *Advancing Sustainable Materials Management,* EPA.gov, July 2018. Accessed 8 Feb. 2019.

Danigelis, Alyssa. "TerraCycle Launches Loop Circular Delivery Service with Major Brands." *Environmental Leader,* 24 Jan. 2019. Accessed 6 Feb. 2019.

East, Becky. "P&G Joins TerraCycle's Loop With 11 Household Brands." *Business Wire*, 24 Jan. 2019. Accessed 11 Feb. 2019.

Makower, Joel. "Loop's Launch Brings Reusable Packaging to the World's Biggest Brands." *Green Biz*, 24 Jan 2019. Accessed 6 Feb. 2019.

Roth, Katherine. "The Return of the 'Milkman Model': Loop Bets on Reusable Containers as Future of Consumption." *Boston Globe*, 24 Jan. 2019. Accessed 6 Feb. 2019.

Sitzer, Carly. "Unilever, Coca-Cola, and P&G Among Brands Partnering with TerraCycle to Eliminate Single-use Plastic." *Green Matters,* 28 Jan. 2019. Accessed 9 Feb. 2019.

Taylor, Mac. "An Analysis of the Beverage Container Recycling Program." *Legislative Analyst's Office*, 29 Apr. 2015, pp. 20. Accessed 9 Feb. 2019.

Wiener-Bronner, Danielle. "How to Solve the World's Plastic Problem." *CNN Business*, 24 Jan. 2019. Accessed 6 Feb. 2019.

Reasoning, Argumentation, and Writing

CONSIDER THIS:

- In research writing, students often note that it's difficult to preserve their own voice when so much of the paper is devoted to evidence and support. Where does this author's voice shine through most clearly? What does this tell you about the ways in which you can keep your own voice in academic writing?

- Because Loop is a company that few people are familiar with, the author needs to provide a fair amount of background in addition to making an argument. How does he keep the essay overall from being more argumentative than informative? What are the key aspects that make an argumentative essay argumentative?

- As we all know, conclusions can be challenging—especially if we're not content with merely restating our supporting points. What are some other things that we can do in a conclusion to make it more effective?

Putting an End to Single-Use Plastics on Campus

Gillian Ippoliti

Reflective Memo: *I enjoyed writing this piece related to a topic I am passionate about, which is ocean pollution. Living at Cal Poly, I have experienced the difficulty of making environmentally-conscious choices on campus, even with the efforts Cal Poly has already made toward sustainability. My main challenge was staying within the length expected for this assignment since this is a broad topic with multiple other solutions that I also would have liked to explore in a longer piece. Overall, I am proud of this essay and how it all came together.*

From what we know, there are currently 5.25 trillion pieces of plastic polluting our oceans ("Plastic Statistics"). Considering the first synthetic plastic was not created until the 1900s, and the material was not even beginning to be widely used until World War II ("The History and Future of Plastics"), 5.25 trillion pieces is an astounding number to enter the ocean over a relatively short period of time. The reason for this rapid rate of pollution is the abundance of single-use plastics. According to UN Environment leader Erik Solheim, "Plastic packaging accounts for nearly half of all plastic waste globally, and much of it is thrown away within just a few minutes of its first use. Much plastic may be single-use, but that does not mean it is easily disposable. When discarded in landfills or in the environment, plastic can take up to a thousand years to decompose" (qtd. in Dal Porto). Plastic pollution is a serious problem facing our planet today, and the abundance of single-use plastic that lasts a thousand years just to be used once is especially wasteful and illogical. This issue is not just a problem to be discussed by world leaders; it is relevant to every person who shares this planet. We at Cal Poly are no exception to the blame for being wasteful with plastic, as it is practically unavoidable on our campus. The amount of single-use plastic provided by Campus Dining is excessive and could be avoided by replacing single-use plastics with compostable paperboard alternatives.

LOOK HERE:

Ippoliti mentions her interest specifically in ocean pollution. Listen to a podcast from the National Ocean Service titled "Garbage Patches: How Gyres Take Our Trash Out to Sea."

Single-Use Plastics: Our Contribution to Global Pollution

The contamination of our environment with plastic products is an issue that we have all played a role in, and it affects every living thing on the planet. Every year, about 300 million tons of plastic is produced, and about fifty percent of it is considered single-use plastic (North & Halden). That includes consumer items such as plastic cups, bags, straws, bowls, boxes, and utensils: many of the things people use in their lives every day and throw away after one use without giving it a second thought. While that may be the end of a plastic object's usefulness as most people are concerned, it is far from the end of its life in the environment. Plastic trash often makes its way to the ocean where it wreaks havoc on marine life. It often entangles marine mammals, leaches harmful chemicals into the water, and is ingested by animals that mistake it for food, often animals that are later eaten by humans (Xanthos & Walker 18). The problem may seem distant from our lives, but it all starts with the single-use plastic items we choose daily. Although it may seem as though most people do not use these items every day, plastic has become ubiquitous, and it is especially unavoidable at certain places like a college campus.

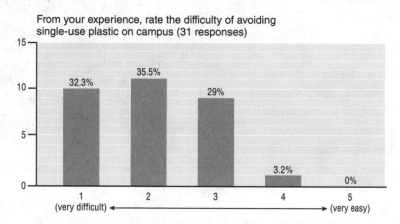

From your experience, rate the difficulty of avoiding single-use plastic on campus (31 responses)

Figure 1. In a survey of students who eat regularly on campus, no students responded that it is very easy to avoid single-use plastic on campus (1 was labeled as "very difficult" and 5 was labeled as "very easy").

Here at California Polytechnic State University San Luis Obispo, almost every option for dining includes some form of single-use plastic without a satisfactory alternative available. In a small survey taken on campus, students who confirmed that they eat on campus regularly were asked to rate the difficulty of avoiding single-use plastic on campus, 1 being very difficult and 5 being very easy (Figure 1). The responses were fairly evenly distributed from moderate to very difficult, but no one responded that it is very easy to avoid plastic on campus.

Figure 2. In one day of eating a typical amount of food on campus, I used 10 pieces of single-use plastic. That may be a small number, but it adds up. (Image by author)

Today's society has made significant progress in environmental awareness, especially in younger generations. Many students here at Cal Poly are conscientious people who would likely make more environmentally friendly decisions if the resources were made available to them. College students are busy and being environmentally friendly requires a conscious effort and is usually not the most convenient option. Therefore, our campus should provide options that allow and encourage students to make environmental choices instead of making it more inconvenient for them.

A common misconception that someone may have on a personal or local level is that their plastic consumption is not enough to pose a significant threat to the environment. This mindset is largely responsible for the excessive consumption of single-use plastics; because so many people believe that their contribution is insignificant, the combined contributions of plastic waste build up on a massive scale. To illustrate how one person's use of plastic even in just one day can contribute to a greater amount of waste, I went through a single school day eating on campus without making a conscious effort to avoid single-use plastic (Figure 2). What I found was that the amount of plastic I used did not seem particularly large or threatening, but it becomes much more significant considering there are approximately 5,250 first-year Cal Poly students who are likely eating on campus frequently, and they are likely to spend approximately 230 days per year on campus ("Cal Poly Quick Facts"). In one day, I used 10 pieces of single-use plastic on campus since I was not actively trying to avoid it. If 5,250 students used that amount of plastic for 230 days, that would mean Campus Dining's to-go options are responsible for over 12 million pieces of plastic waste every school year. That is an unacceptably large contribution to global plastic consumption, but we do not have to let it continue to worsen.

Cal Poly's Steps Towards Waste Reduction: Why We Can Do More

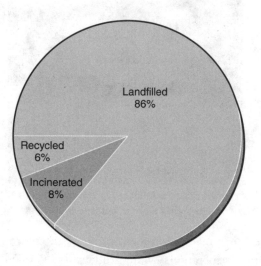

End Result for Plastic in the U.S.

Figure 3. Of all the plastic used in the US annually, only 6% is actually recycled (Data from North & Halden).

Environmental consciousness is not a new concept for Cal Poly. In fact, there are many ways in which the institution has made clear efforts to decrease its waste production. All Campus Dining locations now provide paper straws instead of plastic ones, and their participation in the Zero Waste program diverts significant amounts of trash through composting and recycling ("Zero Waste"). While these steps demonstrate important progress, Cal Poly has still not done everything it can do to reduce plastic waste. According to the Cal Poly Zero Waste webpage, the first steps towards zero waste are rethinking, refusing, reducing, and reusing—recycling comes after all of that. This is because recycling is not actually as simple as one would hope; surprisingly large quantities of plastic are never recycled at all because many plastics are not suitable for recycling and because it is an expensive process. As shown in Figure 3, 86% of plastic waste in the US is landfilled annually, 8% is incinerated (releasing harmful chemicals into the atmosphere), and only 6% is recycled (North and Halden). In terms of waste management, recycling is not as successful as it may seem, so it should not be the primary course of action when considering how to manage plastic waste. It is much more effective to resolve a problem when it is approached from the source, and the source of our problem is the overwhelming availability of single-use plastics. Therefore, our primary approach to reducing plastic waste at Cal Poly should be eliminating that availability.

Alternatives to Single-Use Plastics

There are many alternatives to single-use plastic, and one that would be practical for Cal Poly is paperboard. Paperboard is a thin form of cardboard made from cellulose in wood pulp, and according to the recent UN Environment report on alternative materials, "Kraft paper [paperboard] has been used for many decades to provide inexpensive and effective packaging..." (Kershaw 51). An important point is that the paperboard is inexpensive, so it would not be difficult for Campus Dining to incorporate it. Since it is made from plants, it will not have the harmful effects that plastic has on the environment. Plastics contain many chemicals that can pose risks to human health, but a material made from paper does not have that problem since it is all natural. Just one paperboard option that Campus Dining can consider is Bio Natura Food Container Board, which can be used for hot or cold foods, be microwaved, and withstand moisture (Lingle). It is also compostable, which would accelerate Cal Poly toward its Zero Waste goal.

One issue to address is that students have to be satisfied with the new options, because some may argue that students would prefer the plastic. For one thing, Cal Poly already offers a few paperboard options, such as boxes for salads at The Avenue and at Campus Market, and they are used by students daily. If students are satisfied with paperboard packaging in those places, they will likely feel the same if paperboard is incorporated in other dining locations. To get more information on what students think about this, students were asked, in the same survey referred to in Figure 1, how they would feel about Cal Poly switching to cardboard packaging, 1 being not happy with it and 5 being happy with it (Figure 4). Most students asked (77.4%) responded on the positive side of the spectrum, and 61.3% responded that they would be happy with switching to cardboard. Perhaps eliminating the plastic options would come with some inconveniences; after all, paper packaging is less durable and would not last through the same circumstances that a plastic container might. However, it is not logical to use a material that will last hundreds of years for something that will get thrown away after one use just because it will resist getting squished in a backpack for a couple hours. In a personal interview, Sydney Meertens, member of the Rise Above Plastics campaign for Cal Poly's Surfrider chapter, said, "Specifically at Cal Poly, I see lots of problems regarding the on-the-go lifestyle. It is a norm for us to get plastic cups, bowls, and more on the daily because it is convenient. Our goals for Cal Poly are

Reasoning, Argumentation, and Writing

to move away from what's easiest and more towards what has the greatest impact for the future of our planet." The environmental choice is often not the easy choice, but it is the best choice for taking care of our world and therefore ourselves. If Cal Poly is committed to making a positive change, that must include a change in the habits of plastic use. Making the change to paperboard would be inexpensive as well as satisfactory to most students, help Cal Poly reach its Zero Waste goal, and most importantly, be beneficial to the environment. Therefore, it is in the institution's best interest to swap the single-use plastic for compostable paperboard options.

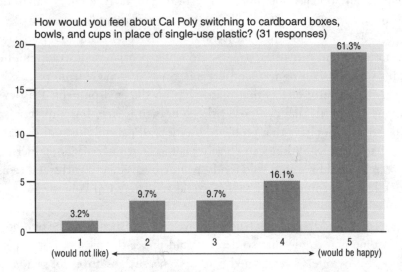

Figure 4. Students were asked how they would feel about switching to cardboard (1 was labeled "I would not like this" and 5 was labeled "I would be happy with this").

Conclusion

Single-use plastic poses a severe threat to the world in which we live, polluting it and causing harm to ourselves and all living things. This threat is not localized to a single source, and no one is excluded from being part of its cause or its effect. As a major institution with thousands of people constantly on-the-go in their busy lifestyles, Cal Poly makes a significant contribution to this problem and is not doing all it is capable of to prevent it. Campus Dining provides too many single-use plastic options, and the best solution to this problem is eliminating the plastic bowls, boxes, and cups altogether. They can easily be replaced by paperboard options, which would have a substantial benefit to the environment and no significant drawbacks. Most students would be happy with eliminating the plastic options. For any students who would not be happy with the change, a continued effort to raise environmental awareness and spread am eco-friendly mindset on campus would encourage more students to be willing to sacrifice convenience for a healthier planet. Making changes to help the environment is no longer an option, it is absolutely necessary; now is the time for Cal Poly to take another step forward in making the right decisions for the planet we all share.

Gillian Ippoliti is a Marine Science major.

Works Cited

"Cal Poly Quick Facts." *Cal Poly University News and Information,* 2019, https://calpolynews.calpoly.edu. Accessed 23 Feb. 2019.

Dal Porto, Lindsay. "Singling Out Plastic." *Quality Progress*, Vol. 15, No. 9, Sept. 2018, pp. 10–12. *ProQuest*. Accessed 23 Feb. 2019.

Kershaw, Peter. "Exploring the potential for adopting alternative materials to reduce marine plastic litter." *UN Environment Programme*, 2017, http://wedocs.unep.org. Accessed 23 Feb. 2019.

Lingle, Rick. "New paperboard packaging material matches foodservice shift in sustainability." *Packaging Digest*, 22 May 2018, https://www.packagingdigest.com. Accessed 23 Feb. 2019.

Meertens, Sydney. Personal interview. 20 Feb. 2019.

North, Emily J. and Rolf U. Halden. "Plastics and Environmental Health: The Road Ahead." *National Society for Biotechnology Information*, 2013, https://www.ncbi.nlm.nih.gov. Accessed 23 Feb. 2019.

"Plastic Statistics." *Ocean Crusaders,* 2019, http://oceancrusaders.org. Accessed 23 Feb. 2019.

"The History and Future of Plastics." *Science History Institute,* https://www.sciencehistory.org. Accessed 23 Feb. 2019.

Xanthos, Dirk and Tony Walker. "International policies to reduce plastic marine pollution fromsingle-use plastics (plastic bags and microbeads): A review." *Marine Pollution Bulletin,*Vol. 118, No. 1–2, 15 May 2017, pp. 17–26, *Science Direct*. Accessed 23 Feb. 2019.

"Zero Waste." *Sustainability*, Cal Poly Administration and Finance, 2019, https://afd.calpoly.edu. Accessed 23 Feb. 2019.

CONSIDER THIS:

- In her reflective memo, Ippoliti mentions that she would like to have expanded this essay. If given more space, what changes could be made to this essay? What other solutions and consequences could Ippoliti then include?

- One of the sources Ippoliti uses in this essay is a survey she conducted of Cal Poly students. What are the benefits and drawbacks to incorporating this type of source? What are some strategies Ippoliti uses to justify the survey's legitimacy?

Plastics Are Out: Reusables Are In

Anna Wannenwetsch

Reflective Memo: I really enjoyed writing this proposal argument because I wrote about a topic I am passionate about—sustainability—and I worked hard to create the final paper you see now. Even though I had a rocky and stressful beginning, in hindsight, I'm glad it was hard for me when I started because it forced me to push myself, to think outside of the box, and to go after the answers I was searching for but not expecting. I was successful in my quest, and I am proud of the result! Hopefully it inspires all of us to lead more sustainable lives because the little everyday acts are ultimately what makes the biggest impact.

Why is it that American culture relies so heavily on single-use plastics to help us get through everyday life, when, according to National Geographic writer Laura Parker, plastics take more than 400 years to degrade? Some plastics can even take up to more than 1,000 years to fully decompose, which means that regardless of how one feels about plastics, the first plastics to ever be created are still sitting in our landfills ("Plastic Planet"). Plastic utensils, specifically, began to be mass produced in the 1950s, after there was a massive shift in families moving to the suburbs. They became a convenient way to feed families on a modest budget, without any of the hassle of clean up (Bernier). The landfill would take over that messy job of cleaning up, and in the process of relying on the expediency of disposable plastics to serve our everyday needs, we as a society have now subjected the earth to catastrophic harm, from the toxic carbon emissions that are produced when plastics are left in the landfills to the chlorinated plastics that contaminate our groundwater ("Plastic Planet").

Two years ago, a ground-breaking study in *Science Advances* measured that "[o]f the 8.3 billion metric tons [of plastic] that has been produced, 6.3 billion metric tons has become plastic waste. Of that, only nine percent has been recycled." (qtd. in Parker). In short, even though many companies boast today that their products are made with recycled plastics, the reality is that only an exceptionally small number of these plastic products will ever be recycled. The other 91 percent will end up in our landfills and oceans. If plastics continue to be produced at the astronomical rates that they are predicted to be, then simply recycling plastic products is not the answer. Though many people seem to prefer convenience over the impact of their plastic use on the environment, we all need to take an extra step to create an environmentally friendly and waste-free world, or at least a world that minimizes waste as much as possible.

LOOK HERE:

 Visit this webpage for more information on Cal Poly's Zero Waste Initiative.

Cal Poly, the large public university that it is, plays an enormous role in contributing to the excessive plastic waste that is produced and manufactured to meet the university's single-use plastics needs. According to Anastasia Nicole, our Zero Waste coordinator, Cal Poly "creates 2,000 tons of garbage a year, [which is equivalent to] 6 tons of garbage a day." To put this amount into context, 6 tons is about the same as the weight of one adult elephant ("How Heavy is 6 Tonnes?"). Clearly, we are part of the problem. As stated on Cal Poly's website on sustainability, the CSU system has mandated that "Cal Poly must reduce per-capita landfill disposal 80 percent by the year 2020, then continue toward zero waste." In 2017, Cal Poly achieved 86 percent of wasted diverted from the landfills ("Zero Waste"). While Cal Poly has met the 2020 reduction requirements, achieving zero waste is still an objective of this campus, and this goal will not be met unless we begin to take further measures in waste reduction.

We, as students and staff, are inextricably linked to the environment in which we live and learn. San Luis Obispo, the beautiful, sunny town that it is, is and will be profoundly affected by the detrimental and toxic effects of plastic waste on the environment. Cal Poly's foundational motto on which its curriculum and practices are anchored to is "Learn by Doing." If this university truly wants to embody the maxim they promote, then we must actively begin making the necessary changes to solve this plastic problem in order to help this campus, San Luis Obispo, and eventually, the world. Therefore, in order to reduce the plastic waste that Cal Poly produces, as well as our reliance on single-use plastics, I propose that Cal Poly Corporation switch to using reusable metal silverware throughout campus dining, instead of continuing to use disposable utensils. This will be a small but significant step in allowing the university to achieve its zero waste ambitions and to continue its commitment to practicing sustainability in our daily lives.

How Cal Poly Can Be a Part of the Solution

Instead of diverting more plastic waste from the landfills, Cal Poly should begin to reduce the amount of waste we produce in the first place, and this project can commence by switching from using disposable, plastic utensils throughout campus dining to providing only reusable silverware. A short-term solution would focus on making this switch primarily in the central University Union dining locations, such as The Avenue, Mustang Station, Poly Deli, and 805 Café, where students, especially first years, frequently sit and eat most, if not all, of their meals. Instead of having plastic utensil dispensers, Cal Poly should provide bins of clean metal forks, knives, and spoons in the aforementioned UU dining locations that can then be returned to a "dirty" bin. The used utensils will be washed, and the reusable process begins again. Furthermore, a long-term solution to work toward would include providing every incoming student with their own set of reusable silverware which they can carry with them. Cal Poly would also continue to make progress in creating every dining location on campus to be plastic utensil free.

Figure 1. The life spans of plastic utensils vary drastically from the life expectancy of reusable silverware. Data derived from Bernier and Cioci.

This university should care about making these changes not only to reach their own zero-waste aspirations but to also further their commitment to encouraging students and staff to lead sustainable and responsible lifestyles. According to Dr. Andrew Bernier, who received his Ph.D in Sustainability Education at Prescott College, a single-use plastic utensil has an approximate life span of "7–10 minutes, however long it may take to eat a piece of someone's birthday cake or potato salad at a barbeque." On the other hand, reusable silverware lasts, on average, three or more years in a school setting, according to the Minnesota Pollution Control Agency. These statistics, as illustrated in Figure 1, put into context just how not environmentally friendly it is to continue to buy and use plastic utensils that have a lifespan of only a few minutes versus reusable silverware that lasts years longer, and only require a single purchase. When considering this information, along with the fact that plastics can stay in our landfills for more than 1,000 years, the university's desire to make the switch to reusable silverware should be resolute. If universities are microcosms of the real world, let Cal Poly lead the way in creating a future in which a reusable mindset, not a disposable one, is the norm.

Why Compostable Utensils Are Not the Answer

When I first set out to find a solution that would alleviate the waste that Cal Poly produces through plastic utensils, I thought that simply switching to a compostable, biodegradable material would be enough. I was shocked to find that substituting compostable utensils for plastic ones is actually a worse solution than simply continuing to use disposable cutlery. Anastasia Nicole, Cal Poly's Zero Waste coordinator, took the time to explain why the answer to my problem is not to change to compostable utensils, but to instead switch to reusable ones.

Allow me to clarify my process for determining the most effective solution to mitigate some of the plastic waste produced by Cal Poly. When conducting preliminary research for this proposal, I discovered that I had a sincere lack of education on what the term biodegradable means and what composting on a massive scale involves. The Federal Trade Commission has defined the term "biodegradable" as a material that will "completely break down and return to nature, i.e., decompose into elements found in nature within a reasonably short period of time (one year) after customary disposal" ("Compostable Plastics 101"). However, as there is no regulation on the word "biodegradable," it can be placed on labels by companies in order to make them sound sustainable, when in reality, the product could degrade in one thousand years in the environment, or in less than one year in an industrial compost facility. Context matters, and this discrepancy is huge, yet unregulated. Thus, even though there may be good intentions in creating biodegradable plastics, if not disposed of properly and with the correct infrastructure, they do more harm than good:

> In order to biodegrade, biodegradable plastics need to be placed into the end-of-life environment for which they were designed. If placed in the wrong environment, not only is a biodegradable plastic prevented from delivering many of its potential environmental benefits, but it can hinder the efforts of composters or recyclers ("Compostable Plastics 101").

Essentially, biodegradable plastics are only better for the earth if these products end up in the environment in which they were intended to end up in after use. In many cases, "the end-of-life environment" is an industrial compost facility, and these are few and far between in San Luis Obispo County. While there is one larger-scale compost facility in Santa Maria called Engel and Gray, it has a maximum contamination rate of 1 percent (Nicole). Meanwhile, "[Cal Poly's] contamination rate regularly exceeds 32% for public trash, recycling, and composting" based on numerous waste audits that Nicole has conducted this past year. Therefore, Cal Poly cannot send any compostable utensils to Engel and Gray, even if they are plant-based, and they are instead sent to the landfills, which leaves us back where we started—with excessive plastic waste.

This is not to say that switching to compostable materials is not a viable solution on some campuses. College campuses in the Bay Area have access to large industrial compost facilities that have the means to sort through the compost sent to them by the universities in order to ensure that the compost is 100 percent clean and will not damage their machines or further contribute to waste production. As mentioned on *SF Environment*, San Francisco's environmental impact website, San Francisco, for example, can compost everything from pizza boxes to orange rinds that they can then send to a compost facility in Vacaville with no further issues (Howard). However, as Cal Poly does not have access to the proper infrastructure necessary to compost these kinds of materials, we must look to reusable options to meet our zero waste goals.

Looking at a Model of Success

In October 2014, the Minnetonka Middle Schools (East and West) located in Minnesota received a grant from the Minnesota Pollution Control Agency (MPCA) in order to take part in a case study that would look at the effects of switching from disposable utensils to reusable silverware and bowls (Cioci 3).

Madalyn Cioci, an environmental specialist who works at the MPCA, explains how the most prized aspect of converting to reusable utensils is how long-lasting they are because durability translates to fewer costs: from shipping the utensils from the manufacturing facility, to packaging the utensils (often in more plastic), to finally replacing the utensils after a single use. Cioci elaborates, "Assuming a 3-year life span of the reusables, even with budgeting for replacement of 20% loss in Year 2 and 3, MPCA estimated the schools would save about $23,000 over three years" (7). This is no small sum of money, and this money could then be invested in other underfunded programs at Cal Poly. While this was the predicted amount of money that the schools would save, the total came out to be "over $26,000 that the schools saved" (Cioci 7). From this case study, one can conclude that even making the initial switch will not be a significant financial burden on Cal Poly, and will ultimately save money, both short and long-term.

The Minnetonka Middle Schools were able to reduce the amount of garbage sent to the landfills by "almost 6,000 lb[s]… in the first year alone. This represents an 89% drop in solid waste by weight" (Cioci 8). If these middle schools can reduce their waste by 6,000 lbs in the first year, just imagine how much waste Cal Poly could avert from the landfills, as we produce significantly more trash to begin with: 6 tons a day, to be exact. Additionally, "the schools purchased 98% fewer individual utensils from the prior year—dropping by over half a million items from almost 700,000 to just under 12,000" (Cioci 8). Within just a few years, Cal Poly Corporation would be able to eliminate much of their efforts on ordering and restocking disposable utensils and refocus their time in other aspects of dining.

Not only can Cal Poly drastically reduce the amount of waste we generate on a daily basis from disposable utensils, but the amount of extra work and energy associated with having slightly more dishes to wash is also nearly negligible, according to both the kitchen staff at the middle schools, as well as Cioci. Cioci explains, "Prior to use of the reusable utensils and bowls, staff ran an average of

38 dishwasher loads each day… Afterwards, the average was 41.5 (increase of just 3.5 loads per day at each school)" (8). While there were more dishwasher loads, the increase was considered insignificant by staff (Cioci 8). Reusable utensils are not bulky, and they therefore take up very little space in a dishwasher and do not contribute to excessive water usage. Furthermore, greenhouse gas (GHG) emissions that resulted from the production of plastic utensils were also widely reduced, once the switch to reusable silverware was made: "By running the purchase cost of just the utensils (forks/knives/spoons), both disposable and reusable, through the Carnegie Mellon EIO-LCA model, [MCPA] estimate[s] that this change, in its first year, reduced GHG by 77% (from 7.61 to 1.74 metric tons co e)" (Cioci 9). Not only is converting to reusable utensils more cost-effective, but it does not significantly increase water usage, and it would even reduce Cal Poly's GHG emissions.

This case study provides base-level cost statistics for how much Cal Poly Corporation could save long term that ultimately illustrate the efficacy of transferring to reusable utensils. While middle schools function differently than universities, the cafeteria aspect of a middle school and the dining aspect of Cal Poly are comparable, and thus this case study provides invaluable insight into how beneficial this switch could be to Cal Poly, on both a financial and environmental level.

Is It Going to Cost More?

The Cal Poly Corporation is likely concerned with how much this switch to reusable utensils would cost the university, and this apprehension is valid. However, after looking up and comparing utensil prices on a restaurant online supply store called "WebstaurantStore," I found that the prices are actually very comparable. For a case of 1,000 heavy weight plastic forks, the cost would be $15.49 per case, which comes out to be approximately $0.015 for each fork. For a case of 50 stainless steel forks, the cost would be $1.09 per case, which comes out to be about $0.02 for each fork ("WebstaurantStore"). The individual price for each fork is remarkably similar. While clearly a case of 1,000 forks is much more than a case of 50 forks, Cal Poly has to replace 1,000 plastic forks hundreds of times in a year versus buying 1,000 metal forks once that can then be used for at least three years, if not longer. Therefore, one can conclude that investing in reusable, metal utensils is extremely cost-effective and will save money long-term.

How the Pros Outweigh the Cons

Some might argue that only providing reusable silverware is inconvenient. However, there are several reasons as to why this is untrue. First, if one does not have access to plastic utensils, they will not use them, and they will proceed to use the silverware that is actually provided for them. Second, for students who need or want to eat on the go, they can simply take the reusable fork or spoon on the go with them. Later, after their class, they can return the utensils to the dirty bin to be cleaned and reused again. Third, Cal Poly has already proven that students can handle a sustainable switch. Last year, Cal Poly eliminated plastic straws and now only provides paper straws. Students adapted to this change, and they can adapt to this new one, too. Overall, the small inconvenience of using a reusable fork versus a disposable does not outweigh the detrimental harm the production of plastics causes to the environment.

Some might also argue that the reusable utensils are just going to get thrown away, along with all the other garbage. While this is certainly true, Cioci advises to "anticipate and budget for 40–50% utensil loss in the first year and for about 20% loss in in future years" (11). Additionally, if middle schoolers can learn to not throw away their metal silverware, I would argue that college students can learn not to, as well. Cioci also notes that buying higher quality, sturdier silverware will increase the lifespan of the utensils and thus further reduce loss and replacement costs in the future (11).

With the Proper Education, This Solution Can Work

As with all major changes, it will take time for people to adapt. In this case, Cal Poly students and staff will need to adapt both their mindset and their habits. In the *BioCycle* article, "Deeper Dive into Zero Waste," Green Business Certification Inc. Zero Waste program director Stephanie Barger explains that "Education and training [are] vital to helping teams work towards Zero Waste" (qtd. in Stanley 22). She continues to describe how achieving zero waste takes a complete "behavior shift" and that the only way to accomplish it is to educate staff on how important the impact they are making is to the well-being of the environment (qtd. in Stanley 22).

There are many students at Cal Poly who are committed to adopting more sustainable practices, from Cal Poly Surfrider, which has committees such as "Rise Above Plastics" and "Beach Clean-Ups" that aim to reduce waste, to Net Impact, which is a club centered on eco-friendly business practices. With their help and the help of the Zero Waste program at Cal Poly, we can educate Cal Poly students during Week of Welcome, for instance, and explain why the adjustment to reusable silverware is necessary, feasible, and manageable. Bill Stonecypher, manager of the solid waste management and university recycling program at LMU, further advocates that "It's important to create a culture that seeks to identify and reduce waste throughout areas of the food service process on campus" (qtd. in Stanley 22). Making the switch to reusable silverware is the first step to making the culture shift at Cal Poly from one of simply convenience to

Reasoning, Argumentation, and Writing

one of sustainability. Let Cal Poly be a model to other universities of what our students stand for and can achieve with a little bit of determination and a desire to do good for the world.

Anna Wannenwetsch is a Liberal Studies major.

Works Cited

Bernier, Andrew. "A Life Cycle Analysis: A Plastic Fork—Sustainability." *Google Sites*, CREST Paradise Valley High School, 2011, sites.google.com/a/pvlearners.net/sustainability/. Accessed 13 Feb. 2019.

Cioci, Madalyn. "The Cost and the Environmental Benefits of Using Reusable Food Ware in Schools." *Minnesota Pollution Control Agency*, Oct. 2014, www.pca.state.mn.us. Accessed 21 Feb. 2019.

"Commercial Restaurant Supplies & Equipment from WebstaurantStore." *WebstaurantStore*, WebstaurantStore Food Service Equipment and Supply Company, www.webstaurantstore.com. Accessed 26 Feb. 2019.

"Compost Locator Map." *US Composting Council*, 2019, compostingcouncil.org/compostmap/. Accessed 21 Feb. 2019.

"Compostable Plastics 101." *US Composting Council*, 2011, compostingcouncil.org. Accessed 13 Feb. 2019.

"How Heavy Is 6 Tonnes?" *The Measure of Things*, 2018, bluebulbprojects.com. Accessed 21 Feb. 2019.

Howard, Brian Clark. "How Cities Compost Mountains of Food Waste." *SF Environment*, San Francisco Department of the Environment, 25 July 2013, sfenvironment.org. Accessed 21 Feb. 2019.

Nicole, Anastasia. Telephone Interview. 14 Feb. 2019.

Parker, Laura. "A Whopping 91% of Plastic Isn't Recycled." *National Geographic*, National Geographic Society, 20 Dec. 2018, news.nationalgeographic.com. Accessed 20 Feb. 2019.

"Plastic Planet: How Tiny Plastic Particles Are Polluting Our Soil." *UN Environment*, United Nations Environment Programme, 3 Apr. 2018, www.unenvironment.org. Accessed 20 Feb. 2019.

Stanley, Sarah. "Deeper Dive Into Zero Waste." *BioCycle*, vol. 58, no. 6, 2017, pp. 21–22. Accessed 20 Feb. 2019.

"Zero Waste." *Administration & Finance*, California Polytechnic State University–San Luis Obispo, 2019, afd.calpoly.edu. Accessed 12 Feb. 2019.

CONSIDER THIS:

- This proposal uses section headings as an organizational tool. What benefits do these headings have on this piece? If they were to be removed, what would the writer have to change?

- Wannenwetsch describes how her thinking changed as she researched this problem. What effects does referencing her changing position directly have on the introduction of her solution?

- Because this essay focuses on Cal Poly's role in sustainability, Wannenwetsch interviews campus staff on the issue. Who else could she have interviewed? What other campus sources could she have included?

Reasoning, Argumentation, and Writing

A Plastic Spoonful of Sugar

Catherine Zadorozhna

Reflective Memo: As a frozen yogurt fanatic and frequent visitor of the on-campus frozen yogurt site, Yogurt Creations, I am requesting that my peers, especially the ones living on-campus, consider bringing their own spoon every time they visit this eating establishment. I recognize the some may not have access to spoons within their dorm or do not wish to carry spoons around with them, but I hope to convince my peers that giving this utensil a second thought is a worthwhile investment in a healthier environment and their daily lives.

What is the price for a couple of ounces of delectable frozen yogurt goodness? Some may reply: around 59 cents per ounce. On a purely monetary level, they are not wrong. However, hidden at the end of this transaction, a simple, often-times unconscious action has a devious environmental cost. At Yogurt Creations (YoCre), the on campus go-to eating establishment for frozen yogurt, a Cal Poly student hands their trusty PolyCard to the cashier. The cashier swipes. The student reaches for a tempting, sinfully colorful utensil: the plastic spoon. The rush to consume this delicious treat is understandable on the most basic level of human desire, yet, as with many sins, it requires a moment of humble reflection. What are the consequences of a single frozen yogurt enthusiast's impatience?

Plastic spoons fall in the category of "non-durable" plastics, meaning they have a lifespan of three years or less. The availability of plastic utensils is a modern hallmark of the rise of fast-food establishments, a societal movement away from dependence on home cooking, and a cultural emphasis on consumption and convenience. This convenience relies on the availability of plastic polystyrene made from the waste products of non-renewable crude oil, with considerable energy input in both manufacturing and transportation in order to produce a spoon used only once. Its upfront cost is masked to the consumer by its complementary nature. There is no environmental guilt included with a bowl of froyo. When I inquired about the frequency at which employees at Yogurt Creations refill their bowl of plastic spoons, an employee replied immediately with "Often! Very often!" This same employee testified that a box of one thousand spoons would usually last two to three days, which is a reasonable statistic when considering our university serves a student population of nearly twenty-two thousand people, not including a faculty of nearly two thousand. The ease with which our community approaches this compromising situation explains why it is possible for thousands of spoons to be thrown away month by month. This is directly in the face of increased environmental awareness, as well as ease of access to environmentally friendly alternatives. This encounter at the YoCre cash register poses an intriguing opportunity for a dramatic turn-around of our Cal Poly student population, a worthy challenge for our student body to prove ourselves as exceptional with one simple action. The next time you visit Yogurt Creations, bring your own spoon.

Whether it is metal or bamboo, part of a handy kit, or taken from 805 Kitchen, the most important quality of the spoon of your choice is reusability. Taking responsibility of a spoon personally is an empowering, accessible decision that any student can make, without actively campaigning for a business to change its policies and/or purchases. Even if Yogurt Creations showed the initiative to switch to a composite plastic spoon made of recyclable materials, this action would still depend on proper disposal of the spoons. According to a United States Environmental Protection Agency report titled "Advancing Sustainable Materials Management: 2015 Fact Sheet Assessing Trends in Material Generation, Recycling, Composting, Combustion with Energy Recovery and Landfilling in the United States," written in 2018, only 2.2% of non-durable plastics were recycled when looking at a generation of these products. These previous observed trends indicate that depending on consumers to recycle is not the most effective way to reduce the amount of plastic spoons entering landfills.

Additionally, there are specific circumstances encountered within our situation living in the city of San Luis Obispo. On the recommendation of the San Luis Obispo Integrated Waste Management Authority, plastic utensils are intended to go to the Cold Canyon Landfill. This is due to a lack of a facility to process the polystyrene after contact with food products ("Plastic Utensils"). They recommend on the plastic utensil reference page of their website to reduce the use of these utensils by carrying your own to-go pack of utensils as well as reusing utensils by washing them. While the encouragement to create a personal collection of washed YoCre spoons is attractive to the hoarders among us, there is a limit to the level of commitment most college students want from their utensils. We have limited storage space within our modest living quarters that does not account for a lifelong pile of used plastic spoons waiting to be reused. Currently, compostable utensils are not a viable option, since there is not an adjacent compost collection service on Cal Poly's campus to accommodate that type of utensil.

There was a previous effort by the university to collect post-consumer compost that failed due to a large amount of contamination in compost receptacles ("Recycling and Composting"). Since compostable utensils and recycling

LOOK HERE:

Watch this video from *National Geographic* on an alternative to plastic spoons.

are not possible currently without the introduction of new local composting or recycling facilities, as a student body, our only solution is to commit ourselves to bringing our own spoons. Our very own waste management authority has advised against using single-use plastic utensils. Their recommendation falls in line with my motion for action, which is to invest in a 99-cent stainless steel spoon for future value and enhanced social standing, in addition to the positive environmental impact.

Possessing a spoon would place an individual in the ranks of all of the other utensil-owning adults, a step toward independency with only a minor spoon-sized increase in responsibilities. Time spent washing one's utensils every week can be limited if one has a select collection of multiple reusable spoons. Taking the three minutes to clean a spoon can be condensed into only one venture to the nearest sink by one's dorm room if one simply owns a month or weeks' worth of frozen yogurt spoons. An additional benefit to this enterprise is control over the sanitation of one's utensils. Free-floating complementary utensils have a risk of contamination dependent upon the responsibility and oversight of the workers of the eating establishment. I challenge you to ask how frequently the inside of a plastic utensil dispenser is sanitized at any favorite eating establishment. Consider also, for example, how an employee might react to dropping some spoons on the floor when refilling the dispenser. Rather than trust the integrity of every employee who ever worked in a place of dining one visits, one can have account-ability over what they choose to ingest. Even if it is knowingly using an unwashed spoon in a fit of sugary midnight cravings, that individual knows exactly how unwashed the spoon is and can reasonably assess the risks they are taking when they use their spoon. With a foreign spoon, these risks are unknown.

Whatever ultimately motivates one to bring about this change in how they treat their trips for treats, they will find themselves in the company of others who have already taken this step as well as further action to reduce their waste output. Not only has Cal Poly's administration taken steps toward sustainable practices within the dining program, there are numerous student-run organiza-tions such as the Real Food Collaborative or Zero-Waste Club that encourage environmentally-conscious practices. The post-Industrial Revolution production of plastic products has sucked away limited natural oil reserves without ample consideration of proper disposal or afterlife for nearly a quarter of a millennium alongside our apathetic complicity. The environmental toll no longer must be the price we pay for our common sweet pleasures; with our own spoons we can enjoy frozen yogurt guilt-free.

Catherine Zadorozhna is an Architecture major.

Works Cited

"Plastic Utensils | SLO County IWMA Recycling Guide." *SLO County IWMA*, Citizen Communications, LCC, www.iwma.com. Accessed 1 July 2019.

"Recycling and Composting." *Sustainability—Cal Poly*, California State Polytechnic University, https://afd.calpoly.edu. Accessed 1 July 2019.

United States Environmental Protection Agency, Office of Land and Emergency Management. "Advancing Sustainable Materials Management: 2015 Fact Sheet." *Advancing Sustainable Materials Management: 2015 Fact Sheet*, July 2018. https://www.epa.gov. Accessed 1 July 2019.

CONSIDER THIS:

- Zadorozhna opens this essay with a paragraph of descriptive detail to entice the audience. What other ways could she open the essay? What are the benefits and drawbacks associated with other types of openings?

- Who is the audience for this piece? How does it differ from the other essays on campus issues of sustainability in this section, Ippoliti's "Putting an End to Single-Use Plastics on Campus" or Wannenwetsch's "Plastics Are Out: Reusables Are In"?

- This essay proposes a practical, local solution to a problem that is of national and international consequence. Zadorozhna references the broader situation, but what elements could she add if she wanted to convert this into a policy proposal? What are the main differences between a practical proposal and a policy proposal?

We Need Them. Period.

Bella Amador

Reflective Memo: *It was difficult at first to choose a topic for my "claim essay" in English 145. The assignment was very open-ended, which is something I wasn't very used to as a writer coming fresh out of high school. My previous essay in that class was a little more on the humorous side, and that was something I wanted to incorporate into this work. In arguing for an end to the "tampon tax," I was able to discuss a facet in the fight for gender equality not often talked about, while also having a little fun highlighting how society views women and their periods towards the end of the essay. I hope you enjoy!*

A smooth female voice says, "Hand set with 156 brilliant cut diamonds. Eighteen-karat white gold. Custom-made bezel set diamond chain. Where else would you keep something that 36 states tax like a luxury?" Then the model on the screen who is flaunting the diamond necklace opens the charm to reveal none other than… a tampon. This was a strategic advertisement released by the organization Period Equity. American women have made great strides in the fight for their fundamental rights, such as the right to vote and the passing of Roe v. Wade; however, the fight is far from over. The advertisement described above, titled "Periods are Not a Luxury. Period," was released to support a recent movement in women's ongoing fight for gender equality: the movement to exempt essential feminine hygiene products (pads, tampons, and panty-liners) from state sales tax. In the interest of gender equality, states should exempt necessary feminine hygiene products from sales tax.

The movement to end the "tampon tax" has gained traction and considerable support in recent years and has resulted in four states passing laws to exclude feminine hygiene products from sales tax (Sanger). Sales taxes are issued at the state level, and out of the forty-five states that do issue a sales tax, thirty-six of them do not exclude tampons and pads. These states justify their decision on the grounds that feminine hygiene products are not a "necessity" needed to treat a medical condition or illness. However, female politicians at the forefront of the "tampon tax" discussion strongly disagree with this practice. These female politicians are working on state legislation that would define feminine hygiene products as medical devices, which would exempt them from state sales taxes.

Those who oppose the movement to terminate the "tampon tax" argue that exempting such products from sales tax would be a great loss in tax revenue for the state. In response to that argument, I argue that the potential loss in state revenues is overshadowed by the benefits of terminating the "tampon tax" and making feminine hygiene products more affordable and available to all women. A 2016 article by NPR states that if California eliminated "its 7.5 percent sales tax on feminine hygiene products, it would be a $20 million loss to the state's general fund." Compared to its proposed 2016–2017 budget of $170 billion, that loss is miniscule (Gass-Poore). The same NPR article offers a quote from California state assemblywoman Cristina Garcia: "Eliminating the tax is a short-term monetary loss that can lead to long-term success for girls."

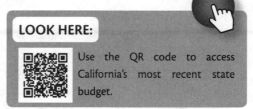

LOOK HERE:

Use the QR code to access California's most recent state budget.

These feminine hygiene products are a necessity for women, not a luxury. The menstrual cycle is a vital part of a woman's reproductive health. Therefore, no woman should be denied access to products that are necessary to maintain her reproductive health. It is a well-known medical fact that women cannot simply turn off their periods; therefore, women need access to feminine hygiene products to safely control their menstrual cycles. Taxing these products, though, makes them more expensive and less affordable, and without access to these products, women can be forced to use unsafe methods or products that can result in illness or infections. For example, Garcia shares that "girls have told [Me] they've missed school because they couldn't afford feminine hygiene products—one even used socks instead" (Gass-Poore). Restricted access to necessary hygiene products is a real problem that affects real women; this problem that reaches so far as to damage women's education is far worse than the state losing a small amount of tax revenue. It is illogical that items like Chapstick, Viagra, and dandruff shampoo are exempt from sales taxes, while tampons and pads remain taxed as a luxury (Sanger). Assemblywoman Garcia explains the argument for terminating the "tampon tax" perfectly: "we are being taxed for being women" (Seibold).

Furthermore, taxing essential feminine products intensifies the already existing economic disparity between men and women. In 2017, women still experience a gender wage gap of 20 percent, making only 80.5 cents to the male dollar ("Pay Equity"). The wage gap affects women of different ethnicities with varying severity; for example, the wage gap for women of Hispanic and African heritage will not close until 2233 and 2124, respectively ("Pay Equity"). The "tampon tax" did not create the economic disparity between men and women, but it intensifies the problem. Huffington Post editor Jessica Kane used information from the US Health department and the American Pregnancy Association along with prices from Walgreens and Target to calculate how much a woman's period will cost her during her lifetime. She estimates that a woman will spend $5,859 on her period in her lifetime, including panty-liners, Midol, tampons, new underwear, acne medication, and heating pads (Kane). It is important to note that her calculation does not include pads or birth control, which is commonly used to treat severe period symptoms. In Kane's calculations, tampons alone will cost an average woman $1,773.33 and with the added sales tax of 7.5% in California, this number rises to $1,906.33 (Kane; Kaeding). It is important to note that sales taxes are regressive (Gass-Poore), and therefore impact low-income and impoverished women more severely. Admittedly, eliminating the tax on tampons will not erase the financial burden of periods completely, but will alleviate it substantially, and allow women easier access to essential items.

In addition to increasing economic inequality, the sales tax on tampons and pads is also an example of taxation without representation. Historically, women in the United States have not been equally represented in government. A female president has yet to been elected into office, and the Inter-Parliamentary Union has ranked the United States 103 out of 193 in women's representation in national legislatures or parliaments. In 2018, women only make up 20% of the seats in the United States Congress ("Women"). Specifically on the state level, the level in which sales taxes are imposed, women make up 22.8% of state senate seats and 26.3% of state house or assembly seats ("Data"). If women were equally represented in government, these percentages would be much closer to fifty. It is simply unjust to continue to tax women for a process out of their control if they are not equally represented in the institution that governs them.

Despite these problems, it would be unfair to say men in government have continued with the "tampon tax" out of pure malice. The root of the issue is that there is a profound misunderstanding in society and among our government representatives regarding women's bodies and reproductive healthcare needs; many elected officials have not made efforts to amend state law to eliminate the "tampon tax" because they have been unaware of the issue. It is easy to find countless videos of adult men mesmerized by how tampons work or what a pad looks like online by simply typing "men" and "periods" in a search bar. Society regards periods as taboo, as this mysterious, yet horribly disgusting "moon cycle" that turns men's female counterparts into hormonal, chocolate-craving she-wolves for a week. Women have also failed to share enough to combat this cloud of ignorance surrounding the female menstrual cycle. If you questioned why new underwear was previously included in the calculations of the overall cost of the menstrual cycle, or are generally uncomfortable with the idea of periods, you're likely the victim of such ignorance. You're not alone. My father, a seasoned firefighter-paramedic who has seen countless gruesome scenes filled with blood and gore, still dramatically cries out and shudders in disgust at the briefest mention of periods by his wife and two daughters. Researchers at Clark University explain the phenomenon: "The mysterious nature of what happens to girls contributes to a gap in boys' knowledge about female bodies and to some negative views about girls" (Schultz). It's important to note that there is no specific "Tampon Tax," but 36 too many states still have not made them exempt from the tax because their elected officials have been blind to the issue affecting half of their population.

The state sales tax on essential female hygiene products should be terminated. Exempting pads, tampons, and panty-liners is not going to close the wage gap, elect the first female president, or dissolve the patriarchy, but it'll bring us one step closer towards gender equality. As a woman, I'll speak for myself when I say I'll take my victories where I can get them.

Bella Amador is an English major.

Works Cited

"The Data on Women Leaders." *Social and Demographic Trends*, Pew Research Center. 13 Sept. 2018. http://www.pewsocialtrends.org. Accessed 22 Oct. 2018.

Gass-Poore, Jordan. "Citing Gender Bias, State Lawmakers Move To Eliminate 'Tampon Tax'." *NPR*. 6 Mar. 2016. https://www.npr.org. Accessed 22 Oct. 2018.

Kaeding, Nicole. "Tampon Taxes: Do Feminine Hygiene Products Deserve a Sales Tax Exemption?" *Tax Foundation*. 26 Apr. 2017. https://taxfoundation. org. Accessed 22 Oct. 2018.

Kane, Jessica. "Here's How Much A Woman's Period Will Cost Her Over A Lifetime." *Huffington Post*. 18 Mar. 2015. https://www.huffpost.com. Accessed 22 Oct. 2018.

"Pay Equity And Discrimination." *Employment, Education, and Economic Change*. Institute for Women's Policy Research. https://iwpr.org. Accessed 22 Oct. 2018.

"Periods Are Not a Luxury. Period." *Period Equity*. 29 Sept. 2017. https://www. periodequity.org/. Accessed 22 Oct. 2018.

Sanger, Ema. "More States Move To End 'Tampon Tax' That's Seen As Discriminating Against Women." *NPR*. 25 Mar. 2018. https://www.npr. org. Accessed 22 Oct. 2018.

Schultz, Colin. "How Men Learn (Or Don't) About Menstruation." *Popular Science*. 6 Mar. 2014. https://www.popsci.com. Accessed 22 Oct. 2018.

Seibold, Holly. "D.C. moves one step closer to menstrual equity." *Washington Post*. 27 Apr. 2016. www.washingtonpost.com. Accessed 22 Oct. 2018.

"Women in National Parliaments." *Inter-Parliamentary Union*, 1 Jan. 2018. http://archive.ipu.org. Accessed 22 Oct. 2018.

"Women in the U.S. Congress 2018." *Center for American Women and Politics*. Eagleton Institute of Politics, Rutgers University. New Brunswick, NJ. http://www.cawp.rutgers.edu. Accessed 22 Oct. 2018.

CONSIDER THIS:

- In this essay, the writer has a clear policy claim, and a policy claim will always have opposition (if only because people are unwilling to change). How does this author deal with some of the various counterarguments? Can you think of another counterargument that the author does not address?

- When incorporating research, it's always useful to establish the credibility of your sources rather than to rely on the in-text citation alone. Where are some instances in which the author does this effectively?

No More 7 a.m. Classes

Juliana Brozio

Reflective Memo: Developing this piece was a two-quarter process for me. My interest in the topic of 7 a.m. classes began during my first quarter at Cal Poly, when i was blocked into a 7 a.m. COMS class. Having personal experience taking a 7 a.m. class and an interest in psychology, I wanted to know the impacts that early classes have on students. I began to do a lot of research on the topic and found studies done on circadian rhythms and early start times in college students. I also met with the registrar to gather data on 7 a.m. classes and looked at Mustang News articles on overcrowding at Cal Poly. I like that it relates to me personally, but also to thousands of other students at Cal Poly, and that it draws attention to the issue of overcrowding and provides am effective solution.

Six a.m. My alarm blares violently as I groan and turn over, not believing that I have to wake up for class at this reproachful hour. Forty-five minutes later I am miraculously shuffling my way to class in the dark like a zombie. As I doze off in class, I realize that I only slept for five hours the night before and will be tired for the rest of the day. This saga was my daily routine for all ten weeks of fall quarter because of my 7 a.m. class.

Unfortunately, this same situation occurs for thousands of students at Cal Poly who are forced to take 7 a.m. classes. Early classes do not align with young adults' circadian rhythms, causing many students to lose sleep and to struggle to wake up and focus in the morning. In addition to causing sleep deprivation, 7 a.m. classes are also detrimental to students' academic success, personal well-being, and social lives. At Cal Poly, students are forced to register for these early classes because they are often the only ones available, due to the fact that Cal Poly is overcrowded—there are too many students and not enough classrooms on campus. In order to eliminate the negative effects that 7 a.m. classes have on students, overcrowding needs to be addressed at Cal Poly so that classes can be held at later times and students can prosper.

The main reason that 7 a.m. classes cause negative effects in college students is because young adults have delayed circadian rhythm cycles that do not align with early college classes. Circadian rhythms are the body's biological clock which helps people fall asleep at night and wake up in the morning. However, according to a study published in the academic journal *Frontiers in Human Neuroscience*, in adolescence and early adulthood, sleep wake cycles shift to be two to three hours later. The peak of this cycle shift occurs at age 19 before it switches back to an earlier pattern in the late 20's (Evans et al). This means that young adults physically cannot fall asleep until much later each night. Shifting the sleep wake cycle by a few hours may seem harmless, but it poses a problem when young adults go to sleep at midnight and then have to wake up at 6 a.m. to go to class. Thus, they only get 6 hours or less of sleep, which over time can be detrimental to their health.

As a result of this shift in circadian rhythms and early classes, students are becoming sleep deprived and tired which is damaging to their health. A study done by researchers from the Department of Neurology at the University of Michigan found that half of college students report daytime sleepiness and 70% of college students get less than the eight hours of sleep that they need per night (Hershner and Chervin). This is an issue because both sleepiness and sleep deprivation have negative effects. For college students, both of these can lead to an increase in depressive symptoms, lower GPAs, increased risk of failing academically, and impaired learning ability (Hershner and Chervin). These negative effects prove how important it is for college students to receive sleep, and having early classes hinders their ability to get this sleep because of the circadian rhythm shift in young adults.

In addition to negatively affecting sleep, early classes can also have a negative impact on students' social lives, which are important in college. In the opinion section of Purdue's student newspaper, columnist Logan Judy writes about his negative experience with taking a 7:30 a.m. class. He explains that he had to sacrifice his social life every night because he would go to bed at 11 p.m. while all his friends stayed up much later socializing (Judy). Social lives are important in college according to Judy because they give students "relief from the stresses of academics and [provide] helpful connections for professional life as well as private life." A study published in an academic journal by the American Psychological Association confirms Judy's statement, explaining that at age 20 the quantity of social interactions is important and can predict "loneliness, depression and psychological well-being 30 years later at age 50" (Carmichael et al., 101). Thus, having a social life in college is important for students' well-being and should be part of their normal lives. However, having early classes in college often forces students to choose between sleep and social activities at night, creating a no-win situation which can be harmful in the long run.

Critics may say that students at Cal Poly should be able to avoid all of these negative effects by simply not taking 7 a.m. classes. However, the solution is not that easy. Currently there are not enough classrooms at Cal Poly to accommodate the number of students, and as a result, classes have to be held earlier in the day. According to a *Mustang News* article by Bryce Aston and Mady Minas, Cal Poly has not expanded its lecture or lab spaces since 2013, yet the total student population has increased by almost 20% since then. Data generated by Aston and Minas from the CSU Space and Facilities Database, which monitors space related issues for all the CSU campuses, also confirms how overcrowded Cal Poly is. Currently Cal Poly's "total lecture and lab space is intended to accommodate

Reasoning, Argumentation, and Writing

about 16,516 full-time equivalent (FTE) students based on state standards," but "there are 21,627 FTE students enrolled" right now, which works out to be about 30% more students than Cal Poly is intended to have (Aston and Minas). This proves that there is a major issue of overcrowding at Cal Poly. Too many students need classes, but there is not enough space, resulting in students being forced to take the classes they need at inconvenient times like 7 a.m. Ultimately, 7 a.m. classes are not something that is easily avoidable for students at Cal Poly due to overcrowding.

In order to solve the issue of overcrowding and eliminate 7 a.m. classes, Cal Poly needs to make more space for classes. There needs to be enough available resources and classrooms for all of the students on campus. If there are enough resources for students, they will not have to take the 7 a.m. classes that are detrimental to their health and well-being. Cal Poly needs to solve this issue and make more space on campus. In order to do this, several different solutions have been proposed.

One suggested solution is to build more classrooms on campus. There is enough space to do so; however, there is not enough funding. Cal Poly just received a $50 million grant to redo the Kennedy Library and another $10 million to build a new research building,

LOOK HERE:

Find the Cal Poly Master Plan here.

which means that more funding will be scarce for at least the next few years (Aston and Minas). In fact, Cal Poly actually has a master plan to expand space on campus, but the funding for this plan was turned down last year and is projected to be turned down in future years as well (Aston and Minas). Acquiring funding and then building more classrooms are both going to take time, but the issue of overcrowding needs to be solved right now so that students do not have to keep suffering from it.

Another possible solution to solve overcrowding is to increase the graduation rate at Cal Poly. Currently the six-year graduation rate is at about 82% (Clark). Cal Poly's goal is to increase the graduation rate to 90%, but this goal has some issues as well (Aston and Minas). One of the reasons why the graduation rate is low at Cal Poly is because students struggle to get the classes they need. Classes fill up and have as many as 50 to 70 students on the waitlist (Aston and Minas). The students that do not get necessary classes are sometimes forced to take different classes, resulting in them falling behind in their major. Therefore, in order to increase the graduation rate, Cal Poly first needs to make sure that students can get the classes they need. However, the only way to do this is to either add more classrooms and professors or to reduce the student population.

Since the solutions above will not solve the issue of overcrowding and are not feasible, other solutions need to be considered. I am proposing that to solve over-crowding, Cal Poly should reduce its student body by 3,000 students. According to Michele Reynolds, the Assistant Registrar, there are 83 classes that start before 7 a.m. this winter quarter. That is only 1.7% of the classes this quarter, but since Cal Poly is a large school, this means that over 3,000 students are in these classes (Reynolds). Therefore, in order to eliminate 7 a.m. classes, 83 classes need to be rescheduled. Considering this and the data from the CSU database mentioned above, I think that if the student population is reduced by 3,000 students to start, it will eliminate 7 a.m. classes and leave extra room so students can get the classes they need. This reduction would bring the student population to around 18,000 students overall. Having the student population at 18,000 is more than Cal Poly's capacity of around 16,500 students mentioned above, but it is still a fairly dramatic reduction from the current population of 21,600 students. This reduction will help significantly with classroom space. To implement this solu-tion, Cal Poly should start admitting less students each year so that in the next five years the goal will be met. Reducing the population over five years ensures that no dramatic changes will occur all at once. After the goal is met, the school should adjust the number of students accordingly, so the student population stays at around 18,000 students. Then, once the school receives more funding and can build more classrooms and hire more faculty, they can start to increase the stu-dent population again based on how many classrooms are built.

By reducing the student population, there will be fewer students that need classes, and therefore less classrooms will be needed. Classrooms could then be available during optimal learning hours, allowing classes to start at 8 or 8:30 a.m. rather than at 7 a.m. Pushing classes back by one hour will make all the dif-ference. Students will be able to sleep in for another hour, allowing them to get more sleep, focus better in class, and have a better social life. Their mental health will most likely improve, and they will be able to enjoy college more. It is entirely attainable for Cal Poly to reduce the student population by 3,000 students, and it would effectively solve the issue of having 7 a.m. classes.

Critics may fear that a reduction would deter new students from applying if Cal Poly's acceptance rate drops significantly. However, this will not occur because the reduction in population will take place slowly. I am proposing that Cal Poly reduce the student population over the course of five years, meaning that this reduction would not affect one incoming class all at once. It would be spread out evenly so that each year fewer students are admitted over the course of the five-year period. This would cause a small reduction in admissions each year that would barely affect applicants.

Another worry critics may have is that reducing the student population would cause the school to lose money, resulting in things like tuition increases. While it is true that cutting the student population would also cut money for the school, it is still a necessary change. Cal Poly is not currently fit to hold these many students, and until the school is fit to do so it should not be admitting as many students. Tuition increases may occur, but that is a small expense when the health and well-being of the student population is concerned. It is just like when students overextend themselves in college. If students take on too much with heavy course loads, jobs, and positions in clubs, they may suffer consequences to their health and success. They may lose sleep, have to work less, have to step down from club positions, and their grades may fall. In the case of Cal Poly, the school's resources are overextended, causing students to suffer the consequences of 7 a.m. classes. Ultimately, Cal Poly should not be overextending the resources it has; instead, it should admit fewer students so students' health and success are a priority, even if that will result in tuition increases.

Seven a.m. classes are detrimental to students' health and well-being at Cal Poly because they cause students to become sleep deprived, and they cause their social lives to suffer. This problem stems from the fact that there is overcrowding at Cal Poly—there are too many students and not enough classrooms to accommodate them. Overcrowding can be solved by reducing the student population and admitting fewer students each year. If the population is reduced, students will enjoy the benefits of later classes, which is something I have experienced firsthand. Compared to having a 7 a.m. class during fall quarter, this quarter my earliest class starts at 9 a.m. This small two-hour change has made all the difference in my life. I am now well rested, have better grades, a better social life, and I am much happier. If 7 a.m. classes are eliminated, thousands of students at Cal Poly will experience this same significant change in their well-being. It is my hope that in the future, Cal Poly students will not have to wake up sleep deprived and sad because of 7 a.m. classes, and that instead they will be able to wake up rested and live happier, healthier lives.

Juliana Brozio is a Psychology major.

Reasoning, Argumentation, and Writing

Works Cited

Aston, Bryce, and Mady Minas. "Class and Office Space Stagnated as Cal Poly Gained More Students and Faculty." *Mustang News*, 12 June 2018, mustangnews.net. Accessed 1 July 2019.

Carmichael, Cheryl L., et al. "In Your 20s It's Quantity, in Your 30s It's Quality: The Prognostic Value of Social Activity Across 30 Years of Adulthood." *Psychology & Aging*, vol. 30, no. 1, Mar. 2015, pp. 95–105. *EBSCOhost*, doi:10.1037/pag0000014.

Clark, Lucas. "Cal Poly Has the Highest Graduation Rates in the CSU, Data Shows." *Sanluisobispo*, The Tribune, 13 Sept. 2018, www.sanluisobispo.com. Accessed 1 July 2019.

Evans, M. D. R., et al. "Identifying the Best Times for Cognitive Functioning Using New Methods: Matching University Times to Undergraduate Chronotypes." *Frontiers in Human Neuroscience*, Frontiers, 30 Mar. 2017, www.frontiersin.org. Accessed 1 July 2019.

Hershner, Shelley D. and Ronald D Chervin. "Causes and consequences of sleepiness among college students." *Nature and science of sleep* vol. 6 pp. 73–84. 23 June 2014, doi:10.2147/NSS.S62907

Judy, Logan. "7:30 Classes Are a Bad Idea." *Purdue Exponent*, 30 Oct. 2014, www.purdueexponent.org. Accessed 1 July 2019.

Reynolds, Michele. "Re: Question about 7 a.m. Classes." Received by Juliana Brozio, 20 Feb. 2019. Email.

CONSIDER THIS:

- Writing on a local or campus-based topic can often be challenging because of the limited amount of research available. How does this author solve that problem? What are some other ways to generate evidence for a local or campus topic?

- The author spends as much time looking at alternative solutions as she does supporting her own. Why might this be a useful strategy?

Solitary Confinement in the U.S. Prison System

Fiona Gleeson

Reflective Memo: In the process of writing this essay, I learned a lot about the prison system as a whole. I was already fairly well aware of overall issues with prison systems and the effects of solitary confinement, but synthesizing all of these sources that combined both concepts gave me a new perspective on the topic.

In the writing process, I spent a lot of time organizing my thoughts, finding evidence to support my claims, and re-writing sections so they would be precise and understandable.

Through the essay, I try to use an academic but approachable tone since this is a very serious subject but one that everyone should be able to understand. I spent a lot of time researching so that I would be able to give a complete picture of the situation, and I think using citations from a number of credible sources makes my argument much stronger.

I worked hard to keep my essay well organized and on topic so there would be a solid structure for the reader to follow. I also kept my sections similarly weighted so there would be a nice flow of the essay.

Solitary confinement is a common practice in the U.S. prison system. A survey with responses from forty-seven jurisdictions across the U.S. found that approximately 6.6% of the prison population was being held in a form of solitary confinement in the fall of 2014 (Baumgartel). The use of solitary confinement has increased in recent U.S. history, and what used to be a few hours to a day has now become anywhere up to decades of time alone in a small cell (Weir). While people may have a picture of what solitary confinement is from what they have seen in movies and other media, the experience of being alone in a small room for prolonged periods of time is much more devastating than it is usually portrayed.

According to the National Criminal Justice Reference Services, prison has four main purposes: retribution, deterrence, incapacitation, and rehabilitation (Kifer). These four measures relate to prisons as a whole, but only retribution and rehabilitation are specifically tied to solitary confinement. Solitary confinement may factor into the deterrence component because it is such a terrible experience that it could scare people into not committing crimes, but any form of punishment would achieve some form of deterrence. Solitary confinement is not necessary to aid in incapacitation because incapacitation is already achieved by placing the criminals in prison. On the other hand, retribution and rehabilitation are integrally intertwined with the practice of solitary confinement. Solitary confinement is extremely counterproductive in terms of these two goals. In this essay, I am going to explain why solitary confinement is doing the opposite of what prison is supposed to do in terms of those retribution and rehabilitation.

Solitary Confinement in Regard to Retribution

People go to jail for a number of crimes. As a society, we have decided that someone who murders, sexually assaults, tortures children, or commits other heinous crimes deserves to pay for those crimes. Forcing these criminals to spend time apart from their family and friends, live with the conditions and the rules of a prison, and sometimes endure solitary confinement is retribution for the terrible crimes they have committed. Making someone who has committed irrefutably awful crimes endure solitary confinement is understandable. But what about the people in prisons who *have not* done truly awful things? For the most part, all inmates have committed crimes, but it is important to note that all crimes are not equally terrible and that there are a variety of crimes that can result in someone going to prison. For example, statistics from the US Federal Bureau of Prisons show that almost half of inmates are in jail because of drug offenses, and 6.5% are in jail for immigration offenses. While it is debatable as to what a "terrible" crime is, punishing everyone who has ever broken a law with something as harmful as solitary confinement is ludicrous and unjust.

It is also important to note that solitary confinement is not used equally within prison populations. An article from *The Atlantic Journal of Communication* about the use of solitary confinement explained, "[solitary confinement is used] as a political tool to control those seen as political threats and [this] practice is broadly implemented as a prison management tool to control minorities, the poor and oppressed, the addicted, and the mentally ill, who increasingly comprise the bulk of the prison population" (Kerness). In reality, solitary confinement is not being used to punish people who have committed the worst crimes, but it is used disproportionately to control groups of people who are already underprivileged.

Solitary Confinement in Regard to Rehabilitation

Solitary confinement is said to be used as a tool to punish prisoners who are acting out; theoretically, prisoners will understand that there are consequences for their actions and become better citizens for it. However, solitary confinement has the opposite effect. A study surveying data from the Florida Department of Corrections has found that individuals in solitary confinement have increased violent thoughts, develop worse self-control, and are more likely to commit violent crimes after being released from prison (Mears).

There are also physical consequences from being inactive, such as abdominal, back, and neck pain. Other physical symptoms include chronic headaches, trembling, sweaty palms, extreme dizziness, heart palpitations, digestive issues, extreme weight loss, and insomnia (Boyd). Additionally, solitary confinement is directly linked with a number of psychological issues. The human brain is made to function with social interactions and different stimuli. Being cut off from those parts of life severely damages the brain. Some of the mental symptoms of solitary confinement include, but are not limited to, auditory and visual hallucination, anxiety, panic attacks, a decline in the ability to think, deterioration of memory, paranoia, lack of impulse control, suicidal thoughts, and a desire to harm oneself physically (Boyd).

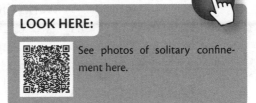

LOOK HERE:

See photos of solitary confinement here.

When the person in solitary confinement is a child, the psychological damage is enormous, and the chances that they will commit suicide increase (Boyd). These symptoms worsen the longer one stays in solitary confinement (Alexander). While negative symptoms of solitary confinement decrease once the individual is reintroduced to social situations, some remain present. Because of this experience individuals often have a very difficult time re-adjusting to normal stimuli. They tend to feel emotionally numb and isolate themselves (Boyd).

The plethora of negative impacts of solitary confinement work directly against the rehabilitation goal of prison as individuals who spend time in solitary confinement are more likely to reoffend and more likely to have symptoms that prevent them from being more productive members of society.

An Unjust System

It is clear that solitary confinement does not align with the retributive and rehabilitative goals of prison. Instead of punishing people who have committed the most heinous crimes, solitary confinement is often used to control minorities, people who are mentally ill, impoverished populations, and people struggling with addiction. Instead of rehabilitating criminals, it degrades mental and physical health while increasing violent behavior against oneself and others. Now that people have studied and understand the usage and effects of solitary confinement, prison systems must stop using it as a correctional technique.

The unjust and inhumane usage of solitary confinement is a terrible issue in the U.S, but it is just one facet of the deeply flawed justice system. In the process of examining and trying to correct the use of solitary confinement, one must also examine the disproportionate incarceration rates for underprivileged people and the general mistreatment of these people within the justice system as a whole. Working to understand what ways the system is unjust and ineffective is the first step to improving the system.

Fiona Gleeson is a Mathematics major.

Works Cited

Alexander, Ames. "Amid Outcry, N.C. to Limit Use of Solitary Confinement for Prisoners." *Charlotteobserver*, Charlotte Observer, 19 July 2017, www.charlotteobserver.com. Accessed 13 Mar. 2019.

Baumgartel, Sarah. "Time-In-Cell: The ASCA-Liman 2014 National Survey of Administrative Segregation in Prison." *The Liman Program*, Yale Law School Association of State Correctional Administrators, 2015.

Boyd, J. Wesley. "Solitary Confinement: Torture, Pure and Simple." *Psychology Today*, Sussex Publishers, 15 Jan. 2018. www.psychologytoday.com. Accessed 13 Mar. 2019.

"Federal Bureau of Prisons." *BOP Statistics: Inmate Offenses*, Feb. 2019, www.bop.gov. Accessed 9 Mar. 2019.

Goode, Erica. "Prisons Rethink Isolation, Saving Money, Lives and Sanity." *The New York Times*, The New York Times, 10 Mar. 2012, www.nytimes.com. Accessed 13 Mar. 2019.

Kerness, Bonnie, et al. "Race and the Politics of Isolation in U.S. Prisons." *Atlantic Journal of Communication*, 2014.

Kifer, Misty, et al. "Goals of Corrections: Perspectives from the Line." *Criminal Justice Review*, vol. 28, no. 1, 2003, pp. 47–69.

Mears, Daniel P., and William Bales. "SUPERMAX INCARCERATION AND RECIDIVISM." *Criminology*, 8 Dec. 2009.

Quillen, Jim. "My 19 Days in Solitary Confinement on Alcatraz." *The Telegraph*, Telegraph Media Group, 6 Jan. 2015, www.telegraph.co.uk. Accessed 13 Mar. 2019.

Weir, Kristen. "Alone, in 'the Hole': Psychologists Probe the Mental Health Effects of Solitary Confinement." *American Psychological Association*, vol. 43, no. 5, 2012, p. 54.

CONSIDER THIS:

- In the introduction, the author says that "the experience of being alone in a small room for prolonged periods of time is much more devastating than it is usually portrayed." What details in the essay were particularly effective in supporting this assertion? Overall, were you convinced of the cruelty of this practice?

- In this essay, the author has chosen to use section headings. Why might they be useful given the nature of the thesis?

- In addition to summarizing the main points, the conclusion also has a call to action. Beyond asking the reader to learn more about solitary confinement, what else could the author reasonably ask the reader to do?

The Death of Marilyn Monroe

Kaylee Earnshaw

On the morning of August 5th, 1962, 36-year-old Marilyn Monroe was found dead from an apparent barbiturate overdose. Though her death was ruled a suicide, conspiracy theorists have argued that Monroe's pervasive knowledge of inside government information, given to her directly by the Kennedy brothers, gave the CIA extensive motivation for murdering her. Due to the disappearance of essential evidence, namely Miss Monroe's red diary, troubles with the police report, the lack of lethal substance in her digestion system, and tapes that showed she was not suicidal at the time of her death, this theory of the CIA murdering Marilyn Monroe is supported.

Marilyn Monroe was an iconic model, singer, and actress in the late forties, fifties, and early sixties. She was commonly displayed in her most famous roles as a ditsy blonde, an act she also integrated into her socialite persona. Though Monroe played the part well, she often expressed uncertainty to friends and family about constantly being portrayed this way in the media (Taylor). She was smarter than people gave her credit for and, due to this, many may have possibly underestimated her power. Notably, Monroe had close relations and alleged affairs with President John F. Kennedy, and therefore, according to the conspiracy theorists, was likely entrusted with state secrets. Suspicions arose about the affair in the late 1950s and were bolstered after Monroe sang her infamous "Happy Birthday, Mr. President" song at Kennedy's 45th birthday party in 1962 (Kelly).

Monroe was found dead in her Los Angeles home at approximately three in the morning by her housekeeper, Eunice Murray, who was spending the night. Murray alerted Monroe's psychiatrist Ralph Greenson when she could

LOOK HERE:

Time investigates the only known photo of John F. Kennedy and Marilyn Monroe together.

not get Monroe to open her locked bedroom door ("Death of Marilyn Monroe"). Based on Monroe's known history of substance abuse and mental instability, and on the substantial amount of drugs in her system when she was found, her death was ruled as probable suicide by the Los Angeles County coroner's office. Many attributed her suicide to the fact that only two weeks prior, Monroe had been dismissed from the movie *Something's Got to Give* and expelled from 20th Century Fox ("Death of Marilyn Monroe"). Soon after her death, Theodor J. Curphey from the Los Angeles Coroner's Office describes her as suffering "from psychiatric disturbance for a long time" and announces her "often expressed wishes [to] give up, to withdraw, and even to die." He highlights multiple previous incidents during which a despondent Monroe had made similar attempts at ending her life with similar drugs. In these attempts, she had called for help and been saved. Curphey noted that Monroe was found with a telephone in her hand, declaring that "the same pattern was repeated, except for the rescue" ("Marilyn Monroe—Death"). This theory makes sense logically due to her known pattern of almost overdosing and calling for help.

The suicide of Marilyn Monroe became a national tragedy because of her high social status and the amount of people who looked up to her. But, was it really a suicide? It didn't take long for conspiracy theories to emerge. The most popular and best supported theory was that Marilyn Monroe was killed by the CIA in order to protect both the Kennedys and the confidential government information to which she had been made privy.

Perhaps the most compelling support for this theory is that Monroe kept a diary, a "little red book," that went missing from the coroner's office the night of her death. Conspiracy theorists believe that the book contains highly confidential government information as relayed by the Kennedys, including details about the government's plot to kill Fidel Castro. Detective Milo Speriglio, a private investigator who worked on the Monroe case, was alerted of the existence of the diary by a man named Robert Slatzer, who was secretly married to Monroe. Slatzer told Speriglio that "Marilyn had shown him the red diary and he had read parts of it which disclosed the (Castro) assassination plot." Lionel Grandson, the deputy coroner who signed Monroe's death certificate, told Speriglio that on the night of the death, "he [Grandson] found the diary was missing and stricken off the inventory as if it never existed" (Rojas). This information was released by the United States Central Intelligence Agency in August 10, 1982, twenty years after Monroe's death. According to the National Broadcasting Company News script, Speriglio announced his offering of a $10,000 reward for the missing diary (Mudd). Speriglio said that he received a call from a New York attorney, in 1982, claiming that his client had the book "but would only turn it over to a living blood relative of Miss Monroe's" (Yates). Unfortunately, Monroe's only living relative at the time was her mother, who was in a mental institution. The disappearance of the diary raises the questions: who stole it? And, why would the diary be stolen in the first place if Monroe had committed suicide? Theorists have posited that the diary contained either information about her killer or incriminating information that someone wanted to keep secret, and I agree with this theory.

On the other hand, in addition to her little red book, Monroe also kept other writings that gave insight into her personal life. After Monroe's death, several of her "previously unseen diary entries, jottings, and poems," not including the contents of the missing red diary, were published into a volume called *Fragments: Poems, Intimate Notes, Letters by Marilyn Monroe* (Taylor). Amidst strong claims about the controversial contents of the red diary, Lucy Bolton, a journalist for British Broadcasting Corporation, wrote about the ordinarily poetic nature of Monroe's other writings, specifically pointing out how these diary entries are "the writings of a poet: a person who is driven to write and to express herself in carefully crafted words" (Bolton). It is possible, but not proven, that these writings were not hidden because they were of a lighter nature whereas her red diary could have included confidential information that the CIA wanted to keep away from public eyes.

The red diary was not the only document to go missing in the immediate days after Monroe's death. Deputy Coroner Lionel Grandison, who signed Monroe's death certificate, notes that "an original autopsy file vanished, a scrawled note that Marilyn Monroe wrote, and which did not speak of suicide also vanished and so did the first police report." Despite these suspicious disappearances, Grandison signed the report of Monroe's suicide, later admitting that "the whole thing was organized to hide the truth." Grandison's close proximity to the case makes him a credible source, but his statements do not help to solve the mystery. Though he hinted at being coerced in saying that he signed his name to avoid "[finding] [him]self in a position [he] couldn't get out of," he never named who threatened him or pointed fingers towards anyone who could have stolen the evidence (Yates).

Though many went along with the suicide report, Police Chief Ed Davis of Los Angeles was bothered by the inconsistencies of Monroe's death. It didn't help that *Oui* magazine published an article that was "highly critical of the Police Department's handling of the case." Following Deputy Coroner Lionel Grandison's announcement about being pressured into signing the autopsy report, "the Los Angeles County district attorney's office in 1982 conducted its own 3 1/2-month investigation. It discounted theories that Monroe had been murdered and that the Police Department had covered up" (Freed). Unfortunately, this reinvestigation yielded no additional evidence, supporting the original conclusion that Monroe died of suicide. One cannot help but wonder what the detectives might have uncovered had they had access to modern technological advancements; after all, law enforcement and criminal investigation have come a long way since the 1980s. There is also the chance that if the CIA did have anything to do with Monroe's murder, they would have kept any findings of the reinvestigation closely under wraps. Even today, there are those that argue for further investigation into Monroe's death. Most prominent among them is American lawyer John Miner, who was the District Attorney of Los Angeles at the time of Monroe's death as well as an assistant in her autopsy. Miner strongly believes that Monroe's body "still holds traces of the drugs used to kill her" (Perthen) and that the only way to settle the suicide versus murder debate is to exhume the body and perform an in-depth autopsy. The fact that exhumation has not occurred again begs the question: could the CIA be involved? After all, if a modern autopsy would solve the mystery once and for all, why hasn't it been done yet? I comply with the many that conclude that Monroe's body remains untouched because there is something to hide.

Another cause for suspicion is the substances found in Monroe's body during autopsy. The official report of chemical analysis done by Deputy Medical Examiner T. Noguchi M.D. at the Los Angeles County Coroner shows that Monroe's blood tested positive for barbiturates and chloral hydrate, and her liver tested positive for Pentobarbital (Noguchi). Alarmingly, her stomach did not test positive for anything: as observed in Los Angeles Times reporter's Dennis McLellan's article "John Miner dies at 92; Investigator of Marilyn Monroe's Death," "the stomach is almost completely empty. No residue of the pills is noted." This is suspicious because, had Monroe ingested the pills orally, they would have shown positive in her stomach as well, which Ronald Yates, award winning foreign correspondent for the Chicago Tribune, Professor of Journalism at University of Illinois, and Dean Emeritus of the College of Media, brings to light in the article "Mystery Still Lingers on Marilyn Monroe" (Yates). However, the analysis of this evidence could be considered as using slippery slope logic, considering the fact that just because they did not find any residue of pills in her stomach, they immediately jumped to the conclusion that Monroe must have been murdered, most likely by the CIA. This leaves many gaps in logic.

Regardless of the substances found in the autopsy, it is important to note that many experts contradict the idea that Marilyn Monroe was suicidal towards the end of her life. In reference to the recordings Monroe's psychiatrist made of Monroe speaking just prior to her death, John Miner claims that "anyone who read the transcript would conclude that 'there was no possible way this woman could have killed herself. She had very specific plans for her future.'" Miner, known for his "keen legal mind," "sharp intellect," and "desire and willingness to learn as much as he could about various forensic scientific specialties as they applied to individual cases," is a highly credible source. Unfortunately, there is no evidence to back his conspiracy theories other than his professional opinion (McLellan). The holes in the individual stories and the conflicting drugs in Monroe's system raise questions which promote the possible theory that she was murdered by the CIA.

Despite the speculations surrounding the causes of Monroe's death, most of her fans trust law enforcement's conclusion that the starlet committed suicide. Many doubt the hypothesis that Monroe could have had access to sensitive information. An anonymous author defends this point in the article "The Red Diary," arguing that the "Kennedy brothers weren't fools. They weren't going to reveal government secrets to an unstable woman, especially one in the habit of using barbiturates." Indeed, John F. Kennedy was an intelligent man, but the point made here is flawed, appealing to false authority by implying that Kennedy wasn't a fool simply because he was the President of the United States. Because the author is unknown, it is impossible to trust his or her authority on the subject of the president's relationship with Marilyn Monroe. There is no way to know what secrets lovers share behind closed doors. Furthermore, though Monroe may have been "an unstable woman… in the habit of using barbiturates," she was also a skilled actress accustomed to assuming the "dumb blonde" persona amongst fans and lovers ("The Red Diary"). One can posit that the Kennedy brothers greatly underestimated her, allowing her to stay in the room as they discussed classified information.

The fact that there are multiple pieces of missing evidence, inconsistencies in the police report, a lack of drugs in her stomach, and non-suicidal tapes all support the theory that Marilyn Monroe was murdered by the CIA. Unfortunately, we may never know the full truth behind this Hollywood starlet's famously tragic death. But there are too many discrepancies in the case to believe that Marilyn Monroe died of a simple overdose. On that fateful night of August 4th, 1962, there was undoubtedly some foul play.

Kaylee Earnshaw is an Agribusiness major.

Works Cited

Bolton, Lucy. "Culture—The Secret Diary of Marilyn Monroe." *BBC*, BBC, 1 Jun. 2016, www.bbc.com. Accessed 1 July 2019.

"Death of Marilyn Monroe." *Wikipedia*, Wikimedia Foundation, 17 Apr. 2019, en.wikipedia.org/wiki/Death_of_Marilyn_Monroe. Accessed 1 July 2019.

Dennis McLellan, "John Miner Dies at 92; Investigator of Marilyn Monroe's Death." *Los Angeles Times*, Los Angeles Times, 4 Mar. 2011, www.latimes.com. Accessed 1 July 2019.

Freed, David. "Police Open the Files on Marilyn: No Bombshells." *Los Angeles Times*, Los Angeles Times, 24 Sept. 1985, www.latimes.com. Accessed 1 July 2019.

Kelly, Lyn. "Marilyn Monroe and John F. Kennedy: A Long-Term Love Affair?" *History 101*, History 101, 12 Mar. 2019, www.history101.com. Accessed 1 July 2019.

"Marilyn Monroe—Death." *Biography.com*, A&E Networks Television, 12 Apr. 2019, www.biography.com. Accessed 1 July 2019.

Mudd, Roger, et al. "Alleges CIA Involvement in Marilyn Monroe Death." *Radio TV Reports*, CIA, 10 Aug. 1982, www.cia.gov. Accessed 1 July 2019.

Noguchi, T. "Official Autopsy of Marilyn Monroe." *Los Angeles County Coroner*, 5 Aug. 1962, www.autopsyfiles.org. Accessed 1 July 2019.

Perthen, Amanda." Lawyer Bids to Prove Marilyn Murder Plot; Marilyn Monroe's Body Could Be Exhumed in a Final Bid to Prove She Was Murdered." *The People*, 13 Oct. 1996, *Nexis Uni*.

Rojas, Aurelio. "A Red Diary Belonging to Marilyn Monroe, Who Died..." *UPI*, UPI, 3 Aug. 1982, www.upi.com. Accessed 1 July 2019.

Taylor, Sophie. "Marilyn Monroe's Writings to Be Published in Autumn." *Reuters*, Thomson Reuters, 28 Apr. 2010, www.reuters.com. Accessed 1 July 2019.

"The Red Diary." *Marilyn Forever*, 4 May 2014, marilyn4ever.wordpress.com. Accessed 1 July 2019.

Yates, Ronald. "Mystery Still Lingers on Marilyn Monroe." *Chicago Tribune*, CIA, 6 Aug. 1982, www.cia.gov. Accessed 1 July 2019.

CONSIDER THIS:

- Kaylee Earnshaw chooses to investigate a conspiracy theory, and as such, she is not working from entirely verifiable facts. What types of sources does she use as evidence? How does that evidence help her pursue her line of inquiry?

- Where does Earnshaw most clearly articulate her thesis? Why do you think she places it there? If it were placed elsewhere, what else would need to change about the essay's organization?

- Images of Marilyn Monroe are iconic. Would incorporating an image distract from this essay's purpose or help develop another angle?

Look to the Appendices for information on:

- Campus Resources
- Plagiarism
- General Education Course Objectives
- Composition at Cal Poly: Catalog Course Descriptions
- The Graduation Writing Requirement
- "Look Here" URLs and QR Codes
- Submitting your work to next year's *Fresh Voices*

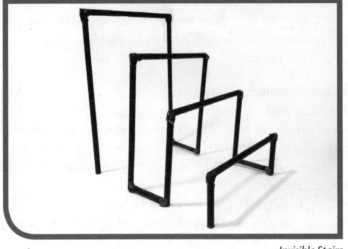

Invisible Stairs
by Laura Nelson

Reflective Memo: *Invisible Stairs was created in the Cal Poly welding shop and is intended to suggest an implied staircase, all conveyed through a single line. It was challenging because I had never welded previously, but I love it because of its simplicity and intricacy.*

CAMPUS RESOURCES: WHERE TO FIND SUPPORT

Your Instructor's Office Hours

If you are struggling to understand a concept studied in class or are simply having a difficult time choosing a topic for an essay, do not hesitate to meet with your instructor during their designated office hours (or make an appointment if those hours don't work with your schedule). Your instructor's office hours will be posted in the course syllabus.

First-year students are often too intimidated or anxious to meet one-on-one with their instructors, yet a short meeting with your instructor can make a major difference when it comes to being successful in a course. Do not wait until you receive low grades on an essay or feel overwhelmed in the course before asking for help. Your instructor will appreciate you taking a proactive stance toward your own development as a writer. Make it a point to ask for assistance when you need it.

LOOK HERE:

Six Harvard faculty members explain why office hours are integral to your learning experience.

Resources for Multilingual Students

The Cal Poly Composition Program is committed to helping students take the writing courses that will best support them. Multilingual students for whom English is a second (or even third) language may want to take one of several multilingual writing courses offered by the English department to satisfy General Education requirements.

ENGL 129, ENGL 130, ENGL 133, and ENGL 312 are all English writing courses, but they are taught from a multilingual perspective. In these courses, you will compose in English for global audiences, all while exploring questions like these:

- How do multilingual speakers use more than one language to keep in touch with networks of family and friends?
- When writing, do you sometimes find yourself searching for just the right way to translate a phrase into English? How can translation work be incorporated into a multilingual writing process?
- What are some of the most popular music, movies, games, and social media being produced outside of the English-speaking world? How is this media influencing global cultures and connections across the world?

Also, if you would like to work with a tutor trained to support students for whom English is not a primary language, please contact the Writing and Learning Center (information below).

Contact Dr. Helmbrecht or Dr. Peters for advice on enrolling in any of these courses.

Mustang Success Center (MSC)

The MSC offers support to all Cal Poly students. More specifically, the MSC "supports undergraduate students with their transition and integration into Cal Poly. The center's staff provides accessible academic advising that guides students to clear pathways of success and timely graduation." Students can sign up for "individual appointments, group advising sessions, and workshops." The center is located in Building 52, Room D37. You can find more information online: https://success.calpoly.edu/.

Veterans Success Center

Cal Poly is a military-friendly campus with an active community of veterans. The campus's Veterans Success Center aims to provide "assistance to prospective and enrolled student veterans and dependents in their transition to college. The center assists in accessing educational benefits, campus resources, leadership activities, and transitioning into the civilian work world." The center is located Building. 52, Room E-4. You can find more information online: https://veteransuccess. calpoly.edu.

Disability Resource Center (DRC)

If you have been diagnosed with a learning disability or are concerned that you may have an undiagnosed disability that is affecting your academic performance, contact Cal Poly's Disability Resource Center for further assistance (http://drc. calpoly.edu/). Students who coordinate with the DRC may receive additional accommodations that can ensure their academic success.

Writing and Learning Center

The university's Writing and Learning Center offers *free,* one-to-one consulta-tions for *any class project* that requires an element of writing and rhetoric: criti-cal thinking, reading, writing, speaking, and developing visual texts. Tutors are undergraduate and graduate students professionally trained both in a 300-level course on one-to-one peer writing consultations and in subsequent workshops on writing and rhetoric in the disciplines. Tutors are available to help all Cal Poly students improve their writing skills.

Students may use the Writing and Learning Center's services at any stage of the writing process, whether they are getting started on a project or editing at the final stages. All writers are welcome!

The Writing and Learning Center serves students at multiple locations on campus:

- Kennedy Library, Room 111C
- Trinity Hall Study Lounge
- Sierra Madre Study Lounge
- Poly Canyon Village Writing and Learning Commons
- Yakʔitʸutʸu Writing and Learning Commons

Thirty-minute and sixty-minute sessions are available by appointment or on a first-come, first-served basis. To schedule a session with a writing consultant, go to www.calpoly. mywconline.com or scan the QR code to the right.

Writing and Learning Center tutors are prepared to assist you with the following:

- Understanding the expectations of an assignment
- Brainstorming and generating ideas
- Generating and organizing your ideas
- Clarifying your purpose
- Developing and supporting your argument
- Researching and documenting sources
- Adhering to a specific format, such as MLA or APA
- Reviewing grammar and punctuation
- Writing in all disciplines (e.g., lab reports, research papers, technical reports)
- Completing senior projects
- Preparing for the Writing Proficiency Exam (WPE)

Keep in mind that the center's tutors do not simply proofread papers or provide students with a stamp of approval on an assignment. Instead, the goal of a writing consultation is to help a student develop writing strategies so that they more successfully complete writing tasks at Cal Poly and beyond.

Right here. Write now!

Kennedy Library: Resources for Research

Personal Help in Kennedy Library
Research Help Desk—room 111: Get in-person help from a LibRAT (Library Research Assistance Technician), a specially trained Cal Poly student who knows how to help you find what you are looking for. LibRATs are very friendly and don't bite!

Phone Support: If you prefer to speak to someone, call 756-2649.

Chat Help: offered by LibRATs, librarians, and Kennedy Library staff.

For help hours, information about the chat box, go to: http://lib.calpoly.edu/ask/.

Research Resources
As a Cal Poly student, you have access to some very extensive resources, and you should take advantage of them while you can. Now is your chance to move beyond Wikipedia.

Appendices

Cal Poly now uses OneSearch, which provides all the search options for online access, requesting items, or borrowing items. It helps to search for items like books and DVDs in Kennedy Library and the other CSUs, but also searches content from a variety of databases.

Research Guides

English 134: Links to catalogs, databases, and resources relevant to this course.

Research 101: General introduction to the library, designed in part for English 133/134. It also includes a tutorial on the research process.

Online Citation Help

Citation examples based on MLA available online at:
http://lib.calpoly.edu/research/citations/mla.html

The OWL at Purdue also provides excellent MLA examples:
http://owl.english.purdue.edu/owl/resource/747/01/

You can also seek individual help with citation at the **Research Help Desk, Room 111.**

Key Research Vocabulary for Writing Courses

Abstract: A brief description of the contents of an article.

Citation: Information about a book or article that minimally includes author, title, date, and publisher.

Citation style: There are many formats for citation, such as MLA, Chicago, APA, etc. English classes use MLA.

Call Number: Library of Congress classification codes. The unique combination of letters and numbers tells you where a book is found among similar items. To find which floor your book is on, look at a library map.

Peer-Reviewed Journal: a journal that publishes articles only after they have been subjected to critique by multiple scholars in that field. Signs that an article is peer-reviewed are the presence of many citations, a text-heavy appearance, and academic affiliations of the editors and authors. If you are uncertain, one way to be sure is to visit the home page of the journal. Peer-reviewed journals are usually proud of the fact and announce it there.

This section was contributed by Brett Bodemer, Humanities and Social Sciences Librarian
at Robert E. Kennedy Library.

DEFINING AND AVOIDING PLAGIARISM

Cal Poly prohibits cheating or academic dishonesty in any form.

Defining Plagiarism

Plagiarism occurs when, without proper attribution, you use another source's words, incorporate images/audio files created by someone else, or restate a source's ideas in your own words. Obviously, purchasing or downloading essays is also a form of plagiarism since the work you hand in is not your own. Yet taking someone's phrasing—even just a sentence or short paragraph—without a proper citation is also plagiarism. You do not have to plagiarize an entire essay for it to "count" as cheating. Your instructor can submit your name to the Office of Student Rights and Responsibilities (OSRR) if only a portion of your paper is not original.

Submitting a paper that you have written for another class (including work written for your high school classes) without the knowledge or permission of your instructors could result in penalty.

Cal Poly's Campus Administrative Manual 684.3 states: "Plagiarism is defined as the act of using the ideas or work of another person or persons as if they were one's own without giving proper credit to the source. Such an act is not plagiarism if it is ascertained that the ideas were arrived through independent reasoning or logic or where the thought or idea is common knowledge. Acknowledgement of an original author or source must be made through appropriate references, i.e., quotation marks, footnotes, or commentary. Examples of plagiarism include, but are not limited to, the following: the submission of a work, either in part or in whole completed by another; failure to give credit for ideas, statements, facts or conclusions which rightfully belong to another; failure to use quotation marks when quoting directly from another, whether it be a paragraph, a sentence, or even a part thereof; close and lengthy paraphrasing of another's writing without credit or originality; use of another's project or programs or part thereof without giving credit."

Examples of Plagiarism

- The submission of another person's work in any medium, either in part or as a whole, without acknowledgement.
- Failure to give credit for ideas, statements, facts, or conclusions that belong to another person.
- Failure to use quotation marks when quoting directly from another source, whether the quotation is a paragraph, a sentence, or a phrase.
- Paraphrasing (putting in your own words) another person's work without acknowledging that person as the author.

- Including images, chart, graphs, etc. in your essay without properly citing the original source material (e.g., Google images).
- Submitting your written work for another class unless you have the express permission of both instructors.

Note that quotation marks, signal phrases, and parenthetical citations generally address these problems.

Reading *Fresh Voices* Essays that Cite Sources

As you read the essays in this collection, focus on how students use sources to support their own ideas. In particular, note how they introduce and quote sources, how they paraphrase, summarize, and integrate quotations with signal phrases. In addition, don't skip over the Works Cited page at the end of essays. Rather, focus on how this page supplements the essay: every source cited in the essay (including images) needs to appear here. Learning how to incorporate and cite sources properly helps to build your credibility (*ethos*) with your readers. While you may learn a different citation style in your major (MLA, APA, Chicago, etc.), the key is to learn how to work with outside sources. Once you understand the basic principles for incorporating source material, you will be able to adapt to any citation style.

The Consequences: The Office of Student Rights and Responsibilities

According to university policy, as a student at Cal Poly, you are responsible for your actions. Instructors will also have clearly stated plagiarism policies on their syllabi. **It is your responsibility to become familiar with the plagiarism policies in your classes.**

Upon discovery of any form of academic dishonesty, you will be subject to a penalty as determined by the instructor (you may fail the assignment; you may fail the entire course). In addition, a report detailing the incident of academic dishonesty, as well as the course's penalty, will be filed with the Office of Student Rights and Responsibilities.

According to the OSRR, "Cheating requires, at a minimum, an 'F' assigned to the assignment, exam, or task, and this 'F' must be reflected in the course grade. The instructor may assign an 'F' course grade for an incidence of cheating." The OSRR reserves the right to discipline a student if a pattern of misbehavior exists, up to the consequence of expulsion. Further, if OSRR and the instructor jointly determine that this instance of plagiarism is severe, a single violation could result in a formal charge of violating the Standards for Student Conduct, which could also lead to a sanction up to expulsion. Sanctions for violating the Standards for Student Conduct include a formal warning, disciplinary probation, suspension, expulsion, tutoring, academic integrity seminar, among others.

Work Cited

"Academic Integrity at Cal Poly." *Office of Student Rights and Responsibilities*, Cal Poly, https://osrr.calpoly.edu/academic-integrity. Accessed 28 June 2019.

GENERAL EDUCATION COURSE OBJECTIVES

The General Education Course Objectives for GE A1 state that as a student enrolled in the course, you will learn to:

- Understand the writing act as a means of exploring and expressing your ideas.
- Approach the act of writing as a recursive process that includes drafting, revising, editing, and proofreading.
- Develop and apply a rhetorical awareness of your audience and use that awareness to assess your audiences and adjust your utterances to that audience.
- Understand major organizational strategies and apply those strategies effectively with reference to your audiences.
- Become aware of the major stylistic options such as voice, tone, figurative language and point of view and apply these options with rhetorical appropriateness.
- Apply the above objectives so as to write essays that are unified, coherent, and free of significant grammar, usage, punctuation, mechanics, and spelling errors.
- Read critically in such a way as to understand and to derive rhetorical principles and tactics that you can apply in writing and in critical reading of other students' papers.

First-year writing classes emphasize a process approach to composition: instructors will engage in a dialogue with you about your writing, providing feedback designed to prompt you to rethink your work. You will gain competence as a writer by learning how to assess your own work. In addition, ENGL 133/134 is rhetorically oriented, which means you will learn to account for the relationship between writer, reader, and text when you write.

English 145 meets the GE A3 requirement.

The General Education Course Objectives for ENGL 145 state that as a student enrolled in the course, you will learn to:

- Recognize lines of reasoning and the precise issues they address.
- Determine the relevance of argument to an issue and the relevance of premises to a conclusion.
- Evaluate the strength of an argument by accurately applying principles of both formal and informal (deductive validity and soundness, inductive argument strength, and common deductive and inductive fallacies).
- Write essays that are well composed by demonstrating a clear sense of the issues and developing cogent lines of reasoning.

- Develop rhetorical awareness that will allow you to adapt your arguments to various audiences.
- Recognize the moral, as well as logical, dimensions of rational discourse.
- Assess the written arguments of others.
- Discern the relevance of premises to conclusions and the relevance of arguments to issues.
- Recognize the uses and abuses of language in written argument.
- Find, evaluate, and incorporate research materials.
- Attribute and document sources accurately.
- Apply principles of fair-minded argument (including how to identify and respond to bias, emotion, and propaganda).

English 145 builds on the rhetorical and persuasive elements of GE A1 courses. Students will learn to work carefully with a wide range of source materials. They will also learn to identify and avoid arguments supported with poor logic and reasoning.

Please note that beginning in Fall 2016, the CSU Chancellor's Office began requiring a grade of C– or better in all Area A classes.

COMPOSITION AT CAL POLY: CATALOG COURSE DESCRIPTIONS, 2019–2020

The following courses constitute the composition curriculum at Cal Poly.

ENGL 129: Multilingual Approaches to Academic Writing Stretch (Part I)

Part one of a two-part stretch course sequence. Introduction to academic writing for bilingual and multilingual audiences. Draft, revise, and edit brief, weekly writing assignments to develop fluency in composing English for academic purposes. Credit/No Credit grading only. 4 lectures.

ENGL 130: Multilingual Approaches to Academic Writing Stretch (Part II) Fulfills GE Area A1

Part two of a two-part stretch course sequence. Rhetorical principles of and strategies for producing effective academic writing for multilingual audiences. Focus on genre awareness, strategic responses to a range of rhetorical situations across multiple languages, cultures, and style issues appropriate for bilingual and multilingual writers. 4 lectures. Prerequisite: ENGL 129. Concurrent: ENGL 135.

ENGL 131: Writing and Rhetoric Stretch (Part I)

Part one of a two-part stretch course sequence. Rhetorical principles of and strategies for producing effective academic writing. Writing as a recursive process that leads to greater organizational coherency, stylistic complexity, and rhetorical awareness. Credit/No Credit grading only. 4 lectures.

ENGL 132: Writing and Rhetoric Stretch (Part II) Fulfills GE Area A1

Part two of a two-part stretch course sequence. Rhetorical principles of and strategies for producing effective academic writing. Writing as a recursive process that leads to greater organizational coherency, stylistic complexity, and rhetorical awareness. 4 lectures. Prerequisite: ENGL 131. Concurrent: ENGL 135.

ENGL 133: Writing and Rhetoric for Multilingual Students, Fulfills GE Area A1

Rhetorical principles of and strategies for producing effective academic writing for multilingual audiences. Focus on genre awareness, rhetorical situations across multiple languages and cultures, and stylistic elements appropriate for bilingual and multilingual writers. 4 lectures. For students admitted Fall 2016 or later a grade of C– or better is required to fulfill GE Area A1.

ENGL 134: Writing and Rhetoric, Fulfills GE Area A1

Rhetorical principles of and strategies for producing effective academic writing. Writing as a recursive process that leads to greater organizational coherency, stylistic complexity, and rhetorical awareness. 4 lectures. For students admitted Fall 2016 or later a grade of C– or better is required to fulfill GE Area A1.

ENGL 135: Writing and Rhetoric Tutorial

Guided discussion and practice of writing strategies for students seeking support for first-year composition-related coursework. Weekly, individualized hour-long sessions with a peer writing consultant offering feedback based on the audience, purpose, and context of a writing task. Open to all students enrolled in ENGL 129, ENGL 131, ENGL 133, or ENGL 134; required of all students enrolled in ENGL 130 or ENGL 132. Total credit limited to 2 units. Credit/No Credit grading only. 1 activity. Corequisite: ENGL 129, ENGL 130, ENGL 131, ENGL 132, ENGL 133, or ENGL 134.

ENGL 145: Reasoning, Argumentation, and Writing, Fulfills GE Area A3

The principles of reasoning in argumentation. Examination of rhetorical principles and responsible rhetorical behavior. Application of these principles to written and oral communications. Effective use of research methods and sources. 4 lectures. Fulfills GE A3; for students admitted Fall 2016 or later a grade of C– or better is required to fulfill GE Area A3. Recommended: Completion of GE Area A2.

ENGL: 148 Reasoning, Argumentation and Technical Writing, Fulfills GE Area A3

The principles of reasoning in technical writing. Discussion and application of rhetorical principles, both oral and written, in technical environments. Study of methods, resources and common formats used in corporate or research writing. 4 lectures. Fulfills GE A3; for students admitted Fall 2016 or later a grade of C– or better is required to fulfill GE Area A3. Recommended: Completion of GE Area A2.

ENGL: 149 Technical Writing for Engineers, Fulfills GE Area A3

The principles of technical writing. Discussion and application of rhetorical principles in technical environments. Study of methods, resources and common formats used in corporate or research writing. 4 lectures. Fulfills GE A3; for students admitted Fall 2016 or later a grade of C– or better is required to fulfill GE Area A3. Recommended: Completion of GE Area A2. For Engineering students only.

ENGL: 150 Writing Tutorial

Guided discussion and practice of writing strategies for students seeking support for writing-related coursework and/or the GWR. Weekly, individualized and group sessions with a peer writing consultant offering feedback based on the audience, purpose, and context of a writing task. Total credit limited to 4 units. 1 activity. Prerequisite: Completion of GE Area A1 and consent of instructor.

THE GRADUATION WRITING REQUIREMENT

In 1976, the Trustees of the California State University System responded to industry and university demands to address the decline in graduating students' writing skills. They mandated that all students seeking a bachelor's or master's degree must "be required to demonstrate their proficiency with regard to writing skills as a requirement for graduation." The Trustees also decreed that assessment of student writing skills take place at the upper-division level. The California State University System thus established the Graduation Writing Assessment Requirement to ensure that students can write proficiently before they enter the professional workforce.

At Cal Poly, all students who are seeking a degree, including master's degrees and teaching credentials, must fulfill the Graduation Writing Requirement (GWR) before a diploma can be awarded. Undergraduate students must complete 90 units before they can attempt to complete the requirement.

Cal Poly has two options for fulfilling the GWR:

1. Pass the Writing Proficiency Exam (WPE), which costs $35 and is administered three different dates each fall, winter, and spring quarter. The WPE is a two-hour exam in which students are asked to write a 500–800-word essay that demonstrates their ability to present an argument in an organized manner with fully developed supporting points expressed logically and clearly.

2. Pass a GWR-designated upper-division course with a grade of C or better based on course criteria that includes multiple writing tasks. GWR-designated courses are searchable through the university's course registration system.

"Look Here": URLs

Each essay in *Fresh Voices* includes links to texts that relate to content of the essays. You can access the websites by either scanning the "QR Code" in the "Look Here" box, or by following the links below. To scan the QR codes, download a free "QR Code Reader" app for your portable device.

Front Matter

In March 2017, the Associated Press included *they*, *them*, and *their* as singular, gender-neutral pronouns to their stylebook:

https://www.washingtonpost.com/news/morning-mix/wp/2017/03/28/the-singular-gender-neutral-they-added-to-the-associated-press-stylebook/?utm_term=.6146efa0dd89

The "Blank on Blank" series offers animated interviews with actors, musicians, writers, and other memorable public figures. Watch a few and pick up some more tips!

http://blankonblank.org/

Some advice from a pro...

In his recently published *New Yorker* article, John McPhee discusses his experiences interviewing people during a fifty-year career as a journalist. He advises:

If I am in someone's presence and attempting to conduct an interview, I am wishing I were with Kafka on the ceiling. I'd much rather watch people do what they do than talk to them across a desk. I've spent hundreds of hours in the passenger seats of their pickups, often far from pavement, bouncing from scribble to scribble. Under a backpack, and hiking behind environmentalist David Brower, I walked across the North Cascades, up and down the switchbacks, writing in a notebook....

Whatever you do, don't rely on memory. Don't even imagine that you will be able to remember everything verbatim in the evening what people said during the day....From the start, make clear what you are doing and who will publish what you write. Display your notebook as if it were a fishing license. While the interview continues, the notebook may serve other purposes, surpassing the talents of a tape recorder. As you scribble away, the interviewee is, of course, watching you. Now, unaccountably, you slow down, and even stop writing, while the interviewee goes on talking. The interviewee becomes nervous, tries harder, spills out the secrets of a secret life, or maybe just a clearer and more quotable version of what was said before. (50)

Work Cited

McPhee, John. "Elicitation." The New Yorker. April 7, 2014. (50–57). Print.

You can find McPhee's entire article here:
http://www.newyorker.com/reporting/2014/04/07/140407fa_fact_mcphee

Check out Kennedy Library's Research Guides for 82 different disciplines:
http://guides.lib.calpoly.edu/

Follow the URL to the "Cocainenomics" advertisement:
http://www.wsj.com/ad/cocainenomics

Interestingly, political satire tends to be biased in favor of liberal politics and against conservative politics. To know more, take a look at the article "Waiting for the Conservative Jon Stewart" published in *The Atlantic* in 2015:
https://www.theatlantic.com/entertainment/archive/2015/02/why-theres-no-conservative-jon-stewart/385480/

Follow the URL to the online satirical news site, *The Onion*:
http://www.theonion.com

Here are a few examples of major news outlets using clickbait strategies for writing headlines for their online stories:

    NBC: "A fifth grader who jumped to his death was upset over this, police say"
    https://twitter.com/NBCNewYork/status/583764222636642304

    The New York Times: "Is Donald Trump a Threat to Democracy?"
    https://www.nytimes.com/2016/12/16/opinion/sunday/is-donald-trump-a-threat-to-democracy.html?_r=0

    CNN: "14-year-old girl stabbed her sister 14 times, police say. The reason will shock you"
    https://twitter.com/cnnbrk/status/426265271914205184

    The Atlantic: "How Trump's Speech to the CIA Endangered America"
    https://www.theatlantic.com/politics/archive/2017/01/in-seconds-at-the-cia-trump-made-america-less-safe/514193/

Here are a few important resources for learning more about the problem of fake news:

    "Inside the Macedonian Fake-News Complex" *WIRED* (February 2017)
    https://www.wired.com/2017/02/veles-macedonia-fake-news/

    "We Tracked Down a Fake-News Creator in the Suburbs: Here's What We Learned" *NPR's All Things Considered* (November 2016)
    http://www.npr.org/sections/alltechconsidered/2016/11/23/503146770/npr-finds-the-head-of-a-covert-fake-news-operation-in-the-suburbs

"PolitiFact's Guide to Fake News Websites and What They Peddle" *PolitiFact* (April 2017)
http://www.politifact.com/punditfact/article/2017/apr/20/ politifacts-guide-fake-news-websites-and-what-they/

Writing with Images
To read more about the relationship between captions and images, check out this Errol Morris essay at the *New York Times* site:
http://opinionator.blogs.nytimes.com/2010/01/12/thought-experiment-2/

Exploring Significant Moments
Watch this video for a demonstration on how to give a handshake that would make Papa proud!
https://www.youtube.com/watch?v=41BdlgNyKFI

The House of Representatives has college internship opportunities.
https://www.house.gov/educators-and-students/college-internships

Every state has its own special qualities. Check out the link below and find out the best things about your home state!
https://www.thrillist.com/travel/nation/the-best-things-about-every-us-state

Architect David Adjaye, who designed the Smithsonian's National Museum of African American History and Culture discusses how place shapes identity.
https://www.youtube.com/watch?v=njBCgXmjCpI

Follow this link for an in-depth look at Yokohama Chinatown in Japan.
https://www.japan-guide.com/e/e3201.html

The mission of Cal Poly's Cross Cultural Centers is to offer services and programs to support our students under the shared values of family, diversity, learning, growth, and advocacy.
https://culture.calpoly.edu

Global Glimpse provides opportunities for high school students to participate in international travel programs that focus on service learning and leadership. Check out Cal Poly's International Center for opportunities to study abroad while attending the university.
https://abroad.calpoly.edu

Appendices

Cal Poly's newest residential community, yakʔitʸutʸu, is named in honor of the indigenous peoples of San Luis Obispo. Check out more information on the Northern Chumash Tribe of this region.
http://www.yttnorthernchumash.org

If you're interested in volunteering at a homeless shelter in SLO County, follow the link below to CAPSLO and see how you can help.
https://www.capslo.org/menus/volunteer.html

Check out the National Center for Transgender Equality.
https://transequality.org

The Trevor Project offers resources on coming out.
https://www.thetrevorproject.org/about/programs-services/coming-out-as-you/

Respecting others' gender pronouns sets a positive example for our campus community. Check out the Pride Center's webpage on why pronouns matter.
https://culture.calpoly.edu/PrideCenter/PronounsMatter

The online science and technology news portal Phys.org summarizes a 2013 study about the effects of the red pen on student learning.
https://phys.org/news/2013-01-red-pen-instructors-negative-response.html

Follow the link below for an article in *Inc. Magazine* that reveals four steps for finding your voice.
https://www.inc.com/rebekah-iliff/finding-your-voice-and-why-it-really-isn-t-about-you.html

For more information about ADD, explore the official website for the Attention Deficit Disorder Association.
https://add.org/adhd-facts/

Follow the link below to learn about the Surfrider Foundation and its efforts to protect the world's oceans.
https://www.surfrider.org/mission

Baker begins his essay with a quote by surfer Mark Foo. Check out more about Foo in an excerpt from the documentary *Riding Giants* through the link below.
https://vimeo.com/49425260

After reading Shepard's essay, take some time to watch her TED Talk:
https://youtu.be/bpJgCTIiTU8

University professor and author Dr. Brené Brown says "sometimes the bravest and most important thing you can do is just show up." For more inspiration, consider watching Brown's Netflix special, *The Call to Courage*.
https://www.netflix.com/title/81010166

Profiling a Person, Place, Trend, or Event
For more information about what declining enrollment in the humanities means for universities as a whole, and why humanities majors may have better job prospects than is commonly believed, read the following essay from the *Atlantic Monthly*:
https://www.theatlantic.com/ideas/archive/2018/08/
the-humanities-face-a-crisisof-confidence/567565/

Find out more about the Sojourn Grace Collective:
https://sojourngrace.com/

For more information on the Leaning Pine Arboretum, including its location so you can see it yourself, see the following website:
http://www.leaningpinearboretum.calpoly.edu/

Find out more about the Second Chance Pell Grant Program that Dr. Alaniz is part of:
http://www.aei.org/publication/
the-second-chance-pell-pilot-program-a-historical-overview/

For more information on how women served in World War II, including in WAVES, take a look at the following website:
https://www.uso.org/stories/118-women-of-world-war-ii

Check out this *Mustang News* article about "The Professor Next Door":
https://mustangnews.net/the-professor-next-door-for-the-first-time-at-cal-poly-three-faculty-members-live-in-campus-housing/

SLOCORE is just one example of a Cal Poly campus club. For more information on clubs you could join to make connections with your classmates, or just to have fun, look here:
https://clubs.calpoly.edu/

Analyzing Rhetorically
Sharma's essay is a rhetorical analysis of a photo of a child bride. To see the image she is referring to, go to the following link:
https://stephaniesinclair.photoshelter.com/gallery-image/Child-Brides-Nepal/
G0000PnUjNfNAJFg/I0000HPBelp34FIg

To see the cover poster described in this essay, as well as the rest of the posters from Shreya Arora's set titled "The Good Victim Starter Pack," visit:
https://www.arorashreya.com/the-good-victim-starter-pack

The documentary *White Helmets*, available on Netflix, chronicles the activities of emergency first-responders in Aleppo, a rebel-occupied area of Syria. Check out the trailer here:
https://youtu.be/3wj4ncIEDxw

Engaging in Public Rhetoric and Argumentation

The British Library's online exhibit contains the original manuscript of Elizabeth's "Speech to the Troops at Tilbury":
http://www.bl.uk/learning/timeline/item102878.html

See a *This Week Tonight* segment about Sinclair Broadcast Group's influence on local TV news broadcasts:
https://www.youtube.com/watch?v=GvtNyOzGogc

If you are a U.S. citizen and a resident of California, you can register to vote through the CA Secretary of State's online voter registration system (you can even pre-register if you're under 18):
https://registertovote.ca.gov

An April 2019 article in *Mustang News* reflects on Cal Poly's campus climate one year after the Lambda Chi Alpha incident:
https://mustangnews.net/its-been-one-year-since-the-blackface-incident-where-is-cal-polys-campus-climate-now/

Check out Cal Poly's quick sustainability guide to learn what waste goes in which bin.
https://afd.calpoly.edu/sustainability/campus-action/zero-waste/what-goes-where

Sal Khan discusses methods for avoiding learning gaps and building subject expertise in this *TEDTalk*.
www.ted.com/talks/sal_khan_let_s_teach_for_mastery_not_test_scores

Film Theory argues for the connected worlds of *IT* and *The Shining*.
https://www.youtube.com/watch?v=IfuKFPMZmyU

See student reactions to Cal Poly's initiative to offer free feminine hygiene products on campus.
www.youtube.com/watch?v=2lmzgxZco9Y

Reasoning, Argumentation, and Writing

Check out the Loop program here:
https://loopstore.com/

Gillian Ippoliti mentions her interest specifically in ocean pollution. Listen to a podcast from the National Ocean Service titled "Garbage Patches: How Gyres Take Our Trash Out to Sea":
https://oceanservice.noaa.gov/podcast/mar18/nop14-ocean-garbage-patches.html

For more information on Cal Poly's Zero Waste Initiative visit:
https://afd.calpoly.edu/sustainability/campus-action/zero-waste/

Watch this video from *National Geographic* on an alternative to plastic spoons:
https://video.nationalgeographic.com/video/
short-film-showcase/00000155-a195-db77-a3dd-b3d7fc4e0000

See the most recent California State budget:
https://www.ppic.org/publication/californias-state-budget/

Find the Cal Poly Master Plan here:
https://afd.calpoly.edu/facilities/project_masterplan.asp

See photos of solitary confinement here:
https://www.gettyimages.com/photos/solitary-confinement?sort=mostpopular&mediat
ype=photography&phrase=solitary%20confinement

Time investigates the only known photo of John F. Kennedy and Marilyn Monroe together:
https://time.com/5354958/marilyn-monroe-john-f-kennedy-photo/

Appendices

Six Harvard faculty members explain why office hours are integral to your learning experience: "Office Hours: 6 Realities":
https://news.harvard.edu/gazette/story/2017/12/professors-examine-the-realities-
of-office-hours/

SUBMITTING YOUR WORK TO *FRESH VOICES*, 2020–2021

Dear Writer:

Fresh Voices **needs your essays and artwork!**

- Are you proud of essays you wrote in your composition course?
- Do you want thousands of next year's students to read your work?
- Do you want to tell future employers you're a PUBLISHED writer?
- Do you want to share your photography, painting, or drawing with the Cal Poly community?

If so, submit your work to *Fresh Voices!*

If your essay or artwork is selected, **you will receive a free copy of the collection and a certificate of achievement.**

What to Submit

- Any essays you completed in ENGL 129, 130, 131, 132, 133, 134, or 145 ranging from 2–10 pages in length.
- All citations associated with those essays; we will not consider work that does not properly cite sources. *Fresh Voices* uses the eighth edition of the MLA Handbook.
- Original artwork (photography, paintings, drawing, etc.) that could be appropriate for the collection.

How to Submit

1. Go to the *Fresh Voices* online submission page at https://english.calpoly.edu/composition/fresh-voices-submission.
2. Download, complete, and sign the "Permission to Publish" release form.
3. Complete the online submission process. Be sure to upload the correct essay file(s) for which you've completed the release form.
4. If you're submitting multiple works, you'll need to complete a separate online form for each submission.
5. Manuscripts should be saved as PDF or Word files only.
6. Artwork files should be print resolution (300 dpi) JPEG or TIFF and color balanced for CMYK printing.

Deadline

Essays must be received by the last day of finals week in spring quarter to be considered for publication. Please contact the English Department if you have questions. *Fresh Voices* editors look forward to reading your work!

Dr. Brenda Helmbrecht
Director of Writing, Department of English